Introducing Chinese Religions

Introducing Chinese Religions is the ideal starting point for students exploring the fascinating religious traditions of China. This introduction covers the whole spectrum of Chinese religious history, from the multi-faceted religious heritage of pre-modern China, to the practice of different religions in China today, as well as the spread and influence of Chinese religions throughout the world.

Mario Poceski, an experienced teacher of Chinese religions, explores the three main traditions of Buddhism, Confucianism and Daoism, as well as the development of Western and popular religions in the region, such as Christianity and Islam. The book introduces students to the richness and diversity of Chinese religious life, pointing out mutual influences and intersections of the religions of the region, and how they interact with other elements of Chinese culture and society, including politics, literature and art.

Illustrated throughout, the book also includes text boxes, summary charts, a glossary and a list of further reading to aid students' understanding and revision. The accompanying website for this book can be found at www.routledge.com/textbooks/9780415434065.

Mario Poceski is Associate Professor of Buddhist Studies and Chinese Religions in the Department of Religion at the University of Florida.

World Religions series

Edited by Damien Keown and Charles S. Prebish

This exciting series introduces students to the major world religious traditions. Each religion is explored in a lively and clear fashion by experienced teachers and leading scholars in the field of world religions. Up-to-date scholarship is presented in a student-friendly fashion, covering history, core beliefs, sacred texts, key figures, religious practice and culture, and key contemporary issues. To aid learning and revision, each text includes illustrations, summaries, explanations of key terms, and further reading.

Introducing Buddhism
Charles S. Prebish and Damien Keown

Introducing Chinese Religions
Mario Poceski

Introducing Christianity
James R. Adair

Introducing Daoism
Livia Kohn

Introducing Hinduism
Hillary P. Rodrigues

Introducing Islam
William Shepard

Introducing Japanese Religion
Robert Ellwood

Introducing Judaism
Eliezer Segal

Forthcoming:

Introducing American Religions
Introducing New Religious Movements
Introducing Tibetan Buddhism

Introducing
Chinese Religions

Mario Poceski

 Routledge
Taylor & Francis Group

LONDON AND NEW YORK

First published 2009
by Routledge

2 Park Square, Milton Park, Abingdon, Oxon OX14 4RN

Simultaneously published in the USA and Canada
by Routledge
711 Third Avenue, New York, NY 10017

Routledge is an imprint of the Taylor & Francis Group, an informa business

© 2009 Mario Poceski

Typeset in Jenson by
HWA Text and Data Management, London

British Library Cataloguing in Publication Data
A catalogue record for this book is available from the British Library

Library of Congress Cataloging in Publication Data
A catalog record for this book has been requested

ISBN13: 978-0-415-43405-8 (hbk)
ISBN13: 978-0-415-43406-5 (pbk)

To my wife Hiroko Poceski
and my students

Contents

Appendix

Illustrations

Chinese dynastic history

	BCE
Xia 夏	2205–1766? (or c. 2100–1600?)
Shang (Yin) 商	1766–1122? (or c. 1600–1046?)
Zhou 周	1122–256 (or 1045/1027–256)
Western Zhou 西周	1122–771 (or 1045/1027–771)
Eastern Zhou 東周	771–256
Spring and Autumn 春秋 era	722–481
Warring States 戰國 period	453–221 (or 403–221)
Qin 秦	221–206
Han 漢	206 BCE–220 CE
Western Han 西漢	206 BCE–8 CE

	CE
Xin 新	9–23
Eastern Han 東漢	25–220
Three Kingdoms 三國	220–265 (or 220–280)
Wei 魏	220–265
Shu 蜀	221–263
Wu 吳	222–280
Western Jin 西晉	265–317
Eastern Jin 東晉	317–420
Northern and Southern Dynasties 南北朝	420–589
Liu Song 劉宋	420–479
Qi 齊	479–502
Liang 梁	502–557
Chen 陳	557–589
Northern Wei 北魏	386–534
Eastern Wei 東魏	534–550
Western Wei 西魏	535–557
Northern Qi 北齊	550–577
Northern Zhou 北周	557–581

Sui 隋	581–618
Tang 唐	618–907
Zhou 周	690–705
Five Dynasties 五代	907–960
Later Liang 後梁	907–923
Later Tang 後唐	923–936
Later Jin 後晉	936–947
Later Han 後漢	947–951
Later Zhou 後周	951–960
Ten Kingdoms 十國	902–979
Wu 吳	902–937
Former Shu 前蜀	907–925
Wuyue 吳越	907–978
Chu 楚	907–951
Min 閩	909–945
Southern Han 南漢	917–971
Jingnan 荆南	924–963
Latter Shu 後蜀	934–965
Southern Tang 南唐	937–975
Northern Han 北漢	951–979
Song 宋	960–1279
Northern Song 北宋	960–1127
Liao 遼 (Khitan)	916–1125
Jin 金 (Jürchen)	1115–1234
Xixia 西夏 (Tangut)	1032–1227
Southern Song 南宋	1127–1279
Yuan 元 (Mongol)	1271–1368
Ming 明	1368–1644
Qing 清 (Manchu)	1644–1911
Republic of China 中華民國	1911–1949
People's Republic of China 中華人民共和國	1949–

Preface and acknowledgments

While there are many specialized studies on various aspects of Chinese religious history, literature, doctrine, and practice, there is a scarcity of books that offer broad treatment of Chinese religions and deal with the big picture. This volume is intended to address a conspicuous need for general surveys or textbooks that cover the whole field of Chinese religions. The book aims at comprehensive and balanced coverage of the main religious traditions that over the centuries developed and flourished in China, presented in a manner that is scholarly, exact and reliable, yet also readable and readily comprehensible. Only a few books with compatible coverage have been published in English over the last few decades. Although commendable for their authors' pioneering efforts, most of the earlier volumes are somewhat dated, adopt debatable approaches, or are limited in their coverage (see Yang 1961, Thompson 1995/1969, Jochim 1985, Overmyer 1998/1986, Ching 1993, and Adler 2002). There are also a couple of collections of translations from primary sources that supplement this volume (Sommer 1995 provides a more balanced coverage; Lopez 1996 contains some excellent materials, although it is somewhat confused in its overall design); the reader might want to consult these in order to gain additional exposure to some of the relevant classical texts discussed in the book's chapters.

The origins of this book can indirectly be linked with my teachings of an undergraduate course on Chinese religions, which I first offered in 2001 at the University of Iowa, and have ever since taught at the University of Florida. Accordingly, I would like to start the acknowledgements by thanking all my students for their keenness and hard work. Special thanks go to my graduate students who read parts of the early manuscript and offered helpful feedback: Sarah Spaid, Kendall Marchman, and Phillip Green. I am also grateful to Ruth Sheng for the Chinese calligraphy that appears in Chapter 3, and for proofreading the Chinese text in the glossary. Among my colleagues at the University of Florida, I am indebted to Richard Wang for providing me with useful comments on Chapters 3, 4, and 7, and to Lai Guolong for doing the same for Chapter 1. Richard Wang also kindly provided me with two of the photos that appear in Chapter 4 (Figures 4.2 and 4.3).

Keith Knapp read Chapters 2 and 8, and offered a number of valuable suggestions that I incorporated into the final manuscript. I also wish to thank Livia Kohn for supplying me with the two drawings that appear in Chapter 4 (Figures 4.1 and 4.7).

The photographs used as illustrations throughout the book are mine, unless noted otherwise. The photographic images from the collections of the Freer and Sackler Galleries (Smithsonian Institution, Washington DC), Bridgeman Art Gallery, and Getty Images are reproduced with their permission, as noted in the pertinent captions.

I greatly appreciate the interest and support I received from Charles Prebish and Damien Keown, the editors of the World Religions series, who first came up with the idea of doing this book. I extend special thanks to Lesley Riddle of Routledge, who from the beginning expressed strong enthusiasm for the book, and who tactfully convinced me to undertake the writing of it. I would also like to acknowledge the dedicated work of Amy Grant and the rest of the staff at Routledge. Finally, as always I wish to express gratitude to my wife, Hiroko Poceski, for her patience, love, and support.

Conventions

Throughout the book all transliterations from the Chinese language follow the Pinyin system, which is official in China and is used widely all over the world, although older works and even some recent publications still use the dated Wade-Giles system. The only rare exceptions to that usage are names that are widely known in alternative spellings, such as Taipei (instead of Taibei). In the Chinese glossary that appears at the end, however, in light of the book's historical orientation I use the traditional forms of Chinese characters. When referring to the geographical locations of various monasteries, temples, mountains, and other historical sites, I use present-day provincial boundaries.

Introduction

China has an exceedingly long, captivating, and multifaceted history. Over a staggering array of dynastic epochs, the earliest of which take us back in time for well over three millennia, religion has always been an important presence in Chinese life and a major force in the shaping of Chinese history. Rich and constantly evolving tapestries of religious beliefs and practices have over the millennia remained integral parts of the social fabrics and cultural landscapes of the various Chinese states and empires. Many of those religious elements have also been exported to other countries that historically belonged to China's political and cultural spheres of influence, most notably Korea, Japan, and Vietnam. Consequently, the story told in this book, while centered on religion in China, is also relevant to the past and present cultural experiences of people in living in other lands. That also includes America and the rest of the Western world, where Chinese temples, concepts, or religious artifacts are becoming increasingly common features of everyday life and popular culture.

At the beginning of the twenty-first century, as it gradually moves in the direction of reassuming its central role onto the world stage—that it has previously occupied for large stretches of recorded history—China seems destined to exert an increasing influence not only on the lives of its citizens but also on the rest of the world. Knowledge and appreciation of China's multifarious religious history should be a central part of any serious effort at sophisticated understanding of both China's past and its present. Traditionally, elements of that religious history have been among the key building blocks of one of the world's most important and enduring civilizations. The intricate and enthralling story of the various religious traditions that developed and flourished in China, the subject of this book, is worthy of study and reflection for its own intrinsic value and interest. The story of Chinese religion is also important for what it tells us about the basic character of a range of cultural forms that developed in a key part of the world, which remain significant elements of an enduring heritage and continue to shape the present. Given the increasingly global nature of our world and the important roles religion plays in it, it is incumbent on us to become better informed about the religious landscape of this immensely large, varied, and important country, which in turn facilitates more nuanced understanding of Chinese civilization, in all of its richness and complexity.

This book is intended to serve as a comprehensive yet accessible historical survey of Chinese religions. It covers the whole spectrum of Chinese religious history—from the Shang dynasty (c. 1600–1046 BCE) to the present—providing a systematic and balanced coverage of major developments, texts, traditions, beliefs, institutions, and practices. The book adopts a combination of diachronic and thematic approaches, starting with an exploration of the earliest forms of religious beliefs and practices in ancient China, and ending with a discussion of present-day trends and predicaments. Much of the book is dedicated to the remarkable and multifaceted religious heritage of pre-modern or traditional China. However, there is also ample coverage of the religious terrain of modern China, which is currently undergoing some new developments and notable transitions, even as it remains deeply rooted in the past.

Study of Chinese religion

The two main terms featured in the book's title—China (Chinese) and religion(s)—are not without ambiguities, and each of them can be problematized to some degree. The notion of China as a unitary nation-state, as presently understood, is of a fairly recent origin, even if it is possible to trace some of its origins or precursors in the ancient past. Over the centuries, the land we know as China has experienced numerous changes in terms of its geographical and political boundaries. These changes reflect constantly evolving patterns of political allegiance, imperial aspiration, and ethnic loyalty. For a substantial part of its history China was not united as a single state, and for extended periods parts or the whole of China were ruled by alien dynasties. Some might even argue that the present-day geographical boundaries of China, fixed as they might appear on modern maps, remain contested or uncertain in some areas. Prime example of that is the indefinite status of Taiwan, although there are also the well-publicized arguments for (and against) Tibetan and Uyghur independence. We also need to be aware that there is a multiplicity of historical narratives about China's past—often configured or presented in relation to its present—which reflect a range of political agendas and ideological suppositions.

Narrowly focusing on China in terms of a particular physical place or geographical area—which in many instances comes across as a perfectly sensible approach—can be problematic because, among other things, it leaves out the religious beliefs and observances of the Chinese diasporas. On the other hand, placing a discussion of the predominant patterns of religious life in contemporary Singapore, for instance, within the broad category of Chinese religion(s) is not without its own problems. One way of partially getting around these concerns is to primarily think of China or Chineseness in cultural terms, namely in terms of constellations of beliefs, customs, social behaviors, and practices that are part of a larger civilizational pattern.

When considered that way, it is possible to isolate remarkable cultural continuities throughout the course of Chinese history—alongside numerous changes and variations—that are observable in the persistence of certain cultural orientations and values, for instance the worship of ancestors and the exaltation of the virtue of filial piety. Nonetheless, we still have to contend with evolving cultural configurations and shifting identities, as well as deal with the occasionally messy and contestable issue of delineating cultural boundaries, which involves defining the parameters of what constitutes (or does not) "Chinese culture." While these kinds of considerations are not of central concern in a general survey volume such as this one, where the main focus is on major developments and mainstream traditions, they should be kept in mind whenever we are dealing with broad characterizations of Chinese beliefs, values, and the like.

Similarly, within the academic discipline of religious studies the defining of "religion" is often deemed to be fraught with difficulties. The various attempts to delineate the contours and define the basic character of religion are complicated by the fact that particular definitions are developed from within specific academic disciplines (sociology, anthropology, psychology, etc.), or in light of particular theories about religion (phenomenological, functionalist, structuralist, etc.). There is also the problem of continued prevalence of Western models, primarily based on Christian ideas and archetypes, in the academic study of religion. Within academic circles we have largely moved beyond patently biased and delimiting definitions of religion along the lines of "religion is belief in God," even if such attitudes remain predominant in many quarters, including the public square and the media. Nonetheless, more inclusive definitions of religion, for instance as "a system of beliefs and practices related to supernatural beings" or some variation on a similar theme, are not without their problems, as we will note in the discussion of Confucianism, whose status as a religion has been the subject of occasional disagreements (see Chapter 2; the teachings of some varieties of Buddhism are also relevant in this context).

In light of latent Eurocentric (or Christian-centric) preconceptions and persistent parochial attitudes, which in many quarters still shape the study and discussion of religion, thoughtful examination of Chinese religions assumes special importance. Knowledge of the multilayered and many-sided patterns of China's religious past helps us to reconsider the dominant theoretical paradigms, as well as expand and enrich our understanding of the basic character and varied manifestations of religion. It also prompts us to rethink the whole range of roles religion plays as an important component of the human experience, past and present. For instance, the study of Chinese religions brings us in contact with a prevalent tendency to construct a range of open-ended or hybrid religious identities, which stand in contrast to the common Western and Islamic patterns of constricted or singular religious identities and affiliations, which are primarily defined by allegiance to a church, a revealed dogma, or a sacred scripture. Exploration of China's religious past also familiarizes us with intriguing models of religious pluralism, in which a variety of religions share common social and cultural spaces. A prime example of that is the Tang era (618–907), when an astounding variety of religious traditions—including Buddhism, Confucianism, Daoism, Christianity, Islam, Zoroastrianism, and Manichaeism—peacefully coexisted in China and engaged in complex patterns of interreligious interaction. Once again, this presents a sharp contrast with the situation that during the same period (and over the subsequent centuries) prevailed in Europe and elsewhere, where there was little tolerance of deviation or dissent from the teachings of the official church.

Main religious traditions

The study of Chinese religion is often approached in terms of the so-called "three teachings," namely the dominant religious traditions of Buddhism, Confucianism, and Daoism. Each of these traditions has a long and distinguished history in China; an important part of that history is the interaction with the other two traditions. Confucianism and Daoism both originated in China. Consequently, they are usually depicted as embodying ideas, values, and orientations that are at the core of Chinese social and cultural constructions of reality. In contrast, Buddhism is a pan-Asian religion that originated in India, although in the course of its long history in China—which spans almost two millennia—it was radically transformed and domesticated. The Chinese adaptation and acculturation of Buddhism was complex and thorough; consequently, in its fully Sinicized form Buddhism also came to represent a religion that is quintessentially Chinese.

Over their lengthy history, each of the three teachings developed sophisticated systems of doctrine, canons of sacred writings, moral injunctions about everyday conduct, distinct institutions, and a range of ritual practices and observances. In the cases of Buddhism and Daoism we also find well developed monastic orders, open to both males and females. Throughout much of Chinese history the three teachings were perceived as being complementary rather than antithetical to each other. This led to the notion of the unity of the three teachings, although ecumenical sentiments were not universally shared. Consequently, Chinese religious history also provides us with notable examples of religious intolerance and fanaticism, albeit not on the same scale and with the same propensity towards violence as we find in many other parts of the world.

While the beliefs, doctrines, and practices of the three teachings cover substantial part of the Chinese religious landscape, focusing only on them is unduly restrictive, as it leaves out other important traditions that have greatly influenced China's religious past and still continue to exert considerable impact on the lives of many Chinese. Among them especially important is popular religion, which in many instances represents the most common mode of worship or predominant expression of religious life, especially at the level of local communities. Popular religion is not an organized form of religion along the lines of Daoism or Buddhism, as it lacks a coherent canon and a system of doctrine, as well organized clergy and ecclesiastical institutions. Rather it is a general category, a provisional designation of sorts, which is used by scholars as a way of arranging a broad range of prevalent and widely diffused beliefs and practices that are not officially part of any of the mainstream religious traditions. To these four main traditions we can also add the two monotheistic religions of Christianity and Islam, which initially entered China during the Tang dynasty; presently both religions (or all three religions, if we follow the official division of Christianity into Catholicism and Protestantism) have substantial presence in China, with the followers of each of them numbering into tens of millions.

Beside the aforementioned taxonomy of the three teachings (or four, or even six teachings if we add popular religion, Christianity, and Islam), scholars have put forward alternative conceptual schemes for organizing the religious terrain of traditional and modern China. One such alternative is the binary division of Chinese religion into two structurally distinct parts: institutional religion (primarily represented by the three teachings) and diffused religion (represented by popular religion). That is similar to the well-known conceptual division between the great and the little tradition, which highlights differences between the distinct patterns of religious participation observable among the social elites and the commoners, as well as between the often divergent concerns of the clergy and the laity. While some scholars have stressed the contrasts and differences between these two broad categories, others have emphasized their interrelatedness and have subsumed them all within a single overarching cultural system. Another possibility is to move away from discussing Chinese religious life in terms of distinct traditions; instead, we can examine general categories that cover a broad range of religious themes and experiences, such as rituals, cosmologies, communities, ethical norms, and the like. While this approach readily lends itself to the utilization of theoretical models and technical vocabulary that is in vogue in Western academic circles, it also poses the danger of leading into vague generalizations that have little to do with the concrete realities of lived religion(s), as experienced by actual individuals and communities, past and present.

The danger of reifying the three/four teachings is real, as it is patently wrong to look at them as closed systems that are hermetically sealed from the other. In reality, throughout Chinese history all the main religious traditions interacted and influenced each other. Moreover, the lines of demarcation around and between distinct religious traditions, especially at the margins, were not always rigidly fixed and they were easily crossed. On the other hand, doing away with distinct traditions such as Daoism and Confucianism is not historically warranted, as each of the main institutional religions had its own readily recognizable and more or less coherent systems of doctrines, texts, rituals, and institutions. Accordingly, in this volume I map the spiritual terrain and approach the study of Chinese religion(s) in terms of the traditional distinctions between discrete traditions. Nevertheless, I also hig light the multifarious patterns of interreligious interaction, point to the copious instances of mutual borrowing or influence, and problematize the drawing of exceedingly rigid sectarian boundaries. For instance, in the chapters on Daoism there are also a number of references to Buddhism, Confucianism, and popular religion, and the same applies to the rest of the book.

Organization of the book

The main body of the book consists of ten chapters of approximately equal length, with the exception of Chapter 10, which is about a third longer. At the end of each chapter there is a bibliography of relevant books written in English. Each chapter also includes additional pedagogical tools that are meant to enhance the book's usefulness to general readers, students, and teachers. First, there are brief excerpts from pertinent primary sources, such as *Mengzi* or the recorded sayings of Chan teachers. Second, there are tables or listings that contain key concepts, names, or taxonomies, such as the three parts of the Daoist canon or the five Confucian classics. Third, there are summaries of the main points or issues explored in each chapter, along with sample discussion questions. I have also included numerous illustrations and photographs, most of them taken during my travels to various religious sites in China and elsewhere. There is also a chronology of Chinese dynastic history at the beginning of the book, and an additional bibliography and Chinese glossary at the end.

A substantial part of the book focuses on the three main religious traditions—Buddhism, Confucianism, and Daoism—each of which is allocated two chapters. The chapters on Daoism and Buddhism are placed consequently (Chapters 3 through 6), while the second chapter on late Confucianism (Chapter 8) is placed towards the end of the book, apart from the chapter on early Confucianism (Chapter 2) that appears in the early part of the book. Such arrangement reflects the fact that the Confucian revival of the Song era and its subsequent elaborations must be considered in relation to the spectacular growth of Buddhism and Daoism that occurred during the medieval period, and the great influence these two religions exerted on the Chinese literati. Other relevant traditions also receive adequate coverage. Popular religion is allocated a separate chapter, while the growths of Christianity and Islam are placed together in a single chapter. In light of prevalent (American) academic conventions, I have not included substantive coverage of Tibetan Buddhism, which is usually treated under the separate (and somewhat nebulous) category of Indo-Tibetan Buddhism.

While separate chapters are dedicated to the main religious traditions, as noted above, throughout the book I also point out the mutual influences and intersections among the different religions. In addition, in the various chapters I relate the interactions of various religions with other social forces and cultural phenomena, such as political authority, literary production, artistic representation, and attitudes towards gender. I also highlight the key models of religious pluralism that evolved in the course of Chinese history, and the ways in which the Chinese constructed their religious identities. As was already noted and we will later see in more detail, often those identities were multifaceted or assumed hybrid forms, in contrast to the familiar paradigms that are prevalent in the Western and Islamic worlds.

I have tried to make the book's organizational structure and its overall presentation suitable for a general audience interested in a readable but academically rigorous introduction to Chinese religions. The book is written in such a way as to make it suitable for use as a primary textbook for semester-long courses on Chinese religions at the college level. Each chapter should cover about a week of instruction. Taken together, the various chapters are meant to introduce students and general readers to the richness and diversity of Chinese religious life, with the intent of stimulating interest and appreciation of the main themes and traditions, within a larger context of humanistic knowledge about religion and spirituality.

As it is primarily directed towards a general audience, and given the parameters set by the book series in which it is included, the book is not annotated (with the exception of occasional inline citations, which are sneaked into some of the chapters). Readers interested in learning more about specific topics or religions are encouraged to consult the secondary sources included in the pertinent reading lists and the bibliography. Throughout the book I have tried to write in a clear and relatively jargon-free manner, avoiding unnecessary inclusion of numerous names, superfluous historical information, and the like; I have also aimed at staying away from dwelling on scholarly minutia. At the same time, I have endeavored to put emphasis on scholarly accuracy, which includes implementation of prevalent academic standards in what are admittedly a number of distinct and still growing fields of scholarly research.

1 *Early patterns of Chinese religious life*

In this chapter

The first chapter surveys the principal religious beliefs and practices that emerged during the formative stages of Chinese civilization. It primarily covers the period from the establishment of the Shang dynasty (c. 1550–1045) until the time of Confucius (551–479 BCE?), although some of it is also applicable to later periods, up to the early part of the Han dynasty (206 BCE–220 CE). During the early formative period of dynastic history it is already possible to discern fundamental religiously inflected cultural orientations, institutional paradigms, configurations of belief, and patterns of thinking that continued to shape the essential character and ongoing development of Chinese civilization. The chapter looks at the earliest sources of information, such as oracle bones and bronze inscriptions, which provide important clues about key features of ancient religious life. This includes ancestor veneration and belief in a supernatural realm populated by various gods and spirits, which is closely correlated with the human world. Several of the religious themes and concepts featured here will reappear in later chapters. Such recurrences amplify some of the remarkable patterns of continuity that underscore the central historical trajectories of Chinese civilization, even if, as we will see throughout the book, such enduring elements invariably went together with momentous changes and notable paradigm shifts.

Main topics

- Brief overview of ancient Chinese history.
- Use of oracle bones and practice of divination under the Shang dynasty.
- Worship of gods, spirits, and ancestors.
- Changing perceptions of divinity and sacrifice during the Zhou era.
- Veneration of the cultural heroes and sagely kings of remote antiquity.
- Basic character and scope of Chinese mythology.
- Political and religious underpinnings of the notion of "mandate of Heaven."

Historical frameworks

China has one of the oldest civilizations in the world. Early predecessors of the modern humans, known as *Homo erectus*, lived in China over 500,000 years ago, perhaps even as early as a million years ago. They are represented by the so-called "Peking man," skulls and bones of whom were discovered in the vicinity of present-day Beijing during the 1920s. As its name indicates, this early relation to our species, the *Homo sapiens*, was able to stand erect, and he was sophisticated enough to be able to use fire and make a variety of stone tools. Modern humans settled in the area of present-day China at the onset of the Paleolithic (Old Stone) period, some 100,000 years ago, possibly even before that. The earliest societies were those of hunters and gatherers, who gradually developed more evolved language abilities. By approximately 10,000 BCE there was a gradual development of agriculture, a point at which we can perhaps begin to speak of the beginning of a proto-Chinese history, although the determination of a particular starting point for "Chinese" history is largely an arbitrary and inherently contestable academic exercise.

By 5000 BCE a variety of localized and heterogeneous Neolithic (New Stone Age) cultures emerged in some of the river valleys in both the northern and southern parts of China. During this period, further developments in agriculture led to the formation of more permanent settlements, which fostered the evolution of more complex forms of social organization. In the north the main grain was millet, while in the warmer and wetter southern regions the main focus of agricultural production was the cultivation of rice. This basic farming pattern remained stable over the subsequent centuries. Advances in agricultural expertise and productivity were accompanied with increased sophistication in the production of pottery, textiles, weaponry, and a variety of tools such as spades and hoes. During this period we also encounter the domestication of animals, including dogs, cattle, and pigs.

A well-known example of Neolithic civilization is the Yangshao culture, which flourished approximately during the 5000–3000 BCE period in the area of North China (primarily corresponding to what are the present-day provinces of Henan, Shanxi, Shaanxi, and Gansu). Its people subsisted primarily by means of farming, and they also engaged in hunting and kept certain domestic animals. Archeologists have discovered a large number of artifacts associated with the Yangshao culture—which they divide in a number of distinctive and overlapping phases—including nicely decorated pottery of various shapes and sizes, with many examples of delicately painted animal motifs and geometrical patterns. Other notable artifacts from the same chronological period—uncovered by archeologists at various burial sites associated with other cultures, primarily located in the eastern part of China—are various jade objects, many of them nicely carved with intricate shapes and designs, which were presumably used in religious ceremonies. Some of the other prominent Neolithic cultures are those of Hongshan, Liangzhu, and Longshan.

Traditional historiography traces the beginning of Chinese dynastic history to the legendary Xia dynasty, whose traditional chronology is usually given as 2207–1766 BCE. That is the first of the "three dynasties" of ancient China (the other two being the Shang and the Zhou). We do not have any hard archeological evidence about this dynasty and historians are uncertain if it really existed. Nonetheless, we can trace the onset of the Bronze Age to this important transitional period, during which we can ascertain the evolution of more complex civilizational patterns. Important advances included the development of a writing system, political and religious institutions, and metallurgical technology. We are on a more stable historical ground with the next Chinese dynasty, the Shang, for which we have ample archeological and textual evidence. The domain of the Shang was in north China, the area known as the Northern China Plain, which is sometimes referred to as the cradle of Chinese civilization. The Shang thus covered only a part of what later came to be known as China proper.

During the Shang period we witness the formation of multifaceted urban centers, more involved stratification and organization of society, and use of horse-drawn chariots. There was also the growth of occupational specializations, which included the emergence of certain kinds of ritual specialists and diviners. Another notable occurrence was the further development and increased use of writing that took a distinctive logographic form, which was a direct precursor to the standard Chinese

Figure 1.1   Banshan type jar; 5,000–2,000 BCE (Neolithic Period) (Freer Gallery of Art, Smithsonian Institution, Washington, D.C.: Purchase, F1930.96.)

script that is still used today. Important artifacts that bear testimony to the relative sophistication of Shang culture are the numerous vessels and other objects made out of bronze, many of them beautifully decorated with animal drawings or abstract motifs, thousands of which survive to this day. Most of the bronzes were used in ritual contexts, which points to the great importance attached to religion in Shang society. A notable part of Shang religion were ritual sacrifices, which besides the offering of slaughtered animals (such as oxen) also often included human sacrifices, as evidenced at various burial sites that date back to that period.

The Shang kings ruled over their subjects from a series of capitals that incorporated complexes of palaces and temples—exemplified by the important site at Anyang (Henan), where we have the ruins of Yin, the last capital of the Shang—by combining both political and religious authority. Anyang is the site of major archeological discoveries, including the sizeable tombs of eleven Shang kings that ruled during the late part of the dynasty. The Shang kings were able to mobilize their subjects into large public projects, such as the construction of military fortifications or elaborate tombs. They were also able to assemble sizable armies and project military power beyond their domain. In the eleventh century BCE they were eventually replaced by

Figure 1.2 Ritual vessel (*chia*); twelfth century BCE (Shang dynasty) (Freer Gallery of Art, Smithsonian Institution, Washington, D.C.: Gift of Charles Lang Freer, F1907.37)

the first Zhou king, who defeated the Shang army and went on to establish his own long-lasting dynasty (traditional chronology: 1122–256 BCE). This was a momentous event in the history of ancient China that brought about significant political and religious changes, although there was also much continuity between the Shang and the Zhou.

Chinese history depicts the early Zhou kings as paradigmatic rulers who established a stable and strong state, with a flourishing culture that over the centuries was celebrated as a glorious model to be followed by later generations of Chinese rulers and officials. As we will see in the next chapter, Confucius and his disciples construed this period as a golden age of Chinese civilization. Accordingly, they actively promoted the idea that the early Zhou reign should serve as a blueprint for the institution of just governance and the creation of harmonious society. The historical memories of the early Zhou era were also put into writing, as the Zhou elites further developed the earlier Shang script and placed greater emphasis on literary culture. Accordingly, this is the first period in Chinese history for which we have important textual sources, written from the perspective of the Zhou state and its ruling elites, some of which were subsequently incorporated into the Confucian canon (see Chapter 2).

The Zhou rulers set up a hierarchical social structure and decentralized system of governance, a central feature of which was the enfeoffment of their key supporters and relatives. The sociopolitical order instituted by the Zhou dynasty centered on the relationship between the lord and his vassals, which is why it is often referred to as a feudal system (notwithstanding the notable divergences from the European model of feudalism, which serves as the main point of comparison). The period of Zhou hegemony lasted until 771 BCE, when the royal capital was sacked by rebellious armies with the help of non-Chinese tribes. Even well before that, there was a protracted period of Zhou decline during which the dynasty lost much of its authority. This was accompanied with a shift in political power towards the rulers of the various vassal states that were incorporated into the Zhou dominion.

The fall of the Zhou capital in 771 was followed by the establishment of a new capital further east, in the vicinity of Luoyang. This move was a turning point in Zhou history, which is thereby divided into two distinctive periods: Western Zhou and Eastern Zhou. The Eastern Zhou era is further subdivided into two epochs: the Spring and Autumn era (722–481 BCE) and the Warring States period (403–221 BCE). The Spring and Autumn era was a time of political strife and realignment, as well as accelerated social change. During this protracted period of fragmentation there was little in terms of strong central authority, as the Zhou kings were relegated to being mere figureheads, with traditional ritual authority but no real power to control the various rulers who effectively acted as heads of independent states. Consequently, the various states jockeyed for power and status, amidst constantly shifting political alliances. Gradually the larger and more powerful states annexed the smaller ones, thus greatly decreasing the number of independent states.

The interstate competition turned increasingly violent during the Warring States period, as is suggested by its name. By this time the large states had evolved bureaucratic structures and were able to field huge armies; some of the large battles involved hundreds of thousands of soldiers. Ironically, the prevalent climate of strife and competition led to significant economic and technological advances, including increase in trade, growth in monetary usage, and development of iron technology. These advances went together with significant developments in the social and intellectual arenas, some of which will be noted in the next two chapters. Eventually one of the big states, the militaristic and authoritarian Qin, emerged victorious and in 221 BCE was able to unite China under single imperial rule. This was a turning point in world history that ushered China into the imperial age, which lasted until the early twentieth century. While the Qin regime lasted for only fifteen years, it paved the way for the stable imperial rule and cultural glories of the Han era, which lasted over four centuries. One of the keys to Qin's success in uniting all of China was its creation of a strong and centralized government, with well-organized bureaucratic structures that proved very effective in the mass mobilization of material and human resources.

Oracle bones and divination

Among the most important archeological discoveries related to the Shang dynasty are the numerous oracle bone inscriptions (see Figure 1.3), which constitute the earliest written records about Chinese religious beliefs and practices. The oracle bones were first discovered at the end of the nineteenth century. According to some estimates, to date over 200,000 pieces have been excavated—many of them extant only as fragments—mostly at the old Shang capital and religious center located in the vicinity of Anyang. Significant discoveries of inscribed oracle bones continue to be made by Chinese archaeologists, including the major unearthing in 2008 of numerous oracle bones at the temple of the Duke of Zhou (Shaanxi), which contain well over thousand inscribed characters. The oracle bones were originally used primarily within the context of divinatory rituals performed by or on behalf of the Shang kings, although there are also examples of oracle bones that are not related to the royal house. The contents of the inscriptions provide us with important data about the activities and concerns of the Shang rulers and the court elites. They are less relevant to our understanding of the daily lives, existential concerns, and religious practices of the common people, which for the most part remain unknown due to the lack of pertinent archeological and textual sources.

The divinatory rituals undertaken by the Shang kings were largely concerned with making sense of the world in which they lived and obtaining knowledge about the future unfolding of events. To that end, the rituals functioned as means for establishing channels of communication with the unseen forces that governed the world and influenced human destiny. That included the supreme god of the Shang people, who in a number of inscriptions is mentioned by the name Di, as well as the royal ancestors and a variety of other spirits (see next section). The inscriptions were essentially brief records of communications or interactions between the humans, principally represented by the royal personage, and the various gods and spirits that populated the supernatural realm. The divinatory rituals also served as occasions to express the desires, hopes, and intentions of the Shang kings. In some cases the inscriptions are phrased in terms of the king's search of approval or validation from a divine power for a particular course of action, rather than as a question about the unknown or an inquiry into future happening.

For the purpose of divination the Shang people used the bones of large animals, especially the shoulder blades (scapulas) of oxen that have been killed as sacrificial

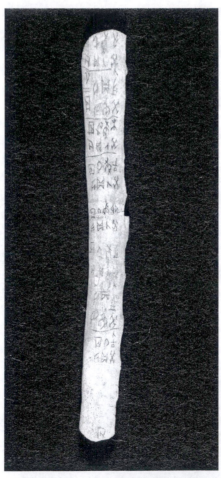

Figure 1.3   Oracle bone with inscription from the Shang dynasty, c. 1,500 BCE (British Museum, London; Bridgeman Art Library)

offerings. Often for the same purpose they also used turtle shells, especially the plastron (the under portion of the shell). Once the shells were carefully prepared, they were heated by the application of hot rods into holes on the bone or shell that had been drilled in advance at specific locations, thereby controlling the positioning of the cracks. The ritualistic application of fire was presumably accompanied with incantations that contained the questions or communications directed towards specific spirits or divinities. It is possible that the ritual also included preparatory stage during which the diviner(s) invoked the spirits and elicited their presence. The application of heat caused the bones or shells to crack, and then specially trained diviners interpreted the cracks as deities' responses to the original questions or topics.

Because of the use of fire, the divinatory techniques performed at the Shang court can be classified under the category of pyromancy, the prediction of the future by means of fire or flames. The Shang king sometimes participated in these rituals, thereby assuming a priestly role that was an important part of the royal persona. The king's abilities to communicate with the supernatural realm and predict the future were key aspects of his priestly charisma and an important source of his political authority. Perhaps more than anything else, it was the royal cult that provided the Shang people with an important sense of social cohesion and gave legitimacy to the existing sociopolitical order. Consequently, the extant inscriptions depict the Shang king as an infallible diviner and prognosticator, someone who is finely attuned to the supernatural realm. There was also a cadre of diviners and ritual specialists that served as officers of the royal court, who officiated during the proceedings and interpreted the results. Notwithstanding the manifest religious character of Shang culture and the religious foundations of its polity, it is also possible to discern a trend towards bureaucratic routinization and rationalization of the state's ritual program, especially during the later part of the dynasty.

After the completion of the divinatory ritual, a brief record of the proceedings, which typically included the communication directed towards the divinity, often accompanied with the result of the divination, was inscribed in an archaic Chinese script on the bone or the shell (see box). The bone inscriptions were archived, thereby functioning as official records that served important bureaucratic and historical functions, in addition to their religious meaning and significance. At times the extant inscriptions also include the names of the diviners and the times when the rituals were performed, following the ancient cyclical calendar that was used at the time.

The contents of the oracle bone inscriptions are usually terse and cryptic, at least to us, although it is safe to assume that they were perfectly understandable to the Shang elites. They provide valuable information about the structure of the Shang pantheon, the activities and prerogatives of the kings, and the general character of courtly life. We can also uncover inklings about an array of concerns that were central to the Shang people, such as agricultural production, meteorological

Oracle bone inscriptions

Will Di order rains that will be sufficient for the harvest? Will Di not order rains that will be sufficient for the harvest?

As for attacking the Qiong tribe, will Di provide us with support?

Shall we pray for harvest to Yue peak with a roasted offering of three sheep and three pigs, and the decapitation of three oxen?

Is it (ancestral) Father Yi who is hurting the king's tooth?

The king made cracks (on the oracle bone) and divined: We shall hunt at Ji; coming and going there shall be no disaster. The king prognosticated, saying, "It is extremely auspicious." Acting on this, we captured forty-one foxes and eight hornless deer.

Excerpts adapted from Robert Eno's translation, in Lopez 1996: 46–51.

events, celestial phenomena, sicknesses, childbearing, propitious or unpropitious times for specific activities, military operations, royal hunts and excursions, building of settlements and edifices, and performance of sacrifices and other forms of worship. For instance, the topics of divination might be concerned with the success of forthcoming harvest or the outcome of military campaign contemplated by the king and his advisors (exemplified by the first two entries in "Oracle bones inscriptions" box). Among the notable features of most of the inscriptions is their prosaic character and utilitarian orientation. There is also a pervasive sense of connectedness between the human and divine realms, which was at the core of Shang approaches to religiosity. For better or worse, human life and destiny were perceived as being inextricably linked with the supernatural world; furthermore, the relationship between the two was not always harmonious, as there were ample occasions for tension, antagonism, or adversity.

Worship of gods and ancestors under the Shang

The Shang pantheon had a hierarchical structure. At its apex was the aforementioned supreme deity, referred to as Di or Shangdi (sometimes translated as the Lord on High; also possible to render as Supreme Lord or High God). Shangdi was believed to have authority and control over both the sociopolitical and natural realms. The origins of this deity are uncertain. According to some scholars, originally Shangdi was perhaps an archaic high ancestor of the Shang ruling house. However, there is little evidence to prove that hypothesis, especially given that in key ritual contexts

Shangdi was treated quite differently from the royal ancestors, as he was not integrated into the official sacrificial pantheon.

Shangdi's power was deemed superior to that of all other preternatural beings, although the range of his powers and the areas of his jurisdiction seem to have been somewhat vaguely defined, as they overlapped with those of other deities and the royal ancestors. From what we can tell, Shangdi was often regarded as being aloof and inaccessible, highly potent yet removed from people's everyday lives and concerns. Consequently, usually no routine sacrificial offerings were made directly to him. Humans had limited ritual means at their disposal—or perhaps even no means at all—by which they could control his behavior, although they tried to approach and mollify him, often with the help of the ancestors.

There was an aura of mystery surrounding Shangdi, who apparently was conceived in fairly abstract terms, with loosely defined qualities and functions. He reigned over all other spirits and divinities, as a king would rule over his royal court. Divine authority was thus conceived in ways that were analogous to the configuration of its early counterpart, and the same applied to the distribution and circulation of power within the two realms, divine and human. Shangdi could be helpful to the Shang people, for instance by providing timely rain and creating favorable climatic conditions, which were essential for agricultural production. When displeased, however, he could also cause lots of trouble, for instance by manipulating the natural world and causing floods or draughts, by sending hail or thunder, or perhaps by causing disastrous epidemics. It was also believed that he could also bring about misfortune by withholding divine assistance during military campaigns, or even by bringing about attacks by outside forces.

The same propensity to dispense both fortune and misfortune was also ascribed to the other spirits or deities, whose relationship with the humans was not always harmonious and could easily take an antagonistic turn. An element of caprice or whim could be discerned in the manner Shangdi and other divinities manifested their power and exerted influence over the human realm. Given such uncertainties, the primary goal of Shang rituals, especially of divinations and sacrifices, was to ascertain, appease, and influence the otherworldly powers, so that they can perchance be persuaded to offer their assistance, or at least to abstain from causing trouble to the king and his subjects.

Shangdi was said to preside over an array of nature deities or spirits, who were responsive to his commands. This included various deities associated with natural phenomena, such as the sun, the rain, and the wind. Prayers and sacrifices were regularly made to these divinities, whose appeasement and help were deemed essential, given the agricultural foundations of Shang society. Similarly, there were deities connected with important features of the natural environment or the local landscape, such as particular mountains and rivers. Within the immediate topography of the Shang dominion, especially important were the deities linked with the Yellow river and Mt. Song, the central sacred mountain, located in the vicinity of Luoyang and Zhengzhou (in present-day Henan province), which centuries later became closely linked with Buddhism and Daoism.

Another important group of divinities within the Shang pantheon were the spirits of the royal ancestors. The belief in their existence was premised on the notion that there is life after death, albeit of a somewhat different kind. The ancestors were common objects of worship and propitiation, and the making of regular sacrificial offerings to them at the ancestral temple was an important aspect of official Shang religion. The items offered to the ancestors during ritual sacrifices included alcoholic drinks, grains, or slaughtered animals (such as cattle and sheep); at certain occasions there were also human sacrifices. Human sacrifices were also part of Shang burial customs. They frequently involved family members and other dependants, who were buried together with their departed lord. The tombs also contained a number of funerary objects, especially various treasures the deceased was supposed to be able to use in the afterlife, such as bronzes, jades, weapons, and ceramics.

Typically the scale of the burial site and the number and refinement of the funerary objects reflected the status and wealth of the deceased, with the largest tombs being those of the Shang kings. The point of death involved important transformation, as the spirits of the deceased turned into ancestors, who were then integrated into a ritual scheme devised and perpetuated by the living descendents. Accordingly, much attention was given to proper burial sites and mortuary practices, which were highly ritualized. The burials of high-ranking women followed a similar pattern to those of their male counterparts, usually reproduced on a smaller scale.

The Shang people believed that the otherworld and this world were coextensive. Not being radically disjointed, the two worlds intimately implicated each other. Consequently, the departed royal ancestors had influence on what was happening among the living. Moreover, as their primary living descendants, the Shang kings had access to them and were able to tap into their knowledge and power. Death essentially marked a change in existential status that to some extent redefined the relationship between members of the same family lineage, namely the lineage of the royal house. Or to put it differently, while death did not alter the fundamental nature of kinship relationships—a person remained the son of his deceased father, for instance—it brought about significant changes in the channels of communication that linked the two parties, as the living had to resort to rituals means such as sacrifice in order to commune with their departed relations. For those reasons, it was important to establish proper links and channels of communication with the royal ancestors, primarily via the performance of divination rituals and sacrificial offerings. By such means the Shang kings were able to secure the aid and blessings of their ancestors—who were also capable of interceding on the kings' behalf with the various preternatural powers, including Shangdi—or at least to appease the ancestors and avoid their censure or wrath.

The relationship between the departed ancestors and the living descendants was conceived in reciprocal terms. Both groups needed each other. The living provided the dead with sumptuous tombs and funeral offerings; they also performed regular sacrifices on behalf of the departed ancestors and paid homage to them. On the other hand, the dead extended their blessings and protection on the living. It is also important to note that the king had a virtual monopoly on the prerogative to commune and interact with the royal ancestors, whose exalted existence and otherworldly power sanctified his rule. The king effectively occupied a special position in the central kinship community of the royal house, which crossed the conventional lines of demarcation that separated the dead from the living. This granted him a unique relationship with a key source of superhuman power, mainly expressed in terms of kinship ties, which in turn bestowed on his reign an aura of socioreligious legitimacy. We can postulate that the ancestral cult was also adopted by the other aristocratic elites in Shang society, who worshiped their ancestors in a similar manner.

Changing attitudes towards divinity during the Zhou era

The cult of ancestors, also dubbed as "ancestor worship," continued during the Zhou dynasty, as an integral part of official rituals and a key aspect of prevalent religious worldview. During this period there was an expansion of the parameters of the ancestral cult, which came to involve the ancestors of the common people as well. The worship of ancestors was also infused with ethical dimensions and given a distinctive moral cast. The ethical underpinnings of ancestral worship primarily centered on the moral concerns of the extended family. Within such framework, the relationship among individual members and the overall structure of authority within the extended family were largely expressed in religious terms. The relationship with the ancestors thus became an extension of the parent-child relationship, which was primarily conceived in patrilineal terms, although female ancestors were also accorded respect and veneration. As a result, the notion of filial piety assumed a central position. The ancestral cult and the virtue of filial piety remained important religious ideals and fundamental cultural values throughout the subsequent history of Chinese civilization, and they still remain important today.

Another important development during the Shang-Zhou transition was the gradual replacement of Shangdi with Tian (lit. "Heaven," also meaning "sky") as the supreme deity of the Chinese pantheon. While there were analogies and similarities between these two conceptions of supreme divinity, a major new element introduced during the Zhou period was the representation of Heaven as a moral force that was unambiguously good. Although Heaven supposedly had control over human life and destiny, within the Zhou scheme it exercised its power according to exacting moral standards, in contrast to the capricious or whimsical behavior that was earlier ascribed to Shangdi. The concept of Heaven carried certain anthropomorphic connotations, especially early on, but it is misleading to equate it with Western conceptions of an omnipotent God who functions as creator of the world, along the strands of belief that developed within the monotheistic religions of Judaism and Christianity.

As a supreme deity or power, Heaven's dominion and authority extended to both the natural and human worlds, which were not perceived as being drastically disjoined. Heaven's functions included those of a creative force that is the origin of the myriad things and beings, an omnipotent ruler of all of creation, and an impartial judge who evaluates and responds to human behavior. Within the Zhou context, especially important was the role of Heaven as the foundation and custodian of the prevalent sociopolitical order. Zhou texts also depict Heaven as being concerned about people's wellbeing and moral character, which led to the setting up of ethical standards that foster virtuous behavior and social harmony.

The significant ethical turn that occurred during the Zhou period was characterized by newly formulated humanistic values and moral concerns which changed the foundations of the human relationship with the supernatural realm and redefined the basic attitudes towards divine authority. From a Zhou perspective, Heaven was not simply content with receiving people's offerings and veneration, but was primarily concerned with their moral character, at the individual and the communal levels. Following the will or design of Heaven brought positive rewards, while transgressing against it resulted in misfortune and punishment. For instance, if displeased, Heaven could affect natural disasters or different kinds of scourge. These kinds of ideas were subsequently expressed in classical texts that became especially influential after they were appropriated by the Confucian tradition, which made them a centerpiece of its canon (see Chapter 2).

These kinds of moralistic concerns and attitudes were also applied to the basic patterns of human interactions with the various spirits and deities, which increasingly became expressed in moral terms (see the quote from the *Zuo zhuan*). This transformed

---

The role of virtue in the human interactions with the spirits, according to the *Zuo zhuan* (Zuo's Tradition)

It is not simply that ghosts and spirits are attracted to human beings: it is virtue that attracts them. Hence the "Book of Zhou" in the *Book of Documents* says, "August Heaven has no partial affections; it supports only the virtuous."... So unless one is virtuous, the people will not be in harmony and the spirits will not partake of one's offerings. What the spirits are attracted to is one's virtue.

Translation adapted from Sommer 1995: 25.

the old way of looking at ritual sacrifices as a system of quid pro quo exchanges, primarily driven by pragmatic concerns, in which the mere performance of rituals was deemed to be sufficient means for the procurement of good fortune and mundane benefits. Instead, there was a shift in emphasis on personal morality, although that does not necessarily imply that utilitarian considerations became less of a concern for the Zhou people. While much of the old ritual façade remained, there was an important reassessment and reconceptualization of the human relationship with the supernatural order. Within the new paradigm, the deities became responsive to the proper moral conduct of those who supplicated or worshiped them, rather than to the offerings that were presented to them. The deities rewarded the virtuous and bestowed good fortune on those who were benevolent, while bringing misfortune to those who behaved in immoral ways.

Such outlook brought about notable changes in the principles of ritual sacrifice. Sacrificial rituals were supposed to be performed with a proper frame of mind, becoming occasions for manifesting the inner virtue of the persons making the sacrifice. They were part of a far-reaching humanistic turn, a this-worldly reorientation with important religious, political, and ethical implications, which blossomed during the Warring States period. A central feature of these developments—at least in certain intellectual milieus, which included the Confucians and other groups discussed in the next chapter—was an overarching concern with social structures and human affairs. Increasingly the central issues related to human existence were discussed in humanistic terms, without undue reference to otherworldly powers and divine authority. That influenced the prevalent conceptions of Heaven, which over time came to be perceived in more abstract terms, as an impersonal principle or a natural law of sorts. A closely related aspect of this general shift in thinking was a tendency to locate divinity within the individual. Human beings came to be perceived as having the spiritual potential to radically transform themselves and assume divine or transcendental qualities: to become sages, immortals, or gods (and eventually also bodhisattvas and Buddhas, once Buddhism entered China).

Cultural heroes and sage-kings

In addition to the three main categories of divinities surveyed above—the supreme deity (Shangdi or Tian), nature spirits, and ancestors—another important group of extraordinary beings venerated by the ancient Chinese were the various cultural heroes and sage-kings. These were mythical figures, believed to have played key cultural roles in remote antiquity, during a primeval age that coincided with the dawn of Chinese civilization. Their remarkable exploits and extraordinary deeds were recounted in a series of myths, which extolled their seminal contributions to the development of culture and highlighted the important benefits they brought to humanity. These myths purport to convey important information about the origins of key aspects of human life and culture, including writing, medicine, agriculture, animal husbandry, sericulture, music, cooking, metallurgy, and forming of sociopolitical institutions. Their main heroes, who are often depicted as multifaceted or multifunctional, were supposedly the first ones to teach humanity some of the key techniques and cultural skills that provided the foundations for the development of enduring civilization.

Among the best-known and most revered of the archaic cultural heroes and sage-kings is the Yellow Emperor (Huangdi), who occupies a lofty position in the divine pantheon, even though his myth is relatively late, probably originating during the Eastern Zhou period. Although early on the Yellow Emperor was not a major figure, gradually his persona and the symbolic imagery associated with him underwent a far-reaching transformation, until eventually he assumed the status of foremost cultural hero. In the process, a copious amount of mythic lore grew around him. Initially the Yellow Emperor was depicted as a warrior figure, albeit with pacifist inclinations, that battled and defeated various evil forces. Later he came to be portrayed as the progenitor of Chinese civilization.

Some myths attribute to the Yellow Emperor the discovery of making fire and the invention of cooking. Others credit him with the domestication of animals and a host of other inventions: the cart, coinage, compass, houses, clothes, devices for measuring weight and time, burial customs, astronomy, medicine; he is even credited with creating a football game. Moreover, the Yellow Emperor is often portrayed as the putative ancestor of the Chinese people—an identity that is still evoked by present-day Chinese, who regard themselves as his descendants—and he is also an important figure in the Daoist pantheon. To this day, myths centered on the Yellow Emperor are transmitted and retold in China. There are also occasional performances of sacrificial rituals dedicated to him, some of them attended by prominent officials of the Communist Party.

Besides the Yellow Emperor, other important mythical heroes are the three sagely kings of antiquity: Yao, Shun, and Yu. Throughout the history of imperial China their successive reigns were commonly invoked and venerated as a utopian golden age, when social harmony prevailed and there was flawless governance. Yao is usually depicted as an enlightened ruler, renowned for his benevolence and concern about the people's welfare. Confucian texts and other writings often evoke him as a paradigmatic example of perfect ruler, a sagely model to be followed by later generations of emperors. He is especially praised for his decision to abdicate the throne and pass the reigns of power to his most worthy and capable subject, Shun, who at the time was a simple farmer.

According to traditional accounts, Shun married Yao's two daughters, who were very virtuous and wise, and who helped him in the management of his domain. Shun is celebrated as a paragon of virtue, particularly renowned for his exemplary filial piety. There are many stories that recount his filial behavior, even though his parents were wicked people who, together with his evil stepbrother, mistreated him badly. Shun followed the precedent set by Yao and bequeathed the throne to the person of greatest virtue and accomplishments among his subjects: the brave, dedicated, and hardworking Yu.

Yu, often called Yu the Great, is best known for his memorable feat of controlling the great floods that allegedly engulfed the ancient world. The central myth that recounts these events and Yu's participation in them is very ancient, as can be seen from an inscription on a bronze vessel from the eighth century BCE. The Chinese tradition celebrated Yu's accomplishment as a prime example of selfless devotion to public service. His noble dedication and strenuous work at battling the devastating floods eventually paid off. Yu was able to restore order into the world and rescue the people, which earned him a special place in the Chinese pantheon of great heroes and worthies.

Various stories recount how Yu ardently continued the strenuous work on controlling the great floods, a colossal project that was started by his father. He allegedly spent thirteen years battling the floods; he was so single-minded in his dedication to the crucial task at hand, the ancient stories tell us, that during the whole period he did not stop even once to visit his home. Eventually he succeeded in his monumental undertaking, primarily by establishing a system of dykes and channels that led the water to drain into the sea. Beside his ingenious use of engineering skill and know-how, in the course of his epic battle with the floods Yu is said to have performed numerous miracles and to have defeated various monsters and other uncanny creatures. Yu is also credited with the establishment of the first Chinese dynasty, the mythical Xia dynasty. According to tradition, he left the dynastic throne to his son, which became a model that was followed by subsequent royal houses.

The three sagely kings of antiquity, together with the Yellow Emperor and his somewhat obscure grandson Zhuanxu, are often grouped together and identified as the Five Emperors (see box). There are also variant versions of this grouping of archaic sage-kings, however, and it seems that the myth of Yu is earlier than the myth of the Yellow Emperor. Another prominent set of divine kings, which according to

The Five Emperors (*wudi*)

- The Yellow Emperor (Huangdi)
- Zhuanxu
- Yao
- Shun
- Yu the Great

The Three Sovereigns (*sanhuang*)

- Heavenly Sovereign (Tianhuang)
- Earthly Sovereign (Dihuang)
- Humanly Sovereign (Renhuang)

popular mythical lore ruled during the prehistoric period, are the so-called Three Sovereigns (see box), although this classification is fairly late, probably from the late Warring States era. Frequently their identities are constructed in terms of the classical tripartite division of the world—heaven, earth, and humanity—but there are variations on this list as well (see next section).

Traditionally, Chinese historical works—such as Sima Qian's (c. 145–86 BCE) immensely influential *Historical Records (Shiji)*—presented these figures as historical personages, especially as sagely kings who ruled during an archaic period and established the foundations of Chinese civilization. Such historicized representations reflect a common tendency to fuse the mythical period and the historical age, as well as to blur the lines of demarcation that separate the mythical and historical modes of narration. Some scholars have suggested that the five emperors and other similar heroic figures originally were archaic gods, who during the Zhou period were subjected to demythologizing and rationalizing processes, as a result of which they were transformed into cultural heroes and bestowed with distinctive human qualities. In scholarly literature this process is sometimes referred to as "reverse euhemerisation."

The notion of euhemerisation was originally applied in reference to a process of deification that is said to have unfolded within the context of ancient Greek mythology. It was initially proposed by the ancient Greek writer and mythographer Euhemerus (fl. late 4th cent. BCE). Euhemerus reinterpreted Greek religion by proposing a new theory about the origin of the gods that constituted the Greek pantheon and the myths that were told about them. According to him, the gods were deified human beings. For instance, Zeus was originally a revered king, who became an object of worship after his death. Similarly, popular mythical accounts that feature various gods are reflections of historical events that unfolded in the distant past, which were subsequently reframed and retold in a distinct, religiously-inflected mode of narration. Accordingly, while in the Greek case we have an argument about human beings being deified and turned into gods, in China we seem to be facing a reverse process of archaic gods becoming humanized and historicized, thereby being transformed into primeval sage-kings.

Chinese mythology

The stories and related imagery about the archaic heroes and sagely kings described in the previous section are part of a larger body of mythical narratives, primarily preserved in ancient texts, some of which are still transmitted and retold in modern China. Generally speaking, there is a lack of scholarly consensus on how to define the category of myth. In part that is due the fact that various scholars approach the study of mythology through the interpretive lenses of diverse academic disciplines, such as anthropology, psychology, literary studies, or history of religions. At the most basic level, myths are ancient stories or archaic narratives, commonly featuring supernatural beings or primordial heroes. Usually they are told in prose, but they can also assume verse form.

Myths often explain in symbolic terms the origins of the world and natural phenomena, shed light on key features of human behavior, epitomize peculiar facets of culture, or convey information about significant features of social life. Myths are sometimes characterized as "sacred narratives," but a number of myths—in China and elsewhere—are not directly concerned with divine beings or other aspects of the sacred realm (and, at any rate, the notion of "sacred" itself is vague and open to diverse interpretations). Some definitions of myth can be somewhat restrictive, while others are broad in scope. Here I am siding with the second view, namely I am employing the category of myth in a fairly expansive sense.

Unlike the people of ancient Greece and Rome, or even ancient Japan, the Chinese did not create an integrated system of myths or a canon of mythological writings; or at least we do not have any evidence of such systematization, in large part because early on the myths were probably transmitted orally. In ancient China myths were constantly-changing narratives, subject to ongoing processes of revision and modification. While the origins of many of the Chinese myths are very ancient, as a rule they are preserved in relatively late texts, in particular from the later part of the Zhou era and the Han dynasty. Moreover, although there is a wide array of Chinese myths, they usually survive in a truncated or fragmentary form. To further complicate things, many myths appear in several different versions, and normally they are incorporated into a variety of larger works, whose authors' for the most part were primarily concerned with other topics and issues.

When looking at the history of early mythical narratives, we can discern ongoing processes of transformation and marginalization, influenced to a large degree by rationalizing tendencies, which were especially brought to the fore with the gradual institution of Confucian hegemony. As part of their ongoing transformation, many myths were historicized and rationalized—or to put it differently, they were essentially demythologized—as we saw in the above discussion about the ancient sage-kings. As they were integrated into larger works, ancient mythological accounts were modified and made to accord with the styles and intents of their host texts.

Often that meant that they were refashioned and presented as integral parts of larger historical, philosophical, or literary narratives.

There are very few early works that provide substantial amount of materials for the study of ancient myths. Notable examples of such texts are the *Classic of Mountains and Seas (Shanghai jing)*, a treasure-trove of mythical lore that was probably composed around the third century BCE, and *Huainanzi* (lit. "the masters of Huainan"), compiled around 139 BCE by the prince of Huainan and his scholarly associates, which unlike most other sources contains complete versions of some early myths. On the basis of these texts and other sources, scholars have been able to study prevalent mythical motifs and characters, and analyze a large assortment of myths composed in ancient China.

Chinese myths feature numerous gods, divine heroes, and other mythical figures, including strange birds and animals. They also cover a broad array of themes and ideas. Prominent examples of mythical themes include the creation of the world and the origins of humanity, the births and acts of the gods, the achievements and tribulations of the semi-divine heroes of antiquity, the unusual character and topography of mythical lands, and the founding of local ethnic groups or dynasties. While for reasons of space we cannot go over the whole range of mythical themes and protagonists, we can illustrate some of the basic features of Chinese myths by having a closer look at three important mythical characters: Shennong, Fuxi, and Nuwa. Sometimes these three are identified as the aforementioned Three Sovereigns, and they are all worshiped to this day.

Shennong (Divine Farmer) is among the most important cultural heroes of China's distant past. He is especially associated with the invention of agriculture. In some stories he is attributed with a miraculous birth and unique physique; one version of his myth represents him as having the head of a dragon, which was purportedly due to the fact that his mother copulated with a divine dragon. As indicated by his name, Shennong is primarily identified as the inventor of farming; he is the best-known among the several gods of agriculture. He is also said to have introduced important farming tools, such as the hoe, the axe, and the plow. Other important discoveries linked with him are the rudiments of irrigation, the first calendar, various cooking implements, and the drinking of tea. He is even said to have devised some of the ancient musical instruments. Furthermore, in ancient China he was credited with the invention of medicine and the use of plants for healing. In that role he was identified as the "author" of an ancient book on medicine and pharmacopoeia, which was among the earliest medical books composed in China. To this day Shennong is worshiped all over China, and there are numerous temples, shrines, and festival dedicated to him (see Figure 1.4).

Fuxi is another prominent mythical figure and key fixture in the ancient pantheon. Archaic myths portray him as many-sided god and seminal cultural hero. He is principally depicted as a prodigious inventor who benefited early humanity

Figure 1.4　Shrine dedicated to Shennong (Baoan Temple, Taipei, Taiwan)

by teaching it a number of important technical skills and cultural practices. For instance, he is linked with the invention of writing, music, and cooking, along with the domestication of animals and the use of nets for fishing and hunting. He is also credited with the invention of divination, in the forms of the "eight trigrams" (*bagua*) that are featured in the *Classic of Change* (*Yijing*, discussed in the next chapter). Some myths describe Fuxi's birth in supernatural terms, while others depict him as possessing extra-human attributes; for instance, his lower body is depicted as assuming the shape of a snake.

Nuwa is among the best-known and most significant female figures in Chinese mythology. Some cosmogonic myths depict Nuwa as a powerful creator deity. She is said to have fashioned the first human beings, molding them with her own hands out of yellow earth and mud (see "Nuwa creates humans" box). The early figures were done carefully and they became the aristocracy, according to a popular version of the story; in contrast, the later figures were done in haste by the exhausted goddess, and they turned into the common people. Another popular group of myths depicts Nuwa as savioress of the world. Once upon a time, there was a disorder of cosmic proportions caused by a breakage of the sky. That happened when (according to one version of the story), in the aftermath of a ferocious fight with another god, a powerful god knocked and damaged one of the four large pillars that holds the sky.

Nuwa makes human beings out of yellow earth

People say that when initially heaven and earth opened and unfolded, human beings did not yet exist. Nuwa kneaded yellow earth and fashioned human beings out of it. Though she worked feverishly, she did not have enough strength to finish her task, so she drew her cord in a furrow through the mud and lifted it to make human beings. That is why rich aristocrats are the human beings she made from the yellow earth, while ordinary poor people are the human beings she made from the cord's furrow.

Translation adapted from Birrell 1993: 35.

Figure 1.5   Nuwa with a serpent body (source: *Myths and Legends of China* [1922; republished by Dover Publications], by Edward Theodore Chalmers Werner; courtesy of Wikimedia Commons)

Nuwa was able to repair the pillar and mend the broken sky, thereby restoring order into the world.

The prominent status of Nuwa points to the importance assigned to the feminine principle in ancient Chinese mythology. Another example of important female divinity is Queen Mother of the West (Xiwangmu), a supreme goddess that purportedly presided over a western paradise. She was later incorporated into the Daoist pantheon, and we will return to her again when we discuss the place of women in religious Daoism (see Chapter 4).

Fuxi and Nuwa are often portrayed together as a pair. In that case, they are known as the progenitors or ancestors of humanity. Their relationship is somewhat ambiguous, as Nuwa is described as both the sister and the consort of Fuxi. According to this myth, the origins of humanity can be traced back to their incestuous relationship: a marriage between a brother and a sister that occurred at the original time of creation, when they were the only two human beings living alone in a primordial world. Like Fuxi, Nuwa's physical likeness is often presented as part woman (which can be either the head or the upper half of the body), part serpent (the bottom part). A common representation of the two as a pair depicts them with human upper bodies, while the lower parts of their bodies are in the form of two serpents that are intertwined.

Mandate of Heaven

We already noted that in addition to their political and social roles, the Shang kings performed important religious functions. Within the Shang context, politics and religion—together with economy, society, and culture—were inseparable and there was no clear line of demarcation between them. In view of that, some scholars have argued about the prevalence of shamanic conception of kingship during the Shang era, with the king functioning as a head of shamanic cult. Such structure was based on a profound sense of connectedness and continuity between the divine and human worlds. In his putative capacity as an intermediary between the two worlds, the king was in a unique position to establish and sustain important links of communication between humanity and the preternatural powers above. That enabled him to intercede on behalf of the people and ask for divine help and protection. The primary means for that were the divinations, sacrifices, and other rituals described above. Such conception of kingship purportedly reflected the central role that shamanism played in Chinese politics and culture during the Shang era, although it is also worth mentioning that some scholars have rejected this argument and have questioned the applicability of the notion of shamanism within the Chinese context.

The establishment of the Zhou dynasty is often regarded as one of the seminal events in Chinese history. After their defeat of the Shang, the early Zhou rulers claimed that they received moral authority to rule directly from Heaven. Their conquest was thus not simply a change of regime brought about by the force of arms; rather, it was the realization of a divine plan. Early historical records, written from a

Zhou perspective, depict the final rulers of the Shang dynasty as incorrigibly corrupt and decadent, while the Zhou conquest of the Shang is presented as a fulfillment of heavenly mandate. The former Shang kings once had the moral right to rule, but due to the loss of virtue their descendants forfeited that privilege, having violated the moral norms of Heaven. Consequently, it was now up to the Zhou kings to rule over earth and serve Heaven, presupposing a peculiar reformulation of the dynamic relationship between the vital agency of Heaven and the king's authority to rule over his subjects. This set of ideas developed into the important notion of "mandate of Heaven" (*tianming*), which became a philosophical foundation of Zhou rule.

The early Zhou kings sanctified their rule and legitimized the new dynasty by claiming a special connection with Heaven, symbolized by their assumption of the title of "Son of Heaven" (*tianzi*), which continued to be used by the rulers of various dynasties throughout subsequent Chinese history. In effect, the Zhou kings came to be perceived as earthly counterparts of Heaven, although they were not deemed to possess divine persona or supernatural attributes. While the kings enjoyed absolute temporal power, they also served as agents of Heaven and exercised their royal authority on behalf of Heaven. In that capacity, each king functioned as a crucial link between Heaven and humanity. He was deemed to possess unique virtue and ability to decipher the grand designs or wishes of Heaven. He also had divine sanction to establish legitimate government and rule over the people. In theory, there was no temporal limitation on Heaven's mandate, as long as the rulers of a particular dynasty were just and behaved morally. However, the mandate could be revoked abruptly if individual ruler became despotic and unjust. According to popular belief, revocation of the heavenly mandate was presaged by natural calamities and other portents that manifested Heaven's displeasure with the current ruler and his dynasty. If that were to happen, Heaven would transfer its mandate to a new ruler with suitable moral character, who would then be able to establish new and legitimate dynasty.

The notion of mandate of Heaven continued to occupy central position in discussions of statecraft and political authority throughout the course of Chinese history, until the modern period. Consequently, Chinese history came to be perceived as a succession of dynasties that have received the heavenly mandate. The early reign of each dynasty, especially the longer lasting ones, was typically portrayed in terms of an auspicious beginning under a virtuous and enlightened ruler, closely followed by an initial period of dynastic growth and consolidation under his talented descendants. After that, there will be a prolonged period of political stability and social equilibrium. Finally, the end of the dynasty typically involves descent into chaos under its final ruler(s), who generally are characterized as incompetent and corrupt, with outbreaks of rebellions and other disasters. The cycle repeats itself with the establishment of new dynasty that had inherited the authentic heavenly mandate, which ushers a new chapter in Chinese history.

In the course of Chinese imperial history the set of ideas associated with the mandate of Heaven continued to function as basic principles that governed the transfer of power and procurement of legitimacy in the political arena, which accompanied the establishment of new regimes. Of course, actual historical reality was somewhat messier, as often there were competing claims to Heaven's mandate. That went together with open uncertainties and willful manipulations of the signs and portents that supposedly communicated Heaven's desires and designs for humanity. On the other hand, the notion that earthly rule derived its legitimacy from a divine source, which was morally good, helped put ethical concerns and moral principles at the forefront of Chinese discussions about the exercise of political power and the structuring of government.

Key points

- China has one of the oldest civilizations in world history. The earliest dynasty for which we have ample archeological evidence is the Shang, which was succeeded by the Zhou dynasty. The end of the Zhou era marks the beginning of Chinese imperial history.
- Divinatory rituals that featured the application of fire on oracle bones were important aspects of political and religious life at the Shang capital. The oracle bone inscriptions provide us with important information about the religious beliefs, existential concerns, and everyday activities of the Shang kings and their people.
- The Shang pantheon was structured hierarchically, with Shangdi, the supreme deity, ruling over a host of nature deities and ancestors. The royal ancestors were important objects of worship and propitiation, as well as a key source of sociopolitical legitimacy for the Shang kings and the royal family.
- During the Zhou period we witness an expansion of the ancestral cult, which increasingly came to incorporate moral concerns centered on the family, including the virtue of filial piety. Another noteworthy development was the replacement of Shangdi with Heaven as the supreme deity, which was given a distinctly moral cast.
- In the course of the Zhou era there was a shift in emphasis towards new humanistic values and ethical concerns, which led to far-reaching redefining of the human relationship with the supernatural realm and change in attitudes towards divine authority.
- The ancient Chinese revered a number of archaic cultural heroes and sage-kings, such as the Yellow Emperor, Yao, and Shun, who were credited with the discovery of key aspects of human life and celebrated for their seminal contributions to the development of culture. Their decisive exploits were

originally told in mythopoeic modes of narration, but gradually they were humanized and historicized.

- While the ancient Chinese did not create a comprehensive system of mythology or a canon of mythological writings, there is a broad array of Chinese myths, usually extant in fragmentary form. Chinese myths cover a range of themes and feature diverse protagonists, such as Shennong, Fuxi, and Nuwa.
- After their conquest of the Shang, the early Zhou rulers asserted their moral authority to govern by invoking the notion of mandate of Heaven. That idea became firmly established and throughout Chinese history it continued to function as an important principle that governed the transfer of political power and the establishment of dynastic legitimacy.

Discussion questions

1. Compare and contrast the Shang versus the Zhou conceptions of the supreme deity, and explain the significance of the differences between the two within the larger context of evolving conceptions of divinity in ancient China.
2. Trace the emergence of ancestor worship in ancient China and explain the rise of filial piety as a central virtue within a distinctive moral universe.
3. Discuss the similarities and the differences between ancient China and Greece that pertain to the function and status of mythology within the two cultures. Additionally, clarify the contrasts between the origins and character of the mythical gods/heroes that developed within the two ancient civilizations.

Further reading

Birrell, Anne. 1993. *Chinese Mythology: An Introduction.* Baltimore, MD: Johns Hopkins University Press.

Birrell, Anne, trans. 1999. *The Classic of Mountains and Seas.* London: Penguin Books.

Chang, Kwang-chih. 1980. *Shang Civilization.* New Haven, CT: Yale University Press.

Chang, Kwang-chih. 1983. *Art, Myth, and Ritual: The Path to Political Authority in Ancient China.* Cambridge, MA: Harvard University Press.

Chang, Kwang-chih, Pingfang Xu, Liancheng Lu, and Sarah Allan. 2005. *The Formation of Chinese Civilization: An Archaeological Perspective.* New Haven, CT: Yale University Press.

Ching, Julia. 1997. *Mysticism and Kingship in China: The Heart of Chinese Wisdom.* Cambridge: Cambridge University Press.

Falkenhausen, Lothar von. 2006. *Chinese Society in the Age of Confucius (1000-250 BC): The Archaeological Evidence.* Los Angeles, CA: Cotsen Institute of Archaeology, University of California.

Keightley, David N. 1978. *Sources of Shang History: The Oracle-Bone Inscriptions of Bronze Age China.* Berkeley, CA: University of California Press.

Keightley, David N. 2000. *The Ancestral Landscape: Time, Space, and Community in Late Shang China (ca. 1200-1045 BC).* Berkeley, CA: Institute for Asian Studies, University of California, Berkeley.

Poo, Mu-chou. 1998. *In Search of Personal Welfare: A View of Ancient Chinese Religion.* Albany, NY: State University of New York Press.

Puett, Michael J. 2002. *To Become a God: Cosmology, Sacrifice, and Self-Divinization in Early China.* Cambridge, MA: Harvard University Asia Center.

Thorp, Robert L. 2006. *China in the Early Bronze Age: Shang Civilization.* Philadelphia, PA: University of Pennsylvania Press.

Xu, Zhuoyun, and Katheryn M. Linduff. 1988. *Western Chou Civilization.* New Haven, CT: Yale University Press.

Yang, Lihui, and Deming An. 2005. *Handbook of Chinese Mythology.* Santa Barbara, CA: ABC-CLIO. Republished 2008, Oxford: Oxford University Press.

2 The classical Confucian tradition

In this chapter

For over two millennia the Confucian tradition occupied a central position and exerted significant influence on the various spheres of life in China, including politics, society, culture, and religion. With the collapse of the imperial state and the customary way of life in the early twentieth century, Confucianism lost much of its traditional prestige and influence, but its basic principles still continue to shape the values and behaviors of many people in China and the rest of East Asia. This is the first of two chapters on Confucianism, covering the formative epoch of the tradition's history: from its early origins during the time of Confucius (c. 552–479 BCE) some twenty-five centuries ago, through the gradual elaboration of its teachings and their codification into a classical form, and ultimately its break into the Chinese mainstream, marked by its acceptance as an ideology of the imperial state during the early part of the Han dynasty (206 BCE–220 CE).

Main topics

- The many faces of the Confucian tradition.
- The "Five Classics" and the historical context behind the rise of Confucianism.
- The life and times of Confucius.
- Basic principles and teachings of Confucius.
- Competing ideas propounded by the Legalists and the followers of Mozi.
- Diversity of perspectives within the early Confucian movement.
- Grand Confucian synthesis of the early Han period.

Various faces of Confucianism

The term "Confucianism" has fairly recent origins. It was invented by Jesuit missionaries upon their arrival in China in the sixteenth century (see Chapter 9). They used it to describe what they perceived to be "the sect of the literati." Confucianism is thus somewhat of a misnomer, or perhaps a useful even if a bit confusing neologism. It roughly covers what in pre-modern China was usually referred to by terms such as the "school (or tradition) of the scholars" (*rujia*) or the "teaching of the scholars" (*rujiao*). The scholarly followers of this tradition were called *ru*, which can be rendered as "literati" or "scholars," but usually it is referred to as "Confucians." The term *ru* initially covered a class of specialists who transmitted the texts and rituals of the ancient Zhou dynasty. Those *ru* who were subsumed within the broader tradition we call Confucianism performed archaic rituals, revered Confucius, were steeped in ancient texts traditionally associated with the great sage, and espoused time-honored values and principles.

Many of the *ru* were also involved in government service, and as a group they esteemed the holding of public office. Renowned for their learning, which often went together with an air of cultural refinement, they constituted an elite segment of Chinese society. Their advantageous status brought many privileges, but also certain responsibilities. Theirs was a somewhat amorphous tradition that lacked many of the trappings and institutions of organized religion, as known and experienced by Europeans at the time when the Christian missionaries entered China. Confucianism was also a many-sided tradition, with many faces. While it concurrently engaged and influenced various aspects of Chinese life—including social organization, political involvement, and educational activities—the Confucian tradition was marked by often fuzzy boundaries and somewhat tentative criteria of membership.

For a very long time, a primary feature of Confucianism was its role as the official ideology of the Chinese imperial state and the ruling elites. In that capacity, it provided a system of political philosophy, bureaucratic models and organizational structures for running the government, and blueprints for organizing the society and the economy. Unabashedly humanistic and this-worldly in its basic orientation— even if usually accepting of various divinities, including many of the gods of popular religion—Confucianism also provided a comprehensive ethical system that shaped public mores and personal behavior. Moreover, Confucian learning was a central part of the educational system in traditional China. Confucius was widely revered as a paradigmatic educator; emphasis on study and educational attainment, inspired in large part by him and his followers, became an essential cultural value. Some also see Confucianism, especially in its later incarnations (discussed in Chapter 8), as a philosophical tradition that engaged in rarefied metaphysical, ontological, and epistemological speculations about the nature of human life and ultimate reality.

In light of the above considerations, it is possible to question the characterization of Confucianism as a "religion." The problem is compounded by the facts that the term religion itself is problematic, especially given that its varied connotations or analytical frames of reference developed within Western milieus that in significant respect differ from the situation that obtained in China. There are many aspects of

Figure 2.1 Stele that contains the text of the *Classic of Filial Piety* (Forest of Stelae Museum, Xi'an)

Confucianism, however, that are either explicitly or implicitly religious, especially if we accept the kind of open-ended and broadminded understanding of religion suggested in the introduction. Throughout the history of Confucianism, there are recurrent expressions of belief in Heaven, often accompanied by efforts to divine its will and act accordingly. There is also a tacit acknowledgement of a supernatural realm, populated with various gods and spirits, along with a pervasive emphasis on ritual.

Furthermore, a central aspect of Confucianism in many of its historical manifestations is the quest for sagehood. Besides the study of canonical texts, this also involves various forms of spiritual cultivation, including contemplative practices. All of this makes it possible to talk of Confucianism as a religion, even if not in exactly the same terms as many might be accustomed from their background or familiarity with the monotheistic traditions of the West. The Confucian tradition's complex character and many-sided applications thus challenges us to rethink the basic contours and character of religion as a pervasive force in human history, as well as a field of academic study.

Another consideration, which sometimes unwittingly complicates the study of Confucianism, is its diffused character and the fact that it is embedded into a broader system of values and a traditional way of life. It is often debatable if particular aspects of Chinese mores or social practices can be traced back directly or solely to Confucian teachings and ideals, as they are also shaped by other systems of values and sources of meaning, which together serve as building blocks of larger patterns of social order and cultural identity. Moreover, as we observe the various changes and adaptations of Confucianism in response to new social circumstances or political demands, we also have to keep in mind the tradition's historical impact beyond China. The influence of Confucianism was especially strong in Korea and Vietnam, and to a smaller degree in Japan, with the conservative and long-lasting Korean Chosŏn (Joseon) dynasty (1392–1910) being arguably the most Confucian state in history.

The five "Confucian" classics

Although the putative founding of Confucianism as a distinct tradition is often traced back to Confucius, there were ancient systems of values, outlooks on life and society, and traditions of ritual that existed before and during his lifetime, which in profound ways inspired and shaped the development of early Confucianism. Some of those ancient perspectives and traditions were written down and transmitted in a variety of textual forms. Gradually they were codified into a coherent canon, with five texts becoming closely associated with the Confucian tradition under the rubric of the "Five Classics" (see box), a designation that is first attested in sources from the second century BCE. Tradition ascribes to Confucius the writing, compilation, or

The Five Classics

- *Book of Songs* (*Shijing*), an anthology of verses from the early Zhou through the Spring and Autumn periods.
- *Book of Change* (*Yijing*), a manual of divination from the Zhou dynasty, with Han-era additions.
- *Book of Documents* (*Shujing*), a chronological collection of speeches, proclamations, and stories about ancient rulers from the pre-Zhou and Zhou periods.
- *Spring and Autumn Annals* (*Chunqiu*), a chronicle of the state of Lu up to the time of Confucius.
- *Three* [*Texts about*] *Rituals* (*Sanli*), discussions of traditional rituals and governmental institutions, from the Warring States and the Han periods.

The *Book of Music* (*Yuejing*) was at some point known as the sixth classic, but it was lost before the Han period.

editing of these texts, although critical scholarship has shown that they had complex literary origins and were assembled together over extended time periods. Some of them incorporate materials that predate Confucius, but others include parts of considerably later provenance, including the Han dynasty.

Although traditionally these texts are interpreted as adopting a single point of view and conveying a unified message, in fact they contain a rich variety of materials, written at different times and in diverse styles. The texts also deal with a broad range of subjects and present a multiplicity of perspectives. One of the pitfalls in the study of these and other related texts is the tendency to categorize and read them in terms of a particular school of thought, namely Confucianism. It is helpful to keep in mind the possibility of interpreting the texts within the context of the intellectual debates that unfolded at the times of their creation, as well as in reference to their subsequent incorporation into the Confucian canon and their important uses as linchpins of Confucian ideology.

The *Book of Songs* (sometimes also translated as the *Book of Odes* or the *Classic of Poetry*) contains folk songs about common people's everyday existence and hymns about courtly life that go back to the Western Zhou period, namely before the time of Confucius. On the other hand, the *Book of Documents* (also called the *Classic of History*) purports to contain governmental documents and records of conversations and proclamations issued by ancient kings and other members of the ruling elites. While some of those materials go back to the early Zhou period, the text has a very convoluted history, and over the centuries it existed in a number of forms and editions. Scholars have established that substantial parts of the text were forged at much later dates, some as late as the fourth century of the Common Era.

The overriding concern with the recording of history that is evident in the *Book of Documents* is also a central element in the *Spring and Autumn Annals*. This text provides a chronological outline of events and activities centered on the rulers of the state of Lu, covering the historical period that obtained its name from the text's title. From early on and throughout successive dynastic epochs, respect for official historical narratives, along with the habitual use (and misuse) of historical records or precedents, became important parts of the classical tradition. Historical events and personages, especially those recorded in these two classics, were frequently evoked in all sorts of predicaments, from court discussions of governmental policy to personal reflections or flights of poetic imagination.

On the other end of the spectrum, the *Book of Change* is basically a manual of divination, over which generations of editors and commentators superimposed philosophical speculations about the manifold phenomenal transformations of the Dao (Way). Conceived as a unitary source of all things, the basic patterns of the Dao are expressed in the text by recourse to graphic symbols. Finally, detailed information about rituals and rules of conduct, along with idealized descriptions of governmental structures and institutions, are covered in the texts of varied provenance subsumed

Realization of the way according to the "Great Learning"

In ancient times, those who wanted to illuminate their bright virtue throughout the entire world first governed their states well. Wanting to govern their states well, they first managed their own families. Wanting to manage their families well, they first developed themselves. Wanting to develop themselves well, they first rectified their own minds. Wanting to rectify their minds, they first made their intentions sincere. Wanting to make their intentions sincere, they first extended their knowledge. The extension of knowledge is grounded in the investigation of things.

"Great Learning" (Daxue), *Record of Rites*; cf. Sommer 1995: 39.

within the three classics of rites, collectively known as the *Three [Texts about] Rituals (Sanli): Ceremonials and Rites (Yili), Record of Rites (Liji)*, and *Rites of Zhou (Zhouli)*. The *Record of Rites* contains the "Great Learning" (see box) and the "Doctrine of the Mean," which became especially popular from the Song dynasty onward with the growing influence of the Neo-Confucian tradition (see Chapter 8; for more on the Five Classics, see Nylan 2001).

Despite the somewhat tenuous connections between particular classics and the early Confucian tradition—and notwithstanding the fact that they were part of a broader cultural heritage and an ancient tradition of classical learning, rather than simply elements of a narrowly conceived Confucian canon—these texts played very important roles in the history of Confucianism. Until the onset of the modern period, they were widely read and were part of the upbringing of virtually every educated Chinese. They were also prominently featured in the curriculum for the state examinations (see Chapter 8). The classics' prominent status as valued repositories of ancient wisdom, as well as conveyors of enduring cultural archetypes and blueprints of civilization with continuing relevance, bolstered Confucian claims about their tradition's role as guardian and transmitter of the essence of Chinese civilization, although of course there were always other voices and perspectives.

Confucius and his times

Confucius was born in the small state of Lu in Northeast China (present-day Shandong province). His original name was Kong Qiu and later he became popularly known as Kongzi or Kong fuzi (Master Kong). The widely-used moniker Confucius is a corrupted Latinized form of the later, introduced by Christian missionaries. Relatively little is known about the life of Confucius and the information we have comes from relatively late sources. He was born in a respectable upper-class family that had fallen on hard times. His father died when he was only three years old and he was brought up in modest circumstances by his single mother. The young Confucius is described as a precocious child and a keen learner.

Confucius got married at the age of nineteen, and he had his first child a year later. He had a few jobs, including a stint as a bureaucrat in the government of his native state. He was member of the class of scholar-officials (*shi*), who held low and middle level positions in the government. While later records state that for a time he occupied the position of justice minister and was successful in instituting good governance, most likely his actual stature and accomplishments in public office were less remarkable than that.

Confucius lived during the Spring and Autumn era (770–476 BCE) of the Zhou dynasty (1122–256 BCE), a turbulent epoch in ancient Chinese history marked by political fragmentation and social upheaval. As the feudal system of government under Zhou rule—that initially worked well and was commendable for ensuring stability—largely collapsed and social order deteriorated, the various feudal states struggled for power and jockeyed for supremacy (or mere survival, in the case of the

Figure 2.2   Painting of Confucius (Confucian Temple, Tainan, Taiwan)

smaller states). Confucius was one of the many innovative thinkers who responded to a prevalent sense of crisis engendered by the chaotic sociopolitical situation. He sought to revive Chinese society and shore up its ethical foundations by reforming the system of government, largely by infusing it with proper ritual and moral frameworks, modeled on those purportedly established by the ancient sages.

The main objective of Confucius was to reinstate the timeless Way (Dao) that was revealed and followed by the ancient sages, which echoed the norms and designs of Heaven and brought perfect harmony between Heaven and humanity. In antiquity the Way supposedly provided a blueprint for just governance and proper ethical conduct, but according to Confucius it was lost in the social disarray and moral confusion of his time. Growing despondent about the prospect of transforming the government of his native state, Confucius is said to have traveled extensively late in life in search of a ruler who would follow his advice and implement his policies, which were meant to establish proper order in the state and the society. This was to serve as a prelude to restoring peace and harmony to "all under Heaven" (*tianxia*), namely the whole civilized world, which in traditional parlance was equated with China.

Confucius's search for a receptive ruler was repeatedly frustrated, and ultimately it proved to be unsuccessful. Late in life he despondently returned to his native state, where he dedicated himself to teaching his disciples. Although Confucius thus failed in his ambition to get a high position under a righteous ruler receptive to his counsel, he was successful as an educator, attracting a sizable group of dedicated disciples that transmitted his teachings after his death. He was an innovator in the area of pedagogy and was the first known individual to make teaching his primary vocation.

Confucius derived the idealistic model for the just and enlightened society he wanted to institute from China's romanticized past. The utopian vision of a perfect society propounded by him was supposedly realized in ancient times: for instance, during the reigns of ancient sage-kings such as Yao and Shun (see Chapter 1), but especially during the glorious rule of the early Zhou dynasty. Confucius considered the early Zhou era to be a golden age of Chinese civilization, a magnificent epoch characterized by peace, social stability, sagacious governance, and cultural effervescence. He unequivocally declared Zhou culture to be "resplended" and

Confucius on his spiritual development

At fifteen, I was intent on learning; at thirty, I had established my stand; at forty, I was without doubts; at fifty, I knew the mandate of Heaven; at sixty, I was in accord with things; at seventy, I could follow my heart's desires without transgressing conventions.

Analects 2:4; trans. adapted from Lau 1979: 63, and Sommer 1995: 43.

proclaimed that he follows the way of the Zhou (*Analects* 3:14; Lau 1979: 69). While the true Way has therefore been realized in the course of human history, it was believed to have been lost by the time of Confucius; that was a cause of profound disconcert and alienation, but also a call for action.

The person that best embodied the exceptional moral standards and wise governance of the Zhou era, according to Confucius, was the Duke of Zhou (fl. 1042–1030 BCE), who ruled as a regent after the death of King Wu (d. 1043 BCE), his brother and the founding ruler of the Zhou dynasty. He was also considered to be an ancestor of the ruling family of the state of Lu, the native place of Confucius. Traditionally depicted as a selfless public servant, the duke consolidated the newly-founded dynasty, and with his wise rule he ushered a celebrated era of peace and prosperity. For Confucius, he served as a paradigmatic model of a wise leader and a loyal subject. Being a paragon of virtue—infallibly humble and with impeccable integrity—the duke refused to usurp the throne and dutifully stepped down when King Wu's son reached mature age and was able to assume the role of a ruler. Because of the respect accorded to him by Confucius and his disciples, the Duke of Zhou became a patron saint of sorts within the early Confucian tradition and for a number of centuries he was worshiped alongside Confucius.

In light of the above, we can say that Confucius saw himself primarily as a restorer and transmitter of ancient values and traditions, not as a creator of a new system of thought, let alone a founder of new religion. Even so, there were undeniable elements of innovation in his inspired reinvention or reimagining of past traditions. In due course, his creative synthesis blossomed into an immensely influential tradition and earned him the status of a seminal thinker. To this day he is widely esteemed as a paradigmatic individual, a visionary figure that occupies central position in the history of Chinese, or more broadly East Asian, civilization.

Teachings of Confucius

It is probable that Confucius never wrote any text, akin to the Buddha and Christ. The main source about his teachings is the *Analects of Confucius* (*Lunyu*), a sundry collection of aphorisms and conversations between Confucius and his followers that lacks clear organizational structure. Legend has it that the text is a verbatim record of the sayings and discussion of Confucius, compiled soon after his death by the surviving disciples. Scholarly analysis of the text has uncovered differences in style, along with internal contradictions and anachronisms which suggests it is a later compilation, incorporating several strata of materials composed at different times, some perhaps as late as the middle part of the third century BCE. On the other hand, some of the material probably goes back to the time of Confucius, constraining the recollections of his disciples; moreover, for the most part the text presents a conceptually coherent point of view. Consequently, the text of the *Analects* is widely used in the study of Confucius's life and thought, even if it is not always easy to distinguish between the ideas of the master and the exegesis of his disciples.

Confucius was primarily interested in human life and social order. Throughout his teaching career, he is said to have spoken about the moral foundations of a just and harmonious society. Notwithstanding his principally humanistic orientation, he believed in Heaven and asserted that the social and political systems he advocated reflected the cosmic patterns of the Dao (Way), which placed human beings in a larger universal order. While like most of his contemporaries he acknowledged the existence of various spirits and divinities, apparently he was keen to keep them at a respectful distance and was mostly disinterested in the supernatural realm (see "Confucius on the supernatural" box). Similarly, he was disinclined to discuss the afterlife. Some passages in *Analects* also suggest that he was critical of those who left society and went on to live as recluses (*Analects* 18:7), a theme that often appears in early Daoist writings, especially *Zhuangzi* (see Chapter 3).

The main concerns of Confucius and the central tenets of his thought converged on the perfection of human conduct in this life, which was to be cultivated within a communal context, involving interacting with other people in an appropriate manner and gracefully mastering the intricacies of complex webs of social relationships. The two principal virtues and fundamental concepts in the moral teachings of Confucius are ritual (*li*)—understood in the sense of ritual propriety—and benevolence (*ren*). For him these two virtues served as indispensable foundations for proper human conduct. When perfected and enacted in the public arena with genuine sincerity, they naturally bring about positive social transformation. The two go together and reinforce each other: a good person who manifests benevolence in all his acts is a person whose behavior is in perfect accord with ritual.

Originally *li* had the meaning of a religious rite or ceremony, especially the sacrificial rites directed towards gods and ancestors in ancient China. Later its connotations were expanded to include formal behavior of any kind, from ceremonies enacted at the court to common patterns of conduct and polite manners of everyday life. Within

Confucius on the supernatural

To work at doing what is right on behalf of the people, and to show reverence to the ghosts and the spirits while keeping a distance from them—that can be called wisdom.

Analects 6:22; cf. Lau 1979: 84, and Sommer 1995: 47.

If you cannot serve men, how can you serve the spirits? ... If you do not know the meaning of life, how can you know about death?

Analects 11:12; cf. Lau 1979: 107.

early Confucianism, the notion of ritual came to function as a primary standard of social conduct, encompassing sacred rituals, ceremonials, and all manners of proper behavior. That, in a sense, implied the introduction of a sacramental dimension in all aspects of human life. The adherence to set guidelines and principles that regulated the various patterns of behavior and social interaction enabled individuals to properly relate to each other in terms of their prescribed social roles and positions. This amounted to the institution of a total sociopolitical order, which Confucius deemed essential for the realization of a harmonious and well-structured society.

According to that point of view, social harmony prevails when each individual dutifully performs his or her appropriate role with authentic sincerity. As famously put in the *Analects* in reference to the realization of proper governance, everything works wonderfully when each member of society acts fittingly within a proper ritual framework: the ruler acts as a ruler should, his subjects behave as they are supposed to, and the same principle is extended to the behavior of fathers and sons (*Analects* 12:11). The society as a whole is harmonious when each individual performs correctly his or her discrete roles, in accord with a specific template of ritual propriety. But Confucius's conception of ritual goes beyond mechanical adherence to prescribed norms of proper conduct: it also requires a proper state of mind to accompany external actions. Accordingly, correct ritual conduct goes together with proper inner disposition. Ideally, it involves spontaneous adherence to preset behavioral forms that is based on real insight into their true meaning and significance. Within this interpretative scheme, proper ritual is internalized: functioning as a blueprint for correct moral action, ritual is primarily expressed in the manifold interactions with other individuals that occur in the course of daily existence.

Ren or benevolence, the other cardinal virtue—sometimes also rendered as "humanity" or "human-heartedness"—refers to an attitude of genuine love for others and compassionate concern for their wellbeing. It is a key virtue in the ethical system formulated by Confucius, anchoring the realization of human excellence and serving as a foundation for the cultivation of other virtues, such as righteousness (*yi*), loyalty (*zhong*), and faithfulness (*xin*). The holistic virtue of benevolence effectively stands for the intimate relatedness of a shared humanity; it accords with the supreme Way of Heaven, its perfection making the individual a truly human and civilized being. Benevolence involves a move away from selfish desires and egoistical obsessions, which are replaced with altruistic concern for the well-being and happiness of others, along with a placid acceptance of both good and bad fortune. Its original crucible and primary sphere of application is the family, where one first experiences or learns about love and nurturing, but it also extends outward to encompass other people.

The cultivation of moral conduct that embraces and exemplifies these basic virtues was intended to take place within the context of social relationships and interpersonal interactions. Confucius basically accepted as a given the class divisions and codified sociopolitical structures of ancient Chinese society, especially as formulated during

Figure 2.3 Calligraphy featuring the Chinese character for filial piety (Confucian Temple, Tainan, Taiwan)

an idealized past, which he took as being sanctioned by Heaven. There is no indication that he considered the possibility of a more egalitarian system of social or political organization, say something along the lines of the democratic principles that were formulated by his contemporaries in ancient Greece. Accordingly, Confucius believed in a natural hierarchy that underlines and configures all social relationships, the most basic forms of which were schematized under the rubric of the "five relationships" (see box). The five relationships presuppose a patriarchal social structure, which is why the basic bond between a child and a parent is expressed in terms of the father-son relationship. The same applies to the relationship between siblings—hence we have "elder brother and younger brother"—although in modern parlance these relationships can easily be reformulated in terms of the bonds between parents and children, or between two (or more) siblings in a manner that includes both genders.

The rigid structure of hierarchical social relationships—in which there is clear distinction between seniors and juniors, superiors and inferiors—typically engenders power dynamics that can easily lend themselves to abuse. Within the Confucian

The five relationships

- Father and son
- Ruler and subject
- Husband and wife
- Elder and younger brother
- Friend and friend

scheme, that danger is partially addressed by the incorporation of discrete mutual responsibilities and personal bonds into each set of relationships. Accordingly, the husband has a superior status vis-à-vis his wife (as men in general have over women), which means that she owes him obedience and respect, but he also has to act in accord with the ideal role of a good husband. That means the husband is expected to treat his wife with kindness and take care of her and the family. The same principle applies to the stratified relationships between ruler and subjects, parents and children, etc.

While early Confucianism was concerned with the whole spectrum of social relationships, the basic pattern of interpersonal interaction was formulated in terms of the parent–child relationship, which became the principal relationship in Chinese society. This was accompanied with a focus on virtues associated with the family, especially filial piety (*xiao*). The virtues that redeem a rigidly stratified society and smooth its rough edges are therefore first learned within the context of the family, where ideally power is exercised primarily on the basis of overt moral expectations and kinship ties, rather than by external compulsion or brute application of force. Accordingly, filial piety was construed as a central virtue and an indispensable initial step in the path of moral cultivation, while family ethics became the foundation of public mores and key element in the realization of an ideal social order.

Although children (and by extension inferiors) were expected to invariably show respect and listen to their parents (superiors), the imposition of those norms and strictures did not necessarily translate into an obligation to engage in or condone immoral behavior instigated by one's parents. The Confucian ethical system had an inbuilt requirement to raise objections when one's parent/superior is behaving in an unethical manner, although of course in most situations that required considerable courage, tact, and poise, which were not always present in abundance.

Government service, cultural virtuosity, and pursuit of sagehood

Throughout his life, Confucius was committed to an ideal of public service and steadfast in his pursuit of government employment as a vocation, although he was not very successful in the latter. These priorities reflected his class background and were in tune with the general tenor of his thought, which aimed to reshape the world by transforming the sociopolitical order. Within his thought there was no clear line of separation between politicking and philosophizing as two discrete spheres of human endeavor. The Confucian Dao primarily was concerned with an all-encompassing normative order that was firmly centered in the human realm. Above all, it was about patterns of human behavior and social institutions, which inevitably brought it into the political arena. The overriding focus on governmental organization and operation, evident throughout the early Confucian tradition, was in tune with the times, and it was also to be expected from a system of thought that first and foremost was concerned with the codification of communal mores and practices, and whose main goal was to bring about a good and harmonious society.

Confucius accepted the legitimacy and moral authority of the Zhou kings, even as he was also eager to offer advice on good governance to the rulers of the various states that existed in his time. According to him, primarily the ruler had to serve as a moral exemplar, inspiring the respect and obedience of his subjects. The best rule therefore has a soft touch, and there is even a natural or spontaneous quality to it. Ideally the government should minimize aggressive intervention; instead, it should primarily rely on moral persuasion and the setting of good example. It is best to avoid imposition of a harsh system of rules and punishments, although there are situations where violence and reliance on penalties might be unavoidable.

While Confucius and his followers frequently evoked concern for the well-being of the common people, they assumed a condescending attitude towards them. They took a somewhat dim prospect at trying to make the common people comprehend the finer points of their moral teachings, which were principally directed towards the elites, even if Confucius was willing to accept as students diverse individuals coming from a range of socioeconomic backgrounds. Because of their limited knowledge and restricted intellectual abilities, common people should be made to follow the Way, but there is little point in trying to make them understand its subtleties (*Analects* 8:9). The setting up of the main agenda and the organizing of the social and political surroundings were the prerogatives of the ruling elites, although ideally they were expected to take into account the needs of the masses they ruled over.

By performing his ritual duties, being concerned with the well-being of his subjects, and manifesting exemplary virtue, the good ruler provided a worthy model and set the tone for his administration. The actual governance, however, was to be done by his officials (*shi*), who formed a distinct privileged group in ancient Chinese society. The prerequisites for governmental service included adherence to established ritual forms, possession of proper moral character, and mastery of specific cultural forms and practices. Within such a framework, exemplary moral character was deemed a more important qualification for governmental service than narrow bureaucratic expertise, which in practical terms meant that the ideal official was somewhat of an upright generalist. The stresses on moral cultivation implied a redefinition of nobility, with far-reaching ramification; being a noble person became a question of character rather than a matter of birth. Accordingly, within Confucian circles nobility came to be construed as a quality attainable by the cultivation of key virtues and the development of wisdom, not as something that is obtained by simply being born into the right aristocratic family, although in practical terms Confucians had to contend with the power and concerns of the established aristocracy.

Confucian moral cultivation was conceived as a path of continuing self-improvement, involving the nurturing of proper conduct and disposition. It was to be undertaken within a clearly defined social context, and it was primarily expressed via humanitarian service. The program of Confucian learning involved study of the classics and technical mastery of appropriate rituals, which were to be accompanied with a constant reflection on their meaning and an effort to apply the lessons learned in the course of one's daily life. It is worth mentioning that self-cultivation also incorporated literature, dance, and music. The integration of music as part of Confucian practice implied a clear distinction between rarefied music that elevates the spirit and has positive influence on proper character formation on one hand, and vulgar music that does the opposite on other hand. The first kind of music was to be promoted, while the second kind was to be proscribed. This suggests that Confucius looked beyond dry moralizing and promoted the development of the whole person, an ideal that encompassed the attainment of a commendable level of cultural virtuosity.

A person of cultivated moral character who exemplified those traits was called a "gentlemen" (*junzi*), while the highest level of moral perfection was that of the sage (*shengren*). The valorization of sagehood as the highest ideal of perfection accessible to humanity opened up the possibility of constituting Confucian practice outside of the customary framework of governmental service and the exercise of political power. While Confucius allegedly humbly declined to proclaim himself a sage, and also spoke about the difficulty of attaining moral perfection (*Analects* 7:34), he came to be widely glorified as the "Supreme Sage," the embodiment of an ideal person to be emulated by all.

Alternative ways of thought

After the death of Confucius his teachings were transmitted by groups of dedicated disciples, who expounded them and tested their application amidst different circumstances. For a long while, however, the early Confucians were just one among the many groups that propounded diverse doctrines, peddling them to various rulers in an ongoing quest for influence and patronage. The few centuries after the time of Confucius, known as the Warring States period (403–221 BCE), are customarily characterized as a chaotic age. As the various Chinese states fought for supremacy or survival, there was a collapse of social and moral order, while great suffering was inflicted on the common people.

Notwithstanding the intermittent warfare and the lack of central authority, the Warring States era was actually a time of intense intellectual ferment and openness to new ideas. Leading intellectuals put forward a number of creative points of view regarding key issues in the social and political spheres, which is a reason why this era is also known as the age of a "hundred schools of philosophy." This was an important transitional period in Chinese history, marked by intellectual and religious pluralism. During it Confucianism interacted and competed with other systems of thought, responding to their challenges or absorbing elements of their worldviews. The two main rivals to the nascent Confucian movement—if we put aside the proto-Daoists discussed in the next chapter—were the Mohists and the Legalists.

Mohism refers to the movement and the teachings of Mo Di (479–381 BCE?), also known as Mozi (Master Mo), and his followers, which are elaborated in the [*Book of*] *Mozi*. Mozi's life in many ways paralleled the life of Confucius. He probably hailed from a family of commoners, but he read widely during his formative years, including the "Confucian" classics and the teachings of Confucius, and became well versed in traditional Chinese culture. He sought a position in government service and traveled in search of a ruler who would be willing to adopt his policy prescriptions. Being largely unsuccessful in that endeavor, he dedicated his energies to teaching his disciples, who became organized into disciplined groups.

Mozi and Confucius shared some basic premises. They both were dedicated to the realization of a perfect society in which prosperity, peace, and harmony would prevail, but they disagreed about the way to achieve that goal and presented different perspectives on the human predicament. The Mohists were sharply critical of Confucian teachings and practices, including the Confucians' belief in destiny and their fascination with music and ritual. They also condemned the extravagant veneration of ancestors, which found its most wasteful expression in the elaborate burial rites practiced by the Confucians.

Mozi and his followers believed in a supernatural world presided over by the Supreme Lord of Heaven, whom some commentators have compared to the anthropomorphic God of monotheistic religions. Many centuries later, that connection endeared the Mohists to Christian missionaries who were active in China. Mozi and his followers also believed in a supernatural realm populated by various ghosts and spirits, who interfered in human affairs. The Mohists are best known for their advocacy of universal love, which was to be extended equally to all people. This novel doctrine went along with their promotion of an egalitarian ethos, which involved advocacy of frugal lifestyle and concern with the well-being of the common people.

The notion of universal love clashed with a prevalent emphasis on the primacy of kinship ties, which as we saw was incorporated into Confucianism with the assumption that partiality towards one's family members is both natural and morally correct. The prototype of universal love advocated by the Mohists was to be found in Heaven's impartial love for all people. Mozi and his disciples were also renowned for their pacifism. In tune with their activist approach and utilitarian spirit, their opposition to war went beyond mere sermonizing: they were energetically involved in war prevention, for instance by lending their considerable military expertise to bolster the defenses of weaker states when they were attacked by stronger states.

The Legalists (*fajia*) had little use for impracticable ideals such as universal love or benevolence. Cognizant of the less savory aspects of human nature and behavior, they also summarily dismissed as naïve the Confucians' beliefs about the realization of harmonious society by the mere adherence to ritual or by the setting of a moral example from above. Legalist thinkers like Han Feizi (d. 233 BCE), a prince and a student of the prominent Confucian philosopher Xunzi (fl. 298–238 BCE), affirmed that people are inherently selfish and harbor antisocial tendencies that need to be corralled and channeled by the institution of a comprehensive system of laws, which incorporated a strict penal code. The Legalists had little interest in individual rights; instead, their foremost concern was preservation and strengthening of the state and expansion of its power.

The Legalist philosophy was unabashedly utilitarian. Its proponents were advocates of practical statecraft, providing methods of management for an efficient administration that relied on the authoritarian enforcement of punitive decrees, along with the recourse to war and violence. In their version of realpolitik, the end justifies the means. Accordingly, they were willing to use the penal system in order to meet their objectives, and to rely on institutional force or violence in order to preserve the state's monopoly of power, as well as prevent the arising of social discord or political resistance. To that end, the totalitarian state controlled knowledge and instilled fear and docility in the population.

The Legalists were criticized by the Confucians for their utilitarian ethos and their lack of concern with morality. They were also discredited by the pivotal role they played in the harsh rule of the Qin dynasty, which in 221 BCE unified China for the first time under the banner of an imperial regime that claimed legitimacy to rule over the whole of China. Nonetheless, the general outlook and even some of the practical prescriptions of the Legalists became incorporated into the Chinese polity. Typically, the hard edges of Legalism became softened, as they were packaged together with lofty-sounding Confucian creeds and intuitions. Ever since, echoes of Legalism have remained readily discernable in the Chinese exercise of political power and authority, down to the present.

Mengzi's and Xunzi's contrasting views of human nature

There were certain ambiguities and creative tensions in the thought of Confucius, which fostered the development of diverse interpretative frameworks and new lines of thought. That is evident when we look at the teachings of the two main Confucian thinkers active during the Warring States period, Mengzi and Xunzi, who are sometimes depicted as representing the idealistic and rationalistic strains (respectively) of early Confucianism. While both of them followed the teachings of Confucius and took them as a key source of authority, they adopted different perspectives and in specific key areas arrived at diametrically opposed conclusions. This is best illustrated when we look at their contrasting views regarding human nature (xing), a central theme in the writings of both thinkers.

Figure 2.4 Children perform a play about young Mengzi's formative education, Zhongtaishan, Taiwan

Relatively little is known about the life of Mengzi (or Mencius, 371–289 or 391–308 BCE?). His father died while he was very young and he was brought up by his wise mother, who supervised his early education (see Figure 2.4). Like Confucius, he traveled widely in search of a ruler willing to adopt his proscriptions about governance and ethics, with little success. He was also involved in the larger intellectual debates and doctrinal polemics of his time, vigorously advocating a Confucian point of view and striving to shore up the legacy of Confucius. Mengzi was opposed to war and promoted humane governance as the best way to deal with the pressing social and political problems of his time. He argued for reliance on the moral charisma and good example set by the ruler, which he believed would naturally win the respect and allegiance of the people. He also spoke against the institution of strict regulations and harsh punishments.

Mengzi propounded a doctrine about the essential and intrinsic goodness of human nature, which accords with Heaven. He believed that all men are basically good, even if they often stray from their basic goodness and act in unwholesome ways. The fundamental goodness of the human heart is evident in the instinctive compassionate response when people are confronted with the suffering of others, for instance when seeing a child falling into a well. Each individual is naturally endowed

The four inborn virtues

- Benevolence (*ren*): caring concern for others.
- Righteousness (*yi*): conformity of thought and action with moral principles.
- Ritual (*li*): ceremonial propriety and proper behavior.
- Wisdom (*zhi*): ability to distinguish right from wrong.

with all qualities needed to actualize moral perfection, as the four basic virtues are already instilled in the mind at the moment of birth and provide each person with an innate moral sense (see box above).

At its core, according to Mengzi, moral cultivation involves recovering and polishing the lost mind of virtue (see box below). That is a gradual process that entails developing one's basic humanity, according to a blueprint that is already inscribed in the mind by Heaven. Successful practice depends on one's personal commitment, but it is also affected by the presence or absence of a social environment conducive to moral cultivation. When one perfects the ability to fully tap into the human potential for goodness and wisdom, that person fulfills his ultimate destiny and becomes a sage.

In contrast to Mengzi's overly optimistic assessment of the human predicament, Xunzi asserted that by nature human beings are fundamentally predisposed towards evil and this leads them to seek satisfaction of their selfish desires by various kinds of unethical and antisocial behaviors, which are readily observable throughout society. Morality and goodness do not come naturally or spontaneously: they are akin to an acquired taste, and their active manifestation presupposes discipline and the application of effort. Xunzi thus started with the premise that human nature is evil, in a sense of human beings lacking an innate moral compass or inborn ability to distinguish right from wrong. But then he went on to emphasize that they can be trained to act in a civilized fashion and in harmony with proper ethical principles. That is precisely the task of Confucian education, which when put into practice

Mencius on human nature being good

Benevolence is the very mind of human beings; righteousness is the path they need to take. To neglect this path and not follow it is to lose one's [original] mind and not know where to find it. What a pity! When people lose a chicken or a dog, they know how to look for them, but when they lose this mind, they do not. The way of study and inquiry is nothing but seeking this lost mind.

Mengzi 6a:11; trans. adapted from Sommer 1995: 58–9.

has the potential to modify human behavior and change society, so that it comes to correspond to the ideal templates presented in the classics and explicated by Confucius.

From Xunzi's point of view, the accomplishment of moral excellence requires a conscious effort and the application of right teachings. He acknowledged an element of artifice in the process of acquiring proper inner virtues and external mores, which are conveyed by a cumulative tradition that was originally formulated by the ancient sages. This is not an easy task, requiring the learning of orthodox doctrines and correct ritual patterns of behavior, under the guidance of learned teachers. Nonetheless, proper education leads to the accumulation of virtue and wisdom, and without it ordinary people remain lost in a state of abject ignorance and moral confusion.

During his lifetime Xunzi was a prominent intellectual, teaching a wide range of subjects at the invitation of various rulers. Often he is linked with the Legalists tradition, because of a realistic streak in his political vision and his connections with prominent Legalists such as Li Si (the prime minister of Qin) and Han Fei, although he positioned himself firmly within the Confucian mainstream. He openly criticized Mengzi's theoretical stance, while he also was greatly concerned with clearly delineating the parameters of Confucian orthodoxy. The intellectual debate between the two is the earliest record of disagreements and fissures within the nascent Confucian movement. During the early Han era and for much of the subsequent millennium, Xunzi was considered to be a more important thinker than Mengzi. However, during the Tang era Mengzi's standing in the pantheon of Confucian sages started to rise noticeably. From the Song era onward, Mengzi was widely regarded as the most significant classical thinker, second in stature only to Confucius, as indicated by the popular appellation of Second Sage that was assigned to him.

Xunzi on human nature being evil

Human nature is evil .... If people follow their nature and indulge their emotions, inevitably there will be struggle and contention, causing them to transgress their proper duties, usurp the correct principle, and turn to violence. Therefore, only by being transformed by the examples of teachers and the ways of ritual and righteousness can they achieve courtesy and civility, so that they can develop cultural refinement and ritual, and return to good order. When looking at it in this way, it is clear that human nature is evil, and that goodness is a product of conscious effort.

"Human Nature is Evil (Xing e)" chapter, *Xunzi*; trans. adapted from de Bary and Bloom 2000: 179–80, and Sommer 1995: 69.

In summary, inspired by the teachings and personal example of Confucius, the two thinkers adopted different premises and arrived at contrasting explanations of human nature. For Mengzi the human propensity for goodness is innate and it is in our nature to try to perfect it, while for Xunzi the impetus for proper behavior and moral cultivation is something that needs to be learned and comes from without. Nonetheless, both of them shared a common belief in human perfectibility and in the power of Confucian teachings to bring about positive change and far-reaching moral transformation. They each sought the institution of a just, prosperous, and harmonious society. Holding similar ideas about the basic framework of the ideal society and the essential character of sagehood, the two Confucians parted ways in their understanding of human nature and in their explication of the process of moral cultivation.

Emergence of Confucianism as official ideology

Confucianism was negatively affected during the rule of the First Emperor of the Qin dynasty (r. 221–210 BCE), when as part of a policy aimed at controlling all knowledge and information in the newly unified empire, the emperor ordered the notorious burning of books not approved by his regime. Some Confucian books were destroyed in the process, although pro-Confucian historians most likely exaggerated the scope of the calamity and its effects on Confucianism. It seems that Confucianism was not singled out for persecution, which perhaps reflected its relative lack of influence at the time. The fortunes of the Confucians changed markedly during the subsequent Han dynasty, when for the first time their tradition rose to a position of unprecedented preeminence. The assigning of a unique status to Confucianism during the Han era was practically tantamount to it becoming an official ideology of the Chinese imperial state.

The early Han dynasty was a period of significant social change and intellectual ferment, as diverse schools of thought interacted with each other and vied for prominence. An early historical work identifies six major schools of classical learning that flourished at the time (see box). Adoption of syncretism was a major tendency at the time, amidst a prevalent climate of intellectual openness and tentative

The Six Schools of Classical Leaning, according to Sima Tan (d. 110 BCE)

- School of Yin and Yang
- Confucians (Ru)
- Mohists
- Legalists
- Logicians
- Daoists

embrace of religious pluralism. There was rich cross-fertilization of diverse political philosophies, systems of ethics, and cosmological theories, with leading thinkers not being shy about incorporating into their theoretical models concepts and ideas derived from other traditions.

The embrace of pluralism and the tendency towards syncretism are evident in the eclectic incorporation of elements derived from other schools of thought into the new and expanded form of Confucianism that was formulated by prominent scholars such as Dong Zhongshu (c. 179–104 BCE), the most famous Confucian of the Han era. Intent on creating a new model for organizing and aggrandizing the Han empire, Dong produced a grand Confucian synthesis that brought together Heaven and humanity in a harmonious relationship of mutual responsiveness, and situated the imperial state into a broad cosmic scheme. In this new theoretical paradigm, he secured a crucial position for the Han state and its sovereign, which were legitimized by being infused with supreme power and moral authority.

Within the context of this new Han version of Confucianism, the ruler was to wield absolute autocratic power as the Son of Heaven, but he was also supposed to serve as a moral exemplar and be open to the counsel of his officials, who were to be recruited from within Confucian circles. The emperor played central role in a larger cosmic scheme, in which Heaven, earth, and humanity formed an essential triad.

Figure 2.5   Main shrine hall, Confucian Temple, Taipei

He was a crucial link that secured their harmonious relationship, aligning his state and his subject with the norms of Heaven and earth. His failure to maintain proper balance and moral order, however, brought all sorts of calamities, including natural disasters, which served as omens of Heaven's displeasure with events on earth.

The initial bestowal of imperial endorsement upon Confucianism occurred during the reign of Emperor Wu (r. 140–86 BCE), who was influenced by Dong Zhongshu's theories, but was also guided by political expediency. The Confucian scholars' expertise was useful in the consolidation of the Han dynasty's power and the development of its state institutions. From the emperor's perspective, the Confucians were especially useful because of their knowledge of religious and courtly rituals, along with their skill in bureaucratic administration. The emperor issued a series of proclamations regarding the role of Confucianism as an ideological basis of imperial rule, starting with the establishment in 136 BCE of official positions to be filed by scholars versed in the Confucian classics. He also established an imperial academy in 124 BCE that used the Confucian classics as its core curriculum. The academy's main function was to produce officials for the imperial bureaucracy, which bolstered Confucians' preeminence in the political arena.

Those policies were accompanied with the institution of an official cult of Confucius as part of the state's ritual program. In the process, the ancient sage became deified, with Dong Zhongshu proclaiming him to be an "Uncrowned King." On the other hand, the emperor was primarily concerned with the prerogatives of the royal house, and he retained some ambiguity about the power and influence of his Confucian scholars and advisers. Accordingly, notwithstanding the unquestionable rise to prominence of Confucianism under Emperor Wu and his successors, the Confucianization of Han imperial ideology and institutions was probably not as thorough as later generations of pro-Confucian historians made it to be.

To conclude, the Han era was a crucial period in the history of Confucianism, an important point when a reinvigorated and transformed brand of Confucianism moved into the limelight and came to occupy central place in the social, political, and cultural spheres. A key upshot of the dynasty's engagement and use of Confucianism was the forming of a long-lasting marriage of convenience, between an autocratic system of imperial governance and a Confucian-centered orthodoxy, with enormous ramifications for the subsequent history of China. Nevertheless, other voices and perspectives continued to flourish, both complementing and competing with the Confucian tradition. Among them, especially important were those of the Daoist tradition, surveyed in the next chapter.

Key points

- While some key aspects of Confucianism, such as its historical uses as political philosophy and blueprint for the organization of society, problematize its categorization as a religion, there are many features in traditional Confucianism that are either overtly or implicitly religious in orientation, for instance the belief in Heaven and some of the forms of spiritual cultivation utilized in the quest for sagehood.

- The various texts included in the so-called "Five Classics" contain a wealth of information about ancient systems of values, outlooks on life, social institutions, and traditions of ritual. Although they had diverse origins, these texts were appropriated by the early Confucian traditions and became the centerpiece of its canon.

- Confucius primarily saw himself as a restorer and transmitter of ancient values and traditions, rather than as a creator of radically new system of thought. While he failed in his quest to find an upright ruler who will implement his teachings and policy proposals, he was successful as an educator, leaving behind a sizable group of dedicated disciples who transmitted his teachings and established the foundations of the early Confucian tradition.

- Confucius was principally concerned with the organization of human life and the structuring of society. In his view, a just and harmonious society must rest on sound moral foundations. That entails the perfection of human conduct within a communal context, via processes of inner cultivation and mastery of predetermined patterns of social interaction, exemplified by the key virtues of ritual propriety and benevolent concern for others.

- Early Confucian teachings about moral cultivation included redefinition of nobility, which came to be understood as a quality attainable by all, via the cultivation of assorted virtues and the development of wisdom. The person of exemplary moral character was called a "gentlemen," while above that was the "sage," who embodied the highest level of moral perfection.

- During the Warring States era the Confucians continued to have limited influence, being merely one among the various contending groups that propounded a wide range of doctrines and practices. Their main competitors included the Legalists and the Mohists.

- Mengzi and Xunzi, the two most important Confucian thinkers of the Warring States era, adopted different theoretical premises and arrived at contrasting views about human nature, even as they shared a belief in human perfectibility and asserted the power of Confucian teachings to bring about comprehensive moral transformation. Mengzi emphasized the inherent goodness of human nature, while Xunzi highlighted the natural

human propensity towards evil and taught that proper moral behavior is
something that needs to be learned.
- The Confucian tradition first rose to great preeminence during the second
  century BCE, when Emperor Wu of the Han dynasty initiated a series of policies
  that were tantamount to establishing the syncretic form of Confucianism
  that flourished at the time as an official ideology of the imperial state.

Discussion questions

1. What was the attitude of Confucius towards the cumulative traditions of the
   past and how he perceived his life mission in relation to them?
2. Describe the views about human nature (*xing*) articulated by Mengzi and
   Xunzi. What were the main points of contrast between the two, and on which
   key issues did they agree?
3. When did Confucianism first officially become the ideological basis of imperial
   rule and what were the long-term historical ramifications of that event?

Further Reading

See also the reading suggestions for Chapter 8.

Brooks, Bruce and Taeko Brooks. 1998. *The Original Analects: Sayings of Confucius
and His Successors*. New York: Columbia University Press.

Chong, Kim-chong. 2007. *Early Confucian Ethics: Concepts and Arguments*. Chicago
and La Salle, IL: Open Court.

Ivanhoe, Philip J. 2000. *Confucian Moral Self Cultivation*. Indianapolis, IN: Hackett
Publishing Co.

Lau, D. C., trans. 1979. *Confucius: The Analects (Lun Yü)*. Penguin classics.
Harmondsworth: Penguin Books.

Lau, D. C., trans. 2003. *Mencius*. Hong Kong: Chinese University Press.

Nylan, Michael. 2001. *The Five "Confucian" Classics*. New Haven, CT: Yale University
Press.

Pines, Yuri. 2002. *Foundations of Confucian Thought: Intellectual Life in the Chunqiu
Period (722-453 BCE)*. Honolulu, HI: University of Hawai'i Press.

Schwartz, Benjamin I. 1985. *The World of Thought in Ancient China*. Cambridge,
MA: Belknap Press of Harvard University Press.

Slingerland, Edward G., trans. 2003. *Confucius Analects: With Selection from
Traditional Commentaries*. Indianapolis, IN: Hackett Publishing Co.

Watson, Burton, trans. 2003. *Mozi: Basic Writings*. New York: Columbia University
Press, 1967.

Watson, Burton, trans. 1996 (1963). *Hsün Tzu: Basic Writings*. New York: Columbia University Press.

Yao, Xinzhong, ed. 2003. *RoutledgeCurzon Encyclopedia of Confucianism*. London and New York: Routledge.

3 Early texts and the emergence of religious Daoism

In this chapter

This is the first of the two chapters on Daoism. The first half of the chapter covers the Daoist tradition's early classical texts, often referred to as "philosophical Daoism." That is followed with a survey of the formative development of Daoism as a distinct form of organized religion, which initially took place in the later half of the second century CE, amidst the gradual decay and eventual collapse of the Han Dynasty. The chapter ends with a discussion of notable trends outside of Celestial Masters Daoism during the third and early fourth century.

Main topics

- Semantic field and varied connotations of the concept of Dao.
- Daoist tradition's basic contours and scholarly perspectives on its historical development.
- The thought of *Laozi* and the text's significance in Chinese religious and intellectual history.
- Central concepts and religious attitudes presented in *Zhuangzi*.
- Key trends and traditions that coalesced during the Han period.
- The Celestial Masters and the emergence of Daoism as an organized religion.
- Perspectives on immortality and alchemy within early medieval Daoism.
- Deification of Laozi within the nascent Daoist movement.

The Dao

The concept of Dao, which literally means "way" or "path," already appeared in this volume. The Chinese word has a long history and covers a broad semantic field (when used as a verb, it also has the meaning of "to say" or "to speak," as well as "to lead"). Dao is a central notion in traditional Chinese thought, appearing in a broad range of

Figure 3.1 The Chinese character for Dao (calligraphy by Ruth Sheng)

texts and being used by various schools of thought. Its multivalent meanings include the impersonal creative force of the universe that is perpetual and engenders *yin* and *yang*, from which emerge the myriad things. Within a Confucian context, the main thrust of Dao's meaning revolves around the proper patterns of human behavior—encompassing formal rituals and everyday activities—that accord with the principles of Heaven (see Chapter 2).

The term Dao was also incorporated into the vocabulary of Buddhism, where it was used to translate from Indian languages a number of technical terms, such as *bodhi* (awakening), *mārga* (path), and Nirvāna. It was also often used in ways that combined its Buddhist and traditional Chinese senses. Nevertheless, the clearest and most sustained focus on the sublime mysteries of the all-pervasive Dao and its diverse manifestation within the human realm can be found within the Daoist tradition, as indicated by its name. The fundamental realm of Daoism is the world of nature—which encompasses additional supernatural or transcendental dimensions—in contrast to Confucianism's preoccupation with the social realm. Because of that, in traditional Chinese culture Daoism is usually seen—together with Buddhism—as complementing Confucianism, rather than standing in an antagonistic opposition to it.

Shifting boundaries and permeable identities

When attempting to delineate the origins and basic contours of Daoism as a distinct religious tradition, one is inevitably faced with a plurality of Daoist orientations or identities. Daoism tends to defy attempts at simple characterization of its basic character and identity, being an open-ended tradition that readily embraces the prospect of ongoing growth and transformation. Its frequently ambiguous stance to the setting up of rigid boundaries, along with its resistance to the marking out of an unequivocal center or essence that remains fixed amidst ongoing transfigurations, has repeatedly frustrated scholarly efforts to arrive at clear definition of what Daoism really is. That is further complicated by the fact that Daoism includes an astounding array of beliefs, doctrines, and practices, written down in a variety of texts and transmitted within diverse religious communities.

The historical growth and evolution of Daoism was never an isolated process: it involved close interaction and cross-fertilization with other religious traditions, especially Confucianism, Buddhism, and popular religion. That was accompanied with a blurring of the boundaries that separate different religious traditions, which is especially evident in the close interactions between Daoism and popular religion on one side, and Daoism and Buddhism on another. As it is often difficult to see where Daoism ends and popular religion begins, some scholars have even proposed that Daoism is a modality of popular Chinese religion. From this perspective, Daoism is an elevated expression of popular religion imbedded or expressed in particular institutional forms (Schipper 1993).

Early scholarly efforts to map the Daoist terrain—which were often undertaken within Christian missionary milieus and reflected Western preconceptions and attitudes—resulted in the creation of a sharp distinction between early "philosophical" Daoism, represented by the classical texts of Laozi and Zhuangzi, and later "religious" Daoism. A number of Western scholars and intellectuals perceived radical discontinuity between the two, which admittedly was not without ample precedents in traditional Chinese scholarship. What were the links that tied together the rarefied thought of ancient philosophers with their subsequent vulgarizations at the hands of religious devotees prone to irrational superstitions, they wondered.

Figure 3.2   Entrance of Baoan Temple, Taipei

Recent scholarship tends to avoid such disparaging dismissal of religious Daoism, which has emerged as the main object of academic research within the growing field of Daoist studies. Departing from their predecessors' prioritization of ancient "philosophical" texts such as *Laozi* and *Zhuangzi*, some scholars turned the tables around and asserted that the designation Daoism should only be applied to the forms of organized Daoist religion that developed from the second century CE onward. Still others have taken an inclusive position, arguing that there is a common thread that runs through the various manifestations of Daoism (e.g. Robinet 1997), while perhaps somewhat glossing over the differences between "philosophical" and "religious" Daoism.

While we should not postulate that Daoism was ever a unified religion (along the lines of Catholicism or Shia Islam, for instance) or try to affix to it a firm identity, it is also true that the diverse Daoist modalities embrace certain common frames of reference that situate humane existence against larger cosmic backdrops and link it with numinous realms of transcendence. Within Daoism we find constellations of symbols, ideas, and ideals that throughout Chinese history channeled spiritual energies and elicited profound emotional responses. In many instances that translated into commitments to ways of life and systems of spiritual practice that met genuinely felt religious needs, which often brought about far-reaching personal and communal transformations. Daoist teachings encapsulated multifaceted systems of meaning and value, which found concrete expressions in colorful rituals and other patterns of sacral behavior that reinforced group cohesion and a sense of belonging, but also opened avenues for individualistic quests for personal development and transformation.

The ongoing formation of multifaceted Daoist orientations and identities therefore involves a continuing process of transfiguration, set amidst a pervasive belief in the lack of permanence and solidity. But even though Daoism is a tradition without a point of origin or fixed boundaries, its manifold manifestations are still imbedded in concrete historical circumstances, texts, traditions, rituals, and communities. At the center, we find lineages of transmission and priestly ordination, along with the presence of monastic orders and a Daoist canon, while on the margins we find diffused forms of popular worship and psychosomatic practices such as Taiji quan and other forms of gymnastics (that may or may not be labeled as Daoist). The spaces they occupy need not be inflexibly demarcated or defined. Accordingly, when studying Daoism in all its richness and variety, we have to keep in mind its porous boundaries and the prominent junctures that bring it in close contact with other religious traditions, as well as its embeddedness into traditional Chinese culture.

Laozi's ruminations on the indescribable Dao

The Figure of Laozi (Master Lao or Old Master) looms large in Daoist history, as he is often regarded as the tradition's founder. According to legend, his name was Lao Dan and he worked as an archivist during the Zhou dynasty (presumably active during the sixth century). Little is known about his life, and some scholars have questioned the historicity of Laozi as an actual person. He is best known as the putative author of the famous text that bears his name, *Laozi*, although later a deified form of him also became an important part of the Daoist pantheon (see below). Laozi's book is also known by the alternative title of *Classic of the Way and its Power* (*Daode jing*), from the opening Chinese characters of its two main parts: Way (Dao) and power (*de*, also possible to translate as "charisma" or "virtue").

Aside from the traditional legend about Laozi's authorship, we have no definitive knowledge about the text's early provenance. The standard edition in use today was put together during the third century CE, although recent archeological discoveries of early bamboo and silk manuscripts indicate that the text already existed by the fourth or third century BCE. It seems probable that *Laozi* is a collection of aphorisms and poetic reflections that represent the ideas of various thinkers that lived at different times. Initially these materials might have been transmitted orally, and they were put together into a coherent form at a later stage of the text's literary evolution.

Figure 3.3 The opening four lines of *Laozi*

The book of Laozi is relatively short—consisting only of around five thousand Chinese characters—but it was an important source of Daoist symbols and ideas, as attested by the numerous quotations and allusions that appear in later Daoist texts. The text also enjoyed broad appeal and influence beyond the confines of the Daoist community, being widely read as one of the great classics of Chinese philosophical and religious literature. Because of the text's poetic ambiguity and the terseness of its language, its contents have been subjected to a wide range of interpretations. Generations of commentators have offered a number of different readings of the cryptic text. Typically *Laozi* is treated as a philosophical and religious classic, with prominent mystical dimensions. However, the text has also been approached as a political work, a treatise on military strategy, or a manual of longevity practices. More recently, *Laozi* achieved broad global acclaim and popularity, which led to it being translated numerous times in many languages, making it arguably the most translated book after the *Bible*. The text's new-fangled fame has led to it being subjected to new uses and interpretations that reflect contemporary values or spiritual predilections, including those put forward by Westerners (some of them with no knowledge of classical Chinese or proper background in traditional Chinese thought).

The central operating concept in *Laozi* is the Dao, the primary principle that remains constant amidst the ever-changing realm of finite and transient phenomenal appearances. The Dao is the one indivisible and underlying reality in the cosmos, the creative source of life in all of its richness and variety that antecedes the formation of heaven and earth. The text's use of the term conveys a sense of belief in an absolute or ultimate truth, a fundamental ground of reality that is beyond conceptualization and transcends the realm of dualistic opposites. The Dao is void, ineffable, and mysterious—the word itself being simply a provisional designation for a trans-conceptual reality that is nameless—yet it is manifest everywhere and permeates everything. The immediate actuality of its sublime wonder is beyond the power of words to describe or conceptualize. Verbal expressions cannot capture its true nature, as ultimate reality by its very nature is inaccessible to language (see box). The Dao is an impersonal natural principle, operating constantly and spontaneously, irrespective of purposeful human action and impervious to pious supplication.

Dao's indescribability

The Dao that can be expressed in words is not the timeless Dao;
The name that can be named is not the name of the timeless.
The nameless is the beginning of heaven and earth;
The namable is the mother of the myriad things.

> The opening lines of *Laozi/Daode jing*.

Like the saying of Confucius, *Laozi* presents us with an idealized vision of a perfect world, albeit of a different kind. This implicitly conveys a critique of the deficient or corrupt world of everyday reality, as it was experienced by the ancient thinkers that created these texts. However, the world of the Daoist sage comes across as a reverse image of the cultured world of ritual propriety and social engagement envisioned by Confucius. This vision is part of a non-theistic understanding of the universe, which is conceived as constantly changing and evolving, naturally going through stages of growth and decay, without the presence or intervention of an anthropomorphic creator or controlling deity. The sage who has realized harmony with the Dao is situated in a serene realm, which possesses an unstructured quality and is in tune with the spontaneous flow of nature.

Such portrayal of the realm of the sage seems to echo a primitivistic tendency in the text to idealize the simple life of an early agrarian society, in which people lived close to the natural world. Such idyllic existence contrasts with the social patterns and cultural schemes characteristic of an evolved human civilization, which inevitably bring about deviation from the pristine Dao. The sage withdraws from mundane affairs and engagements, distancing himself from the bustle and artifice of "civilized" life—which includes the familiar prototype of civilization articulated by Confucius and his disciples—as it inevitably leads to mindless competition and obsession with wealth and power. He stands for a way of life infused with spontaneity and genuine freedom, based on a cogent spiritual vision that values peacefulness and wisdom, while rejecting blind adherence to established norms and values.

While the intellect might not be able to fully grasp the ineffable reality and subtle functioning of the Dao, it is possible to realize a union with it by becoming seamlessly attuned to its unaffected manifestation and operation in the world. The best approach to realizing such harmonious state, according to *Laozi*, is the cultivation of *wuwei* (lit. "non-action"), a key term that implies uncontrived or effortless behavior that is free from grasping and fixation (see box). While *wuwei*

Laozi on virtue and non-action

The supreme virtue (power) comes across as not being virtue, which is why is has virtue.

The inferior virtue does not let go of it being virtue, which is why is has no virtue.

The supreme virtue is non-active, being without ulterior motives.

The inferior virtue is consciously active, being based on ulterior motives.

The supreme benevolence is expressed via action that is free from ulterior motives.

Laozi 38; cf. Lau 1963: 45, and Ivanhoe 2002: 41.

entails avoidance of unnecessary efforts and self-centered activity, it does not denote a state of thoroughgoing passivity. It stands for a method of spiritual cultivation and a way of being that brings the individual in holistic harmony with the universe. By becoming empty of egotistic desires and self-centered obsessions with status, fame, wealth, and the like, the sage accords with the natural flow of things and realizes their essential oneness.

From the *Laozi* authors' point of view, adherence to the principle of *wuwei* also happens to be an effective way of transforming the world for the better—or rather bringing it closer to a primordial state of harmony—especially when compared with the obsessive fostering of ritualism and the social ordering advocated by the Confucians. Therefore, it is possible to see *wuwei* not only as a soteriological paradigm that operates at the individual level, but also as a potentially effective method of sagacious governance that adopts a laissez-faire approach. Those implications are already evident in *Laozi*, where we find a seeming conflation of the images of the sage and the king, which resonates with a tendency prevalent in ancient China to blur the lines of demarcation between politics, ethics, and religion. As we will see, the ideas surrounding the notion of sagacious governance that relies on non-action were subsequently picked up and amplified by later thinkers concerned with the political implications of Daoist thought.

Zhuangzi's imaginative vistas and carefree wanderings

Like Laozi, Zhuangzi refers to both a book and a person, although in this case modern scholarship accepts the historicity of the person and his connection with the book. Little is known about Zhuangzi (Master Zhuang; also known as Zhuang Zhou) as an historical person. Presumably he was an upper-class southerner with unique talents as a creative thinker and writer, who lived during the fourth century BCE (an unconfirmed set of traditional dates for his life is 368–286 BCE). The book that bears his name is a composite text, with only the first seven chapters—the so-called "inner chapters"—usually associated with the historical Zhuangzi. The rest of the book's thirty-three chapters are hybrid narratives, containing the ideas of a number of unknown authors who lived between the time of Zhuangzi and the third century CE, when the standard version of the text in use today was created. Some parts of the text were perhaps composed by disciples of Zhuangzi, but others represent a range of different strains and perspectives subsumed within the nebulous (proto-) Daoist movement.

The text of *Zhuangzi* is of a high literary quality and is widely recognized as one of the great classics of the Chinese literary tradition. It is infused with rich symbolism, makes recurrent use of ingenious allegories that often reveal fascination with the natural world, and frequently exudes an understated sense of humor. The author(s) take the reader on inspired flights of poetic imagination that open up expansive mythopoeic vistas, transposing him or her to new realms of reality populated with strange creatures (including animals that can talk), ethereal sages, and wise men of yore, including Laozi and Confucius. While the stories that feature Confucius usually caricature him as a stiff moralist and compare him unfavorably with the wise and sagacious Laozi, at times he also assumes the unexpected role of spokesperson for a Daoist point of view.

Zhuangzi is a considerably longer and more complex text than *Laozi*. It takes on the main themes broached in *Laozi*—such as the unity of the Dao, the valorization of serenity and withdrawal, and the celebration of nature—while systematizing and elaborating them, but it also moves in significant new directions. Throughout the text there is a palpable tendency towards interiorization. The main focus of attention time and again shifts to the inner world and the various states of consciousness, especially those engendered via mystical experiences. That is accompanied with an unconcealed aversion to involvement in the sociopolitical arena. Political entanglement is seen as a hopeless enterprise, with little prospect of doing any good or bringing about any meaningful change. The main task of transformation lies within: larger social pathologies are merely external manifestation of a basic human propensity to get caught up in petty desires and self-centered attachments, thereby losing sight of the true nature of reality and falling out of harmony with the all-pervasive Dao. The text promotes questioning and subversion of established systems of values and conventional ways of understanding the world; it also advocates empting of the mind, which must precede the intuitive insight into the ineffable and formless Dao.

The path of individual transformation envisaged by Zhuangzi paves the way for a radically different way of being in the world, as the spiritually accomplished adept lets go of the last vestiges of self-centered awareness and adopts an all-inclusive standpoint. Being free from the self-imposed limitations that characterize the workings of small minds, the sage's holistic perspective affords a vivid and free-flowing experience of the world in both its totality and its infinite variety. The sage realizes union with the Dao, without getting stuck in narrow dogmatism or reification of the absolute truth. Zhuangzi takes an issue with the dogmatic tendencies evident in the intellectual debates between partisan proponents of different doctrines that tried to establish the correctness of their views and the wrongness of their opponents' ideas, prime examples of which were the Confucians and the Mohists. The wise person avoids intellectual and moral rigidity, adopting a relativist standpoint that allows for viewing the world from a potentially limitless variety of angles and perspectives.

Throughout *Zhuangzi* we come across images of the sage as a charismatic figure that embodies the Dao, which paved the way for later conceptions of holiness and sanctity that became emblematic of religious Daoism. Obliterating the deluded consciousness and its egotistical impulses, the perfected person (*zhenren*) realizes his full spiritual potential by achieving physical mastery and mental freedom. Having risen above the ethical, political, and social concerns of conventional human

Zhuangzi's butterfly fream

Once Zhuang Zhou dreamt of being a butterfly. The butterfly was flitting and fluttering around, happy in its freedom to do as it pleased. It was not aware of being Zhou. Suddenly Zhou woke up and there he was: unmistakably Zhou himself. But he did not know if he was Zhou who has dreamt of being a butterfly, or a butterfly dreaming it was Zhou. There must be a distinction between Zhou and a butterfly. This is called the transfiguration of things.

"Discussion of the Equality of Things" chapter, *Zhuangzi*; trans. adapted from Sommer 1995: 81, and Moeller 2004: 48.

existence and having reached union with the Dao, he (or perhaps she) wonders around in a carefree manner—occasionally caching a ride on the wind, according to the text. Joyfully traversing the universe, he takes delight in nature's never-ending transformations. He readily accepts constant change as a basic fact of earthly existence and goes along with what life brings to him, remaining composed and equanimous when confronted with pain and pleasure, gain and loss, life and death.

Such sense of inner serenity and equanimity in the face of adversity is illustrated by the well-known story about Zhuangzi's peculiar response to his wife's death, narrated in a chapter titled "Utmost Happiness." In it we find Zhuangzi sitting on the floor in the wake of his wife's demise, beating a tub and singing. After being reprimanded by one of his friends for not grieving in a socially acceptable manner, Zhuangzi explains that although he was naturally sad at first, he quickly realized that like all things in the universe, his wife's life unfolded in accord with a natural process: initially she emerged from the undifferentiated Dao, the ultimate source, and now she is simply returning to it.

Along with conveying memorable images of perfected persons endowed with supernormal abilities, *Zhuangzi* also raises the prospect of immortality and makes mention of techniques for achieving longevity, such as dietary regimes and breathing exercises. In addition, the text alludes to altered mental states and ecstatic spiritual experiences, which perhaps evoke popular traditions of shamanic vision quests and journeys into other spiritual dimensions. Within the text we also find echoes of early Chinese interest in quietism and contemplative practice, which in some ways parallel the meditative practices that were later imported into China with the arrival of Buddhism. Scattered throughout the text we find references to the practices of "sitting and forgetting" (*zuowang*), "preserving (or guarding) the One" (*shouyi*), and "fasting the mind" (*xinzhai*, i.e. emptying it of all thoughts and images).

Although the text attributed to Zhuangzi was clearly not envisioned to serve as a manual of Daoist practice or meditation, it shows developing concerns with exploration of the inner world and the process of personal transformation. Those preoccupations gradually came to incorporate distinctive contemplative techniques as central elements of an integrated system of spiritual cultivation, which aimed at bringing the individual closer to unity with the Dao. In that sense, *Zhuangzi* is an early forerunner of the later traditions of meditation that came to a full blossom during the medieval period (see next chapter). Such contemplative practices were integrated into larger templates of Daoist practice, broadly conceived as a spiritual quest that is pursued at the individual level.

The Huang-Lao Movement and other Han-era transitions

Some of the wide-ranging contents of *Zhuangzi* reflect influences of varied proto-Daoist elements or traditions that flourished within the pluralistic intellectual and religious milieus of the late Warring States and early Han periods. These proto-Daoist elements interacted with each other, as well as with other major traditions such as Confucianism, Legalism, Mohism, and the school of Yin and Yang. Their coalescing set the stage for the emergence of Daoism as an organized religion. While for reasons of space we cannot go into details, it is useful to briefly note some of the major trends and schools of thought that were subsequently absorbed into religious Daoism: various cosmological theories, the Huang-Lao tradition, the diverse shamanic networks and practices, and the cult of immortality.

Prevalent cosmogonic theories at the time traced the origins of the universe to the "primordial force" (*yuanqi*, also possible to translate as "primal breath/energy"). Initially the primordial force divided into two complementary elements: *yang*, the pure and light element that moved upward and formed heaven, and *yin*, the dense and heavy element that moved downward and became earth (see box). The human world is in-between the two, made of varied combination of *yin* and *yang*, which imply each other; through their constantly changing patterns of interaction these two engender

Figure 3.4   The Taiji diagram (or yin-yang symbol)

> ## Basic connotations of *yin* and *yang*
>
> *Yin:* shady side (of mountain), negative, feminine, soft, submissive, destructive element.
> *Yang:* sunny side, positive, masculine, hard, forceful, constructive element.

the myriad things. All things are in essence transfigurations of *qi* (elemental force or energy), the basic creative element or force that underlies all existence.

The *yin-yang* centered cosmology was combined with the five elements (or agents) theory (see box below). This provided a conceptual framework for mapping the world in temporal and spatial terms, in ways that accounted for continuing change and transformation, according to which all things move along or go through different phases. Such theoretical scheme implied a cyclical understanding of time and history. Time was believed to unfold on a cosmic scale, in which each of the five elements comes to predominate in a fixed rotational sequence. Such conceptual configuration made it possible to establish correlations between the basic structures and events of the human realm on one hand, and the cyclical patterns of the natural world on another.

In contrast, the Huang-Lao school was primarily concerned with issues of governance, advocating a pragmatic approach to rule based on the principle of *wuwei*. This tradition originated in northern China and took its name from the juxtaposition of Huangdi (Yellow Emperor) and Laozi, whose classic was a major source for its theories. Another reading of the name Huang-Lao can be derived from a deity named Lord Huanglao (or Huanglao jun), which came to occupy an important place in the Daoist pantheon. The Huang-Lao school reached the apex of its influence during the early decades of the Han dynasty. According to its political model, the sagely king embodies the Dao. He rules by retaining his inner quietude and manifesting charismatic authority that is grounded in a potent state of inaction. Relying on an inner insight into reality and concerning himself with the large picture, the wise ruler delegates the day-to-day running of governmental affairs to his officials, and he does not interfere in people's daily life or try to impose a restrictive ideology.

> ## The five elements
>
> - Wood
> - Fire
> - Earth
> - Metal
> - Water

The shamanic traditions that flourished during this period were led by groups of practitioners of magical arts and esoteric lore, represented by the *wu*, many of whom were female, and especially by the *fangshi*. They formed shamanic networks that functioned outside of the confines of official religious cults, although their services were sometimes used by the royalty. They were inheritors of very ancient shamanic traditions, some of which went back to at least the Zhou dynasty. Echoes of such shamanic beliefs and traditions are readily observable in the poems of Qu Yuan (c. 340–278), one of the most famous poets of ancient China whose tragic death is to this day commemorated with the Dragon Boat Festival. Ancient records tell that the *wu* performed spirit sacrifices and rain dances, while the *fangshi* worked as healers, astrologers, fortunetellers, exorcists, and magicians.

Some of the *fangshi* were also practitioners of techniques and exercises that aimed at achieving immortality—or at least the prolonging of life, in a healthy and vital state. It included the utilization of alchemy, dietary regimes, physical exercises, and meditation. These preoccupations reflected the growing influence of an ancient and largely informal immortality cult, which is also echoed in *Zhuangzi*. The immortality cult celebrated mysterious sages who supposedly achieved physical immortality and possessed various supernatural powers, such as the abilities to make their bodies disappear or to predict future events. The immortals were said to shy away from the ordinary human world, preferring the solitude of mountains and caverns, or the more refined abodes afforded by various celestial realms (see below).

The Celestial Masters and the advent of Daoism as an organized religion

The emergence of Daoism as an organized religion can be traced back to the second century CE, during the social turmoil and political disintegration that marked the final decades of the Han dynasty. The pivotal year in that process is 142, when Zhang Daoling, hereto an obscure practitioner of *fangshi* techniques, purportedly had an inspired vision of Laozi in a deified form. Laozi allegedly transmitted to him new teachings that could deliver people from the adverse circumstances brought by the decadent Han dynasty and serve as a proper alternative to the debased cults prevalent at the time. Zhang went on to preach the newly-found doctrine, which was tinged with millenarian overtones and was directed toward chosen people, attracting numerous followers with a utopian vision that held the promise of a new sociopolitical order and better future.

Eventually Zhang's expanding following was transformed into a highly organized and influential religious movement, the first of its kind in the history of Daoism. The movement was called the Way of the Celestial Masters (Tianshi dao). The term Celestial Masters was already known during the time of Zhang Daoling, and later became an imperially-bestowed title given to Zhang's descendants as heads of an officially recognized Daoist church. Early on the movement was also known as the Five Bushels of Rice, a designation introduced by outsiders that referred to a rice tax that was levied to all followers; yet another alternative name is the Way of Orthodox Unity (Zhengyi dao), which became more broadly used in later periods. Upon Zhang's death the movement's leadership passed on to his son and later to his grandson, who with their followers established a theocratic state that enjoyed de facto autonomy.

The Celestial Masters tradition was one among the popular messianic or millenarian movements that emerged during the unsettled social and political conditions of the second century. Another comparable group in eastern China was the Yellow Turbans, whose name came from the symbolic headscarves worn by its followers (yellow being the color associated with earth and the Yellow Emperor). The members of this movement called themselves the Way of Great Peace (Taiping dao). Their main aim was to usher a sociopolitical utopia characterized by peace, stability, truthfulness, and harmony, a new age called Great Peace (Taiping). The Yellow Turbans adopted similar organizational structures and practices as the Celestial Masters. They promoted the idea of a sagely ruler who combined religious and secular roles, supported by a well organized ecclesiastical hierarchy. The movement's followers engaged in healing rituals and communal worship that featured the chanting of sacred texts. The Yellow Turbans movement was destroyed by the Han military in 184, after it staged an unsuccessful uprising against the reigning dynasty with intent to overthrow it and bring about the new reign of Great Peace. This armed revolt was a culmination of a series of peasant-centered uprisings that occurred over several decades.

The self-rule of the theocratic state established by the Celestial Masters was made possible by their location in the southwestern province of Sichuan, far away from the imperial capital, and by their shrewd decision not to directly challenge the ruling dynasty. Its leaders instituted a peculiar form of governance that mixed familiar Han bureaucratic intuitions with novel ecclesiastical structures. The families of the faithful were organized into twenty-four parishes, led by priest-officials known as libationers, who performed a combination of civil and religious functions. An important part of the libationers' duties was their mediating between the parishioners and the various gods and spirits. They also kept household registers of the faithful, which were periodically undated to keep them in accord with a similar set of registers that were supposedly held by the gods of the celestial bureaucracy, who watched over each individual and recorded his or her misdeeds. As we will see in the next chapter, the Celestial Masters also adopted egalitarian attitudes that included the acceptance of women as full-fledged members of the religious community.

Within the context of Celestial Masters Daoism, the communication and supplication of the various celestial powers was supposed to go via proper bureaucratic channels, with a priest submitting a written petition to the appropriate celestial bureaucrat in the same manner as a government official would present a memorial to the court. The whole Celestial Masters movement was permeated with a bureaucratic outlook that extended to the terrestrial and celestial realms, which became a prominent feature of Daoism and popular religion. The keeping of registers was linked with an injunction that the faithful should live virtuous lives: practicing charity, not being greedy, avoiding conspicuous consumption and gluttony, etc. On the whole, the movement conceived of morality in fairly conventional terms, which included adherence to basic Confucian virtues such as benevolence and filial piety.

The religious observances of the Celestial Masters incorporated many elements of popular religious practice and had a pronounced communal orientation. The faithful performed public confessions of wrongdoing, in conjunction with penance that involved communal service. Their group ceremonies included the chanting of sacred texts; typically they were accompanied with communal feasts that reinforced social ties and group solidarity, as well as marked special events such as new births and marriages. Members of the movement were also expected to maintain shrine rooms in their homes, where daily rituals and supplications of divine beings were to take place.

Other practices mentioned in early sources include breathing exercises, observance of dietary regimes that included assistance from gains, and sexual rites. The sexual practices were apparently carefully monitored and performed under the guidance of a Daoist master, incorporating various ritual procedures and symbolic elements, such as choreographed dance-like movements that represented the coming together of yin and yang. That opened the movement to external criticism, however, as its sexual rites were condemned as immoral. In the eyes of Daoism's detractors, they constituted licentious behavior, being tantamount to religiously sanctioned orgies that contravened established morality, although it is probable that the critics often overstated the nature and prevalence of the sexual rites.

The identity of the Celestial Masters as a distinct religious group was established in part by carefully delineating its relationship with popular religion. While the Celestial Masters adopted many popular religious beliefs and observances, they bolstered their legitimacy and authority by attacking what they labeled as heterodox cults and practices. The movement's leaders issued prohibitions against popular magical/religious practices such as divination, sacrifice, and certain forms of healing. They thus established explicit parameters of orthodoxy that separated the purportedly genuine gods they worshiped and the correct practices they performed from those of various religious impostors, false healers, and others linked with various shamanic groups or practices. Aside from concerns about religious purity and orthodoxy, the proscription of their rivals' rituals and practices can be seen as the priesthood's way of dealing with those who competed for their services. Establishing the singular authority of their tradition in effect vouchsafed the efficacy of the rituals performed by its clergy, while denigrating the correctness and potency of those performed by their competitors.

That Celestial Masters' experiment with running a theocratic state ended in 215, when the grandson of Zhang Daoling submitted to one of the powerful warlords who rose to power in the aftermath of the Han dynasty's collapse, in exchange for official recognition and patronage. That paved the way for the movement's spread throughout northern China. During the early fifth century the movement morphed into an elite court-oriented tradition, even briefly achieving the status of a state religion under the Northern Wei dynasty (386–534). Subsequently it seems to have gone somewhat into a period of decline, as it was eclipsed by new Daoist revelations and traditions (see next chapter), which occurred alongside the growing influence of Buddhism. The Way of the Celestial Masters managed to stage comebacks during the Tang and Song eras. Then it became the dominant Daoist order under the Ming dynasty, and to this day it remains one of the main traditions of Daoism.

External alchemy and the quest for immortality

Notwithstanding the emergence of organized groups like the Celestial Masters, much of early Daoist belief and practice circulated outside of the narrow confines of organized religion. A good deal of it was diffused along unofficial channels, including informal networks of elite practitioners, many of whom came from aristocratic backgrounds. A good example of that is Ge Hong (ca. 280–343), who left valuable writings that illustrate important trends within the burgeoning Daoist movement. His texts also provide us with insights into the subjective views and personal perspectives of an important historical figure within early medieval Daoism.

Ge was a scion of southern aristocratic family. He grew up in a religiously-oriented milieu, having started to study with a Daoist master at an early age. Although he secured a position in the imperial bureaucracy, he gave that up in order to live as a recluse and dedicate himself to the study and cultivation of Daoist teachings and techniques. His writings include the *Master who Embraces Simplicity* (*Baopuzi*, title based on Ge's literary sobriquet), an influential text that deals with a host of themes central to Daoist practice and serves as a compendium of techniques employed in the quest for immortality. Ge was an inheritor of ancient religious traditions that went back to the Han era, but apparently he was not directly influenced by the advent of the Celestial Masters tradition, which at the time had not yet become influential in southern China.

As part of his social background, Ge Hong was familiar with the teachings and observances of Confucianism. He regarded Confucianism as useful source of templates for organizing the sociopolitical realm and guiding human behavior and interpersonal interaction, and he wrote about it in some detail in the first half of the *Master who Embraces Simplicity*. For him Confucianism was complementary to

Daoism, which preached detachment and transcendence, although in his scheme of things the esoteric knowledge of Daoism was clearly superior in its profundity. He conceived of their relationship in terms of a basic dichotomy that entailed two complementary traditions: Confucianism dealt with the external world of political institutions and social interactions, while Daoism addressed the inner world of spiritual exploration and transformation.

The relationship between the two teachings was also expressed in terms of the common root-branches metaphor: Daoism was the root (and thus more essential), while Confucianism was identified with the branches. The inner–outer dichotomy became a predominant framework for locating and ordering the three teachings in mediaeval China, with Buddhism joining Daoism in the "inner" camp. Ge also embraced the diversity within Daoism, which he approached in a fairly eclectic manner. He acknowledged the "philosophically"-oriented Daoism of Laozi and Zhuangzi, with its conception of the ineffable Dao and its doctrine of "non-action." At the same time, he pursued an unabashedly activist approach that relied on deliberate effort and the application of a variety of spiritual techniques, many of which can be traced to earlier shamanic practices.

Ge Hong's main personal interest, and the central theme in his conception of a Daoist path of practice and realization, was the quest for immortality. He took as a given the existence of advanced spiritual adepts who have achieved physical immortality, although Ge acknowledged that they are difficult to trace or see, especially if one does not have faith. Within Daoism such spiritual virtuosi form a special class of numinous beings known as immortals (*xian*, sometimes also rendered as "transcendents"). By perfecting various spiritual techniques, advanced Daoist practitioners were supposedly able to gradually purify and transmute their bodies, an arduous process of transformation that involved elimination of all impurities and culminated in the procurement of an immortal body.

In medieval Daoist literature the immortals are depicted as dwelling in a perpetual state of freedom and spontaneity, exhibiting a number of sublime physical and mental qualities, including extraordinary physique, ability to withstand the elements and forces of nature, and calm demeanor. They were also believed to be endowed with magical or supernatural abilities. For instance, ancient texts describe them as being able to subsist on air or dew, move through space, or make their bodies invisible. There was gradation among the various types of immortals: some immortals were believed to inhabit this world, albeit in remote regions away from the everyday commotions of human habitation, while a superior class of immortals lived in the higher celestial realms. The highest type of immortal was able to leave behind his ordinary body and this world by ascending into the heavens in broad daylight, in a newly-forged immortal body that was light and pure.

Ge Hong celebrated an already established cult of immortals and idolized the putative sages of yore. Some of the prominent immortals were based on historical persons, while others were mythical creations endowed with individual identities. As they became quasi-historicized, the most prominent among the immortals were accorded hagiographies that became an important part of Daoist literature and lore. A prominent example of that process from later periods are the Eight Immortals, whose ubiquitous images can be found in temples, business, and private homes alike; they include Lü Dongbin (see Figure 3.5), arguably the best known of all immortals (for more on him, see Katz 2000). Nonetheless, Ge was primarily interested in the procedures and techniques that allowed him and other practitioners to actually realize the state of immortality. The path of practice was not easy, and required firm faith and expert guidance from a teacher well versed in Daoist theory and praxis. The aspiring adept was expected to adhere to basic ethical principles, as well as having to adopt a balanced and healthy lifestyle. That involved performing various physical exercises that helped regulate the flow of *qi* within the body, being ritually attuned to the cyclical flow of nature with its changing time periods and seasons, and paying attention to food intake. Ge also provided practical advice about controlling the various gods and spirits, who could either help or hinder the adept's efforts.

In terms of their diet, Daoist adepts were generally advised to eat in moderation, consume fresh, balanced, and well-cooked meals, and avoid strong spices and

Figure 3.5   Shrine dedicated to Lü Dongbin, Sanyuan gong, Guangzhou

grains (which were seen as coarse and heavy, and thus facilitating the processes of physical decay). This kind of diet usually went together with the consumption of herbal supplements, which points to the significant intersection of Daoism with Chinese medicine. Serious practice was best done in quietude and amidst natural surroundings, away from the bustle, impurities, and distractions caused by ordinary people and society. Secluded mountain abodes were perceived as being especially conducive to spiritual cultivation (which is indicated by the Chinese character for immortal, which consist of two graphs meaning "man/person" and "mountain").

Generally speaking, Ge Hong advocated a path of practice directed towards the attainment of immortality that was multifaceted and comprehensive. On the other hand, his exposition of the Daoist path was unstructured, which suggests that there were no fixed templates that determined how the various elements should be combined or integrated. The path encompassed all of the above components, along with other common Daoist practices such as sexual rites, breathing exercises that facilitated the harmonious flow of life energy within the body, meditative visualizations, and usage of talismans (see Robinet 1997 for more details). Nonetheless, Ge is perhaps best known for his advocacy of alchemy.

Daoist alchemy is divided into two broad categories: inner and external. The first focuses on internal processes of transforming the life energies within the body, while the second involves the chemical preparation and ingestion of elixirs that supposedly effect the gestation of an immortal body. Ge Hong was a prominent advocate of external or laboratory alchemy, the earlier of the two, mentions of which already appear in records from the early Han era. In his *Master who Embraces Simplicity* we can find descriptions of various substances—such as cinnabar, gold, and mercury—and chemical processes of purification and transmutation that were involved in the concoction of elixirs of immortality. Some of the substances he and others used had toxic properties (e.g. mercury). That made the experimentation with them a precarious enterprise, since when used improperly or ingested in large doses they could be dangerous, even fatal, as can be seen from documented cases of seekers of immortality dying from poisoning. While aware of such dangers, alchemists like Ge Hong believed that the creation of an elixir—perceived as a perfectly pure substance that corresponded to the original pure element that emerged at the point of cosmic creation—was a goal that was well worth pursuing: it held the promise of transforming the body to a primordially pure state that ensured immortality (for more on Ge Hong and the cult of immortals, see Campany 2002).

Laozi's transfigurations

The variety of perspectives and approaches subsumed within the broad and somewhat nebulous Daoist movement is illustrated by the multi-faceted depictions and imagery ascribed to Laozi, some of which were mentioned in passing in the preceding pages.

Ge Hong's writings are once more useful for that purpose, this time in the form of a hagiography of Laozi included in his *Biographies of Divine Immortals* (*Shenxian zhuan*, translated by Livia Kohn in Lopez 1996). At a basic level, Ge relates a common understanding of Laozi as a historical Figure. Here we are confronted with the familiar image of an ancient philosopher and author of the famous text that bears his name, whose cryptic teachings included instructions about governance by means of non-action, along with insightful pointers about methods of self-cultivation.

Another prevailing transfiguration of Laozi is that of an anthropomorphic embodiment of the ineffable and mysterious Dao. In this deified version Laozi appears as a powerful divinity known as the Highest Lord Lao (Taishang Laojun), member of the trinity of highest gods in the Daoist pantheon (see Figure 3.6). In this form he is worshiped as a salvational figure, manifesting his divine presence and dispensing salvific blessings to anguished humanity. This is the divine incarnation of Laozi that allegedly manifested to Zhang Daoling, the first Celestial Master, as well as to other past rulers and sages, such as King Wen, the founder of the Zhou dynasty. While Ge Hong readily accepted the image of Laozi as a historical person, he was incredulous and critical of the deified image of Laozi transmitted via cultic practice and popular lore. On the other hand, this was the representation of Laozi that most captured the religious imagination of people within the broader Daoist community, and the deified Laozi continues to be worshiped to this day.

Ge Hong assumed that Laozi was a historical person who fathomed the depths and mysteries of the Dao, even as he rejects the notion that he was a supernatural

Figure 3.6   Shrine dedicated to Taishang Laojun, Sanyuan gong, Guangzhou

deity. But the image of Laozi that was closest to Ge's heart was the one that depicted him as a consummate practitioner and purveyor of immortality techniques. In this form Laozi appeared as embodiment of the highest principles and ideals esteemed by reclusive adepts like Ge, who cultivated longevity practices and considered immortality to be the apex of religious life. Serene and free from desires, after arduous practice this Laozi perfected the Daoist path and became a true immortal, setting a glorious example to be emulated by later generations of spiritual seekers.

The various transfiguration of Laozi—ancient philosopher, supernatural deity, and immortal—illustrate the breath of visions and the variety of approaches that were already present at the early stages of the growth of Daoism as a distinct yet open-ended religious tradition. That went together with the turning of *Daode jing* into a sacred text, which came to occupy a place of honor in the burgeoning Daoist movement. By the time of Ge Hong, the cumulative traditions associated with Daoism were fairly complex, encompassing the philosophical reflections of Laozi and Zhuangzi, the sociopolitical ideas of the Huang-Lao school, the beliefs and practices of the Celestial Masters, the ancient shamanic techniques of the *fangshi*, and those of their later successors, including the seekers of immortality like Ge Hong. Yet, Daoism was still on an upward trajectory in terms of its historical growth, on the cusp of the epoch-making revelations and other developments discussed in the next chapter.

Key points

- Dao (the Way) is a central concept in Chinese thought, with complex history and varied connotations. Although the notion of Dao is especially important in Daoism, it is also widely used in other religious and intellectual traditions, including Buddhism and Confucianism.
- Daoism assumes a number of identities and defies attempts at straightforward characterizations or rigid delineations of its boundaries, as it embraces continuing growth and transformation. Scholars have for a long time discussed the distinctions between philosophical and religious Daoism, but there is no consensus regarding such broad categorizations of Daoism.
- While the historicity of Laozi is disputed, for over two millennia the laconic text that bears his name has exerted large influence on Chinese thought and has been subjected to a broad range of interpretations. Some of the key concepts discussed in it, such as Dao and *wuwei*, became essential parts of the religious worldview and vocabulary of later Daoist traditions.
- The text of *Zhuangzi* is celebrated for its innovative use of language and unique literary quality. Building on some of the themes and ideas introduced in *Laozi*, it offers exceptional reflections about the inner world,

including various states of consciousness; it also expounds on a path of spiritual cultivations that entails contemplative withdrawal from society and culminates in the realization of unity with the Dao.

- By the early Han period there were a variety of religious strands and proto-Daoist schools of thought that eventually became incorporated into religious Daoism. That included specific cosmological theories, the Huang-Lao tradition, varied shamanic practices, and the belief in immortality.
- The first emergence of Daoism as an organized religion is linked with the formation of the Way of Celestial Masters, which was the most successful among the popular messianic or millenarian movements that emerged during the second century CE. The early Celestial Masters established a theocratic state with its own ecclesiastical bureaucracy, and they also introduced a rich array of teachings, rituals, and practices.
- During the third and fourth centuries much of Daoist practice in the South was broadly diffused and lacked fixed institutional forms, as illustrated by the writings of noted Daoist adepts such as Ge Hong. Ge was conciliatory towards Confucianism, followed the cult of immortality, and was dedicated to the practice of external alchemy.
- With the growth of religious Daoism there were important changes in the representations of Laozi, who gradually came to be deified. In addition to being perceived as a noted philosopher, he also assumed the forms of an immortal and a popular Daoist deity.

Discussion questions

1. What are the main issues related to the defining of Daoism or the delineating of its intellectual and religious parameters, and what they tell us about the construction of religious identities and orthodoxies in traditional China?
2. What are the earliest historical origins of Daoism as an organized religion, and what were the central beliefs and practices of the principal Daoist group that is most closely tied up with those origins?
3. What are the different ways that Laozi was portrayed within the various religious milieus of early religious Daoism?

Further reading

See also the reading suggestions for Chapter 4.

Campany, Robert Ford. 2002. *To Live as Long as Heaven and Earth: A Translation and Study of Ge Hong's Traditions of Divine Transcendents*. Berkeley, CA: University of California Press.

Hendrischke, Barbara. 2006. *The Scripture on Great Peace: The Taiping jing and the Beginnings of Daoism*. Berkeley, CA: University of California Press.

Graham, A. C. 2001. *Chuang-tzŭ: The Inner Chapters*. Indianapolis, IN: Hackett Publishing Company.

Katz, Paul R. 2000. *Images of the Immortal: The Cult of Lu Dongbin and the Palace of Eternal Joy*. Honolulu, HI: University of Hawai'i Press.

Kohn, Livia, ed. 2000. *Daoism Handbook*. Leiden: Brill.

Kohn, Livia. 1993. *The Taoist Experience: An Anthology*. Albany, NY: State University of New York Press.

Lau, D.C., trans. 1963. *Lao Tzu: Tao Te Ching*. London: Penguin Books.

Miller, James. 2003. *Daoism: A Short Introduction*. Oxford: OneWorld Publications.

Oldstone-Moore, Jennifer. 2003. *Taoism: Origins, Beliefs, Practices, Holy Texts, Sacred Places*. Oxford: Oxford University Press.

Pregadio, Fabricio, ed. 2006. *The Encyclopedia of Taoism*. London: RoutledgeCurzon.

Robinet, Isabelle. 1997. *Taoism: Growth of a Religion*. Trans. by Phyllis Brooks. Stanford, CA: Stanford University Press.

Watson, Burton, trans. 1996. *Zhuangzi: Basic Writings*. New York: Columbia University Press.

4 *Daoist traditions and practices*

In this chapter

This chapter continues the historical survey of Daoism that began in the previous chapter, covering the medieval and late imperial periods. The first two sections focus on Shangqing (Supreme Clarity) and Lingbao (Numinous Treasure), the main scriptural corpuses and traditions of medieval Daoism. That is followed by coverage of other key traditions and elements of Daoism, including ritual, sacred texts, political involvement, monasticism, and contemplative practice.

Main topics

- Origins of the Shangqing revelations and the teachings of the Daoist tradition that grew around them.
- Emergence of the Lingbao tradition and the scope of Buddhist influences evidenced in its texts.
- Codifications of Daoist ritual and contributions made in that area by the Lingbao tradition.
- Formation of the Daoist canon and functions of the texts contained in it.
- General patterns of imperial patronage and the relationship between Daoism and the Chinese state.
- Interreligious debates and interactions among representatives of the three teachings.
- Formation of Daoist monastic orders and the basic character of their institutions and ideals.
- Prominent roles of women and their status in Daoist history.
- Practice of meditation and cultivation of interior alchemy.

The Shangqing revelations

During the 364–370 period a medium called Yang Xi (330–386) reportedly received a series of divine revelations, which became foundations for a new school of Daoism. The divinities, said to have appeared to Yang at night, were members of a celestial class of beings superior to the legendary immortals of earlier Daoist lore. They were new-fangled celestial spirits or "perfected" beings (*zhenren*) that descended from a high heaven named Supreme Clarity (Shangqing, also known as Highest Clarity or Highest Purity). That became the name for the whole corpus of revealed scriptures and the school of Daoism that grew around them. The celestial spirits that purportedly communicated to Yang a variety of novel Daoist teachings included Lady Wei, who in her last earthly existence was a libationer in the Celestial Masters tradition with the name Wei Huacun (251-334), while others among them had never experienced imperfect human existence. Yang, who was a talented calligrapher, then wrote down the revealed teachings in a form that could be shared with the rest of humanity.

Yang Xi was employed by the Xu family, which was a member of the southern aristocracy and was related to the family of Ge Hong (see previous chapter). The Shangqing revelations were initially communicated via Yang to the Xu family, whose members addressed a variety of queries—some spiritually oriented, by others of a more prosaic or pragmatic nature—to the divine beings that revealed themselves to Yang. Eventually other families of similar standing became involved in the same process. Accordingly, the new movement initially grew within a fairly narrow social milieu constituted by elite southern families. While proud of their illustrious ancestry, at the time these families felt marginalized by the recent arrival of emigrants within elite backgrounds from the North, who moved south together with the imperial court of the Jin dynasty after the fall of its capital to foreign invaders in 316 CE.

As the northerners established their political control in the South, they also set up their own cultural traditions and religious institutions. That included Celestial Masters Daoism, which initiated a program of suppression of local religious movements. The initial rise of the Shangqing tradition can be seen as a particular mode of Southern response to the loss of sociopolitical power and the encroachment of alien culture. By introducing new Daoist teachings, allegedly revealed by superior deities than those of the Celestial Masters, segments of the southern aristocracy turned the tables around. Effectively, they upended the northern interlopers by establishing themselves as possessors of a superior Daoist lore.

Notwithstanding claims made regarding the newness of the revelations, the Shangqing scriptures did not represent a revolutionary break from preceding Daoist traditions. Basically they incorporated a range of teachings and practices derived from the major strands of Daoism that existed at the time. That included doctrines and techniques associated with seekers of immortality such as Ge Hong, although with a changed emphasis, as external (laboratory) alchemy was deemphasized at the expense of contemplative practices or reinterpreted in a metaphorical manner. There were also substantial borrowings from Celestial Masters Daoism and popular religion. There were even traces of Buddhist influences, which are indicative of the growing clout of the foreign religion. The Buddhist influences, however, were relatively superficial, especially when compared with the extensive borrowings of Buddhist elements evident in later Daoist texts and traditions.

The scriptures of the Shangqing corpus—which collectively represent a coherent body of canonical literature—were at the center of the Shangqing school. The texts' popularity was to a large extent based on their considerable literary value, which reflected the importance and high respect attached to writing within elite Chinese culture. As Yang Xi attempted to replicate in literary Chinese idiom the arcane and rarefied speech of his celestial interlocutors, he created ingenious literary works that are remarkable for their poetic language, abstruse vocabulary, resourceful use of metaphors, and rich symbolism. The texts' literary qualities inspired and influenced later generations of poets and writers, as can be seen from the copious allusions that appear in a range of writings composed during the medieval period.

At its core, the Shangqing school was a tradition of Daoism based on sacred texts, which were deemed to have divine origins. At first the scriptures were carefully transmitted from master to disciple within a limited socioreligious milieu, primarily constituted by persons with upper-class background. They were meant only for a select group of people, who by virtue of possessing the texts were given access to the sacred realms of the perfected. Consequently, there were rules that regulated their transmission, which contained prohibition of their dissemination to unworthy recipients. These select groups of well-educated individuals, often linked by family ties, gradually evolved into religious confraternities dedicated to study of the scriptures and cultivation of the practices explicated in them. The expansions of the movement led to increased institutionalization. That encompassed the development of distinctive rituals, ecclesiastical hierarchy, and monastic communities supported by the faithful, all of which became integral parts of the Chinese religious landscape. By the sixth century the Shangqing school became the most influential and respected tradition of Daoism, and it retained that status well into the tenth century.

Among the leading figures within the early Shangqing movement was the famous scholar Tao Hongjing (456–536)—sometimes depicted as the de facto founder of the school—who collected, edited, and disseminated the Shangqing scriptures, as well as writing commentaries on them. Coming from the familiar social milieu of southern aristocrats—his family was related to the Ge and Xu families—Tao led a monastic community, whose organization was loosely modeled on that of the Buddhist monasteries, at Mao mountain (Maoshan). His friends and supporters included Emperor Wu of the Liang Dynasty (r. 502–549), the prominent pro-Buddhist monarch. Located in the vicinity of Nanjing, Maoshan became a famous center of Daoist practice (the Shangqing school is also known as Maoshan Daoism, from the name of the mountain). Tao was concerned with establishing criteria for authenticating genuine Shangqing scriptures, as the popularity of the corpus, along with the high value attached to the possession of individual texts, led to the production of spurious scriptures. That went along with the circulation of fraudulent and unauthorized copies, some of which were stolen or sold for profit.

By rearranging and modifying the constituent parts of medieval Daoism, the Shangqing school presented a fresh approach to spiritual cultivation, marked by an overriding concern with exploration of the inner world. Communal observances and rituals largely gave way to contemplative practices and visualizations performed by individual adepts, preferably in the solitude of mountains or in meditation chambers. The interior practices described in the texts of the Shangqing corpus supposedly mirrored those performed by the perfected beings, who as a result of their spiritual cultivation acquired sublime bodies and came to reside in rarefied celestial abodes. The meditative visualizations (often accompanied with invocations) engaged the Daoist adepts' faculties of religious imagination and mental pliability. They involved the conjuring up of eidetic images of various gods and divinities, including those that reside within the body and control its functions (see box below and Figure 4.1). The ultimate goal of salvation entailed removal of all boundaries between the individual and the universe, as the adept's inward journey culminated in his/her coalescing with ultimate reality.

The spiritual practices depicted in Shangqing literature also include spiritual journeys that evoke the ecstatic wonderings described in *Zhuangzi*. Advanced adepts are allegedly able to travel to mythical places, such as the famed "islands of immortality," or Kunlun (the *axis mundi* according to Chinese tradition) and other sacred mountains. During these journeys they encounter an assortment of divinities and uncanny creatures, many of them previously depicted in Chinese mythology. Moreover, on occasion these inspired mental or mystical journeys take

Shangqing depiction of the spirits inhering inside the body

The body of a person contains the spirits of the Palaces of the Three Primes. Within the Gate of Destiny are the Grand Sovereign of the Mystic Pass and the spirits of the three cloudsouls. Altogether there are seven spirits within the body who desire that the person live a long life. These are the greatly propitious sovereigns of kindness and benevolence. The seven white souls are also born within the same body, but they are thieves who attack the body. That is why they must be controlled.

The Upper Scripture of Purple Texts Inscribed by the Spirits;
translated in Bokenkamp 1997: 326.

Figure 4.1   Meditating adept visualizes the arrival of celestial deities

the adepts beyond the reaches of the terrestrial realms, as they sojourn to the sun, the moon, the stars, and variously heavenly realms. According to canonical accounts, there they commune with the gods and obtain celestial nourishments that foster bodily sublimation, leading to the procurement of a subtle and luminous body of an immortal.

The Lingbao Scriptures

Within a few decades after the advent of the Shangqing scriptures, around 400 CE, a new corpus of Daoist texts appeared in southern China. Declared to be divine revelations and collectively known as the Lingbao (Numinous Treasure) scriptures, these disparate texts initially surfaced in the vicinity of Nanjing. Not only was their place of origin not far from the site of the earlier Shangqing revelations, but the new texts also initially circulated in similar aristocratic circles. The emergence of these texts can be seen as another attempt at reformulating or reforming Daoism.

The core of the Lingbao corpus contains some earlier materials, generally ascribed to notable Daoist adepts of previous eras, most notably Ge Hong's relative of an earlier generation Ge Xuan (164–244), as well as scriptures composed during the early fifth century. In these texts we find a noticeable shift in attitudes and priorities: a move away from the elitist concerns with interior exploration typical of the Shangqing revelations, which are largely replaced with a focus on communally-oriented, liturgical forms of worship. These ritualistic features are somewhat analogous to the ceremonial practices of the Celestial Masters, which had broad appeal and resonated with the religious needs and predilections of wider audiences.

The Lingbao scriptures represent a prominent synthesis of the major traditions of medieval Daoism, including those of the Celestial Masters and the Shangqing school, which were combined with copious borrowings from Buddhist texts and practices. The Buddhist influences are especially noteworthy, as this was the first wholesale introduction of Buddhist ideas and imagery into mainstream Daoism, with lasting ramifications for the subsequent religious history of China. From a traditionalist or normative perspective, the majority of the texts in the Lingbao corpus were earthly manifestations of celestial writings, based on revelations primarily communicated by a high divine being known as Heavenly Worthy of Primordial Origin (Yuanshi Tianzun). In some contexts, the primordial genesis of this powerful divinity is associated with the creation of the universe. Similarly, the cosmic point of origin is depicted as a principal source for the Lingbao scriptures and the talismans associated with them. From a historical point of view, the initial revelation of the texts—and perhaps also their compilation—is attributed to Ge Chaofu (fl. c. 400 CE), an obscure member of the southern aristocracy, who was a descendant of Ge Hong.

A major step towards the formation of a distinct tradition of Daoism centered on the Lingbao scriptures and took place during the middle part of the fifth century, when the prominent scholar and ritual specialist Lu Xiujing (406–477) organized the disparate scriptures and systematized their teachings. An important part of that process was Lu's compilation of the first catalogue of the scriptures and his standardization of the rituals depicted in them. His efforts paved the way for the creation of a coherent school of Daoism, renowned for its codification of communal rituals. That was accompanied with the production of additional scriptures and the writing of commentaries.

Although subsequently it was largely overshadowed by the Shangqing school, the Lingbao school continued to occupy an important position within Daoism. Its elaborations and codifications of Daoist liturgy were especially significant, as they became the predominant liturgical frameworks and ritual templates for the whole of Daoism. The lasting influence of Lingbao Daoism is still evident in the common forms of ritual practiced within contemporary Daoism.

As was the case with the Shangqing school, the amalgamation of diverse elements of medieval Daoism into the Lingbao texts and the teachings associated with them involved notable shifts in emphasis and that implied selective rearranging of the priorities of religious life. The Lingbao school continued a trend towards relegation of physical exercises, use of herbs and potions, and laboratory alchemy to a relatively marginal position within the broad array of Daoist practices, even if the quest for immortality remained a predominant theme, albeit in a reformulated form. The solitary meditations and visualizations of the Shangqing school were also not a major focal point of attention. Instead, the Lingbao school is renowned for its

Benefits of possessing and reciting a Lingbao scripture

Whoever possesses this scripture is able to mobilize its powerful merits on behalf of heaven and earth, the thearchial rulers, and the masses of people. When, in times of calamity, you arouse your faith and practice retreats, burning incense and reciting this scripture ten times, your name will in all cases be recorded in various heavens and the myriad spirits will guard you. In contradiction to the aforementioned whose grasp of the Dao is shallow, those who excel in its study will serve as ministers of the Sage Lord in the Golden Porte.

The Wondrous Scripture of the Upper Chapters on Limitless Salvation;
translated in Bokenkamp 1997: 430.

pervasive emphasis on ritual as the primary form of practice and the central element of Daoist religious life. The liturgical framework adopted and promulgated by the tradition's adherents was predominantly communal in character, even though some of the original scriptures might have been meant for solitary recitation performed in a meditation chamber.

One of the novel ideas brought into Daoism by the Lingbao schools is the notion of universal salvation, which is a prime example of the previously noted Buddhist influences. Other notable developments were the introduction of the Buddhist concepts of merit, reincarnation, and karma, which came to exert great influence on Daoism and popular religion. Buddhist ideas also creep into discussions of morality, where they are typically mixed with traditional Confucian virtues. Furthermore, concepts derived from Buddhist texts play a role in the reconfiguring of Daoist cosmological schemes, including the depictions of various hells and heavens, some of which are given Buddhist-sounding names.

For instance, the threefold division of the heavens introduced in Lingbao texts was based on the Buddhist notion of three realms (or worlds): the realm of desire, the realm of form, and the formlessness realm. Even the main deity associated with the Lingbao scriptures, Heavenly Worthy of Primordial Origin, had notable Buddhist overtones. Not only was his title derived from Buddhist sources, but the deity himself can be seen as a Daoist recasting of the cosmic Buddha Vairocana. Moreover, in a manner reminiscent of the Buddhist scriptures, Heavenly Worthy was provided with a disciple who also served as his interlocutor, a potent deity called Supreme Lord of the Dao (Taishang Daojun).

The authors or editors of some Lingbao scriptures took the additional step of directly appropriating whole sections from Buddhist canonical texts. In addition, the mysterious celestial language reproduced in some of them is modeled on Chinese transliterations of Sanskrit words found in Buddhist scriptures, effectively functioning as a pseudo-Sanskrit concoction that is meant to evoke a sense of otherworldliness. Nonetheless, the infusion of Buddhist ideas and imagery into Daoism needs to be put into a proper perspective. There are palpable elements of superficiality in many of the borrowings, which were primarily based on popular forms of Buddhism, rather than on the rarefied intellectualizations of the clerical elite.

The process of appropriating Buddhist elements within Lingbao Daoism was complex and multifaceted. Buddhist ideas were often subjected to significant modifications as they were integrated into indigenous theoretical and ritual templates, and they were often used for somewhat different purposes. Even so, the pervasive influence of Buddhism, readily observable throughout Lingbao literature, marks an important point in the ongoing reconstitution of the Chinese religious landscape. The infusion of Buddhist concepts and imagery enriched and expanded the contours of Daoism, precisely at a point when Daoism was entering a golden age of unparalleled flourishing and influence, which reached its apogee during the Tang era.

Codification of Daoist ritual

Daoist ritual is essentially concerned with bringing about social harmony and cosmic accord. It is meant to foster integration with the Dao, at the individual and the communal levels. On the whole, the liturgical observances formulated and enacted by the Lingbao school were marked by structural complexity and multidimensionality. They simultaneously operated at three different levels: the heavens, the earthly realm, and the individual person. The primary focus on ritual also brought about significant institutional changes. Most notably, it facilitated the growth of Daoist priesthood that specialized in the performance of rites and ceremonial functions. The members of the clergy secured their privileged status—which also carried notable economic benefits—by adopting the prominent role of mediators between the gods and humanity.

The main element of the Lingbao school's liturgical program was the communal recitation of sacred texts, which to this days remains a focal aspect of Daoist practice. Central to the ritual observances were intricate purificatory rites (*zhai*), of which there were nine main categories. Together with the "offerings" rites (*jiao*), sometimes also referred to as "rituals of cosmic renewal," these rites form the two main categories of Daoist ritual. Staged in carefully designated sacred space that contained a central altar, the rites involved public confession of past transgressions, as well as communal chants, prayers, and petitions directed towards the heavenly realms and the gods that reside there (see Figures 4.2 and 4.3).

The main part of the ritual was preceded by preliminary purification observances, including bodily cleansing and fasting. The formal ceremonies were often followed

Figure 4.2   Daoist priests perform ritual bows, Hong Kong

by communal feasts. The assorted ritual observances adopted a solemn tone and were supposed to mirror central Daoist principles. Key ritual elements were purportedly grounded in contemplative experiences; to that effect, short periods of silent meditation were imbedded in some of the rituals. At the same time, the rituals also possessed striking theatrical traits. They featured conspicuous dramatic elements, such as dance movements and the playing of musical instruments, and made extensive use of ceremonial paraphernalia that included colorful banners and incense. These exterior traits, along with the belief in the spiritual potency of the rituals, doubtlessly contributed to their remarkable popularity and staying power.

In terms of their primary function, the rituals of Lingbao and other Daoist traditions were understood as potent vehicles for return to a primordial order, in which the faithful arrive at a union with the Dao. Within this soteriological scheme, the primary means for the attainment of salvation was ritual practice grounded in sacred texts, situated into a larger cosmological framework. The texts were also credited with talismanic power, as they were believed to bestow protection and possess salvific efficacy. Because of their importance, the sacred texts were to be carefully safeguarded by assuring that they only landed in the hands of legitimate owners. That meant they were to be transmitted only in a properly authorized manner.

Figure 4.3   Daoist priests participate in the Grand Ceremony of Luotian, Hong Kong

The Lingbao rituals were often used for the achievement of prosaic goals, such as the prevention of natural calamities. However, their self-professed ultimate aim was the salvation of all beings. The salvation of the individual (and by extension the group) was therefore closely linked with the salvation of all beings in the universe, an idea adopted from Mahāyāna Buddhism. The prospect of collective salvation from the suffering and imperfection of earthly existence was also extended to the dead. In an apparent bow to Chinese traditions and prevailing sensibilities, the Lingbao texts and rituals make special references to the salvation of the ancestors. That seemingly superfluous move points to an ongoing preoccupation with ancestor worship, which reflected deeply felt religious needs and prevalent cultural sentiments.

Canon formation and functions of texts

One of the defining features of Daoism is that it is a religious tradition grounded in texts or writings. At the core of its textual corpus are scriptures alleged to be revealed by gods and other celestial divinities, which are meant to disclose the inner structure of reality and the mysterious workings of the Dao. Daoist myths of origin trace the initial formation of the scriptures back to the primordial time of cosmic creation, as the original logograms were formed spontaneously from primal breaths or vapors. The gods then wrote down the celestial prototypes of the scriptures—on jade tablets, according to some accounts—which refracted and crystallized the fundamental cosmic patens of the Dao. The scriptures revealed to humanity are deemed to be second-order versions derived from the heavenly archetypes, but they are still greatly revered as sources of sublime knowledge and immense power. This kind of accounting of scriptural genesis resonates with deeply-ingrained notions about the mystical origins of the written graphs that comprise the Chinese script, reflected in the reverential attitude towards writing that infuses Chinese culture.

When used properly, the scriptures are believed to be able to bring about reordering of the world, at the everyday and the otherworldly levels, as well as lead to the realization of sublime states of transcendence. In accord with prevalent beliefs about their primeval and divine origins, the texts are seen as ageless repositories of precious knowledge, with universal import and common meaning, intended for all of humanity. Consequently, their creation is traditionally decoupled from the temporal contexts and historical exigencies that were implicated in their initial manifestations and ensuing modifications. In contrast, critical scholarship sees the Daoist scriptures predominantly as products of the religious and social worlds of medieval China, akin to the canonical collections of other religious traditions. That makes the texts fascinating sources of information about the social worlds and the religious milieus that produced them.

With the ongoing increase in textual production in medieval China, exemplified by the divine revelations surveyed above, there arose a need to assemble together the expanding body of Daoist writings and organize it into a coherent canon. Significant efforts in that direction were the compilations of early catalogues of Daoist texts, such as a catalogue compiled by Ge Hong during the third century. The basic structure of the Daoist canon is already evident by the time of Lu Xiujing, who created an inclusive catalogue of Daoist texts, the second version of which he presented to the imperial throne in 471. Lu divided the catalogue into three broad categories, called "caverns" (*dong*). The gradual process of canon formation was an important step in the creation of a common Daoist identity, as diverse groups were brought together within the broad confines of a relatively cohesive religious tradition. The process of common identity creation was influenced by the increased popularity of Buddhism, whose religious and institutional identities were fairly stable, and to a substantial degree were linked with the prominent status of its voluminous canon.

Besides their normative roles as repositories of timeless knowledge, guides for spiritual cultivation, and manuals for liturgical practice, Daoist scriptures were also perceived as powerful talismans. Some texts were deemed appropriate for broad dissemination (e.g. *Laozi*), but many texts were meant to only have limited circulation. With the increased institutionalization of Daoism, the later group of texts was supposed to be transmitted in carefully defined ritual contexts. That

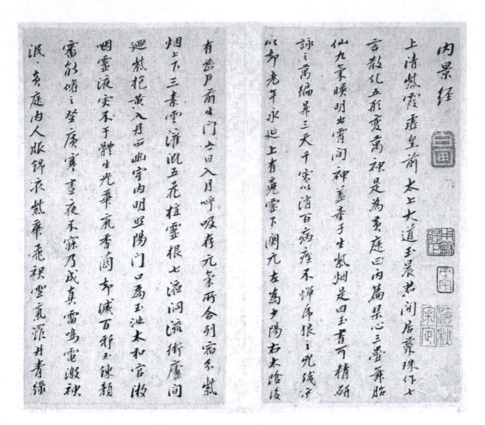

Figure 4.4 *Huangting neijing jing (Scripture of the Inner Radiance of the Yellow Court);* calligraphy by Bada Shanren (1626–1705) (Freer Gallery of Art, Smithsonian Institution, Washington, D.C.: Purchase- E. Rhodes and Leona B. Carpenter Foundation in honor of the 75th Anniversary of the Freer Gallery of Art, F1998.29.1-12)

contributed to the formation of transmission lineages, which to a large extent served to solidify the power and authority of clerical elites. Consequently, scriptural transmissions became key elements in the ritual initiations and ordinations of Daoist priests, some of which were also extended to other practitioners. Daoist adepts were able to go over a series of increasingly higher ritual empowerments and ordinations, each linked with the transmission of a particular scripture. The process ended with the transmission of texts recognized as forming the apex of the canonical hierarchy, which usually meant scriptures belonging to the Shangqing corpus.

The Daoist canon is known as *Daozang* (Repository of [texts about] the Dao), a designation that was originally based on its Buddhist counterpart. Within the threefold division of Daoist texts introduced by Lu Xiujing, the scriptures of the Shangqing school were placed in the first cavern, those of the Lingbao school in the second cavern, while the third cavern comprised a smaller body of texts centered on

The "Three Caverns" of the Daoist canon

- Cavern of Perfection (Dongzhen)—Shangqing scriptures
- Cavern of Mystery (Dongxuan)—Lingbao scriptures
- Cavern of Divinity (Dongshen)—Three Sovereigns (San huang) scriptures

the *Three Sovereign Scripture* (see box). This kind of arrangement involved hierarchical ordering of the various traditions of Daoism, with the Shangqing school occupying the highest position. Gradually this arrangement grew in complexity, as each of the caverns was further divided into twelve sections. The tripartite division of the canon was probably based on Buddhist models: either the original threefold division of the Buddhist canon (scriptures, texts about monastic discipline, and scholastic treatises), or the three vehicles of Mahāyāna Buddhism (those of hearers, pratyekabuddhas, and bodhisattvas). It is notable that the three vehicles model in Buddhism involves hierarchical ordering of teachings that is analogous to the one implicit in the Daoist canon.

The Daoist canon was an open collection of sacred texts. Consequently, it continued to grow over the centuries, as newly-composed texts were added to it, while older texts were subjected to alterations and ongoing exegesis. In light of such growth, the original division of the canon into three caverns proved inadequate. Consequently, four supplements were added to it during the sixth century. The fourth supplement, named Orthodox Unity (Zhengyi), contained the scriptures of the Celestial Masters school. In addition to the aforementioned scriptures, the Daoist canon came to include a wide range of other materials: scholastic and exegetical treatises, historical texts (including collections of hagiographies), and above all ritual manuals, which in terms of their number became the largest genre of texts in the canon.

The production of various editions of the canon was customarily undertaken under imperial auspices, as was also the case with the Buddhist canon. During the early eight century, Emperor Xuanzong (r. 713–756) ordered the collection of all Daoist texts circulating throughout the vast empire. The texts were then put together into a canonical collection, copies of which were distributed to Daoist temples across the country. Similar undertaking was ordered by emperor Taizong (r. 976–97), as part of efforts to consolidate central imperial authority after the reunification of China under the Song dynasty. The version of *Daozang* used today was compiled in 1445 under the imperial auspices of the Ming dynasty; it is thus known as the *Ming Canon of Daoist Scriptures* or the *Zhengtong Daoist Canon* (from the name of the reign era during which it was published). It is a vast collection of texts, numbering some 1,500 separate titles, to which a supplement was added in 1607.

Daoism as official religion

We already noted a few instances of the long-standing connections between Daoism and the exercise of political power in ancient China. Pertinent examples include the political readings of *Laozi* and the ideas about rule by the way of non-action articulated by the Huanglao movement in Han times. The incipiency of Daoism as an organized religion had prominent sociopolitical dimensions, as evidenced by the formation of a theocratic mini-state in Sichuan by the Celestial Masters. The subsequent move of the Celestial Maters to the North was accompanied with their official recognition in the early third century. That represented a momentous shift in political and ideological orientation, a clear move away from the origins of religious Daoism in millenarian movements, which were predominantly peasant-based and thrived at the social margins.

From the third century, the adoption of court-oriented outlook became a predominant concern within the nascent Daoist church, paving the way for rapprochement between the religion and key power-brokers in medieval Chinese society. An early culmination of that process was the institution of Daoism as de-facto state religion under the Northern Wei dynasty (386–534), whose Toba rulers were of non-Chinese extraction. At the time, the promotion of Daoism was perceived within elite circles as a way of Sinicizing the Toba. The central figure in this transformation of Daoism into an elite religion closely alighted with the imperial government and the aristocracy was Kou Qianzhi (365–448). He was a prominent Daoist leader with aristocratic background, who claimed to be a recipient of divine revelations. This procurement of elevated status as Northern Wei empire's official religion was a first event of its kind in the history of Daoism, sometimes interpreted as the establishment of Daoist theocracy.

As a reward for Kou Qianzhi's valuable efforts at providing religiously-based sanction to the Northern Wei dynasty, he was awarded the official title of Celestial Master. The Daoist endorsement and legitimization of dynastic rule, reflected in the emperor's adoption of a Daoist title for himself and the official institution of Daoist rituals at the court, sanctified Wei's authority and bolstered the dynasty's claim to be the rightful inheritor of the Mandate of Heaven. Under Kou's leadership, the Daoist church expanded its footprint and influence at the court, adopting a conservative ideological stance and aligning itself closely with the interests of the state and the ruling elites. The consolidation of Daoism as an official religion under Wei rule was accompanied with the surfacing of exclusivist attitudes. That was given concrete expression in a government-sponsored persecution of Buddhism and other religious groups that were labeled as heretical cults.

The Northern Wei experiment with the institution of Daoism as state religion was short-lived, roughly taking place during the 425–450 period. Following Kou Qianzhi's death, by the mid-fifth century the dynasty shifted its main focus of religious allegiance and political patronage to Buddhism. Nonetheless, on the whole Daoism continued to prosper during the subsequent centuries, as Daoist institutions were recipients of state support under a number of dynasties. That was especially the case during the Tang era, when Daoism achieved the peak of its development and influence on Chinese culture and society. The Tang dynasty afforded great prestige to Daoism and extended generous patronage to the Daoist church. At the same time, the dynasty relied extensively on Daoist ritual, imagery, and cachet to bolster its prestige and enhance the legitimacy of its rule.

The roots of the close connection between the Tang dynasty and Daoism go back to the early seventh century, when the imperial family tried to bolster its standing vis-à-vis the better established aristocratic families of northern China by tracing its ancestry back to Laozi. This ploy at aggrandizing the ancestral pedigree of the new imperial family, as part of an overall strategy of bolstering its claim to have received the Mandate of Heaven, was based on the fact that their family name Li was the same as the one that was traditionally ascribed to Laozi. The purported familial connection with the ancient sage was also linked with a popular prophecy about the pending rule of a sagely ruler surnamed Li, which circulated within millenarian circles. Accordingly, in 625, seven years after the official founding of the dynasty, its first emperor proclaimed that Daoism will be officially ranked first among the "three teachings," ahead of Confucianism and Buddhism.

Picking up on the notion of ancestral connection with Laozi, subsequent Tang emperors offered substantial political and economic patronage to the Daoist clergy and their temples, although the level of official support varied according to political circumstances and reflected the personal pieties of individual emperors. The Tang era is usually celebrated as a remarkable period in Daoist history, marked by imposing consolidation of principal Daoist teachings, practices, and institutions. From a religious perspective, it was a golden age that saw the formation of a grand Daoist synthesis, formed to a substantial degree by the incorporation of copious elements from Buddhism.

Key aspects of the ingenious Tang synthesis were manifested in rarefied philosophical speculations, splendid rituals, and vibrant religious institutions, which secured Daoism's prominent position and its central role in the transmission of traditional Chinese culture. At the same time, throughout this period Daoism had to contend with the greater popularity of Buddhism, whose clergy and religious establishments greatly outnumbered those of the Daoists. The parallel flourishing of both religions is a testimony to the grandeur and openness of Tang culture, in which all three teachings participated and interacted with each other. On the whole, the cosmopolitan and pluralistic outlook generally characteristic of the Tang era proved well suited for the flourishing of multifaceted religious and intellectual life, marked by their sophistication, creativity, and embrace of diversity.

During the Tang era, the height of the status of Daoism as official state religion occurred under the rule of Emperor Xuanzong, which was marked by unparalleled economic prosperity and cultural effervescence. Although like other Tang rulers Xuanzong continued to support Confucianism and Buddhism, throughout his reign he exhibited distinct pro-Daoist sympathies. His extensive patronage of Daoism was to a large extent grounded in personal beliefs and predilections, although pragmatic political consideration also played an important part. The emperor was a student of Daoist literature—he even "authored" a commentary on Laozi's classic—and was an ardent believer in miracles and omens. He associated with a number of prominent Daoist prelates, especially those affiliated with the dominant Shangqing school, often inviting them to lecture and perform rituals at the imperial court. In addition, Xuanzong received a Daoist ordination.

Xuanzong's support of the Shangqing school is evident in a decree that the local gods associated with the five sacred mountains, traditionally linked with the state cult, were to be put under control of Shangqing divinities, who were to be worshiped at temples situated on each of the five mountains. Xuanzong also established a system of state-supported Daoist abbeys, which were required to perform officially-sanctioned liturgies for the benefit of the imperial family and the state. His patronage of Daoist learning included the setting up of Daoist schools and the institution of official Daoist examinations, which made mastery of the Daoist classics an alternative avenue for entry into the imperial bureaucracy. These policies went along with the already-mentioned compilation of a Daoist canon and its distribution throughout the empire.

Following a recognizable historical pattern, this kind of generous patronage was linked with policies aimed at controlling the religion. For instance, Xuanzong and other Tang emperors issued decrees and instituted regulations that restricted the clergy's freedom of movement and the scope of its activities, aimed at the Daoists and the Buddhists alike. Clerics had to register with the government, which also controlled the system of monastic ordinations and influenced the selection of abbots. Their freedom of movement and association were also restricted, and the government had a system of punitive laws and harsh punishments for those who misbehaved or violated its directives. Various emperors also asserted the governmental prerogative to adjudicate the inclusion (or exclusion) of texts into the canon, which gave them an important say in the delineation of religious orthodoxy. From the Song dynasty onward, another aspect of the relationship between Daoism and the imperial state was the Daoist canonization of popular cults that were recognized by the state.

Interreligious debates

One of the remarkable features of religious life in medieval China was the staging of interreligious debates that featured prominent representatives of the three teachings. The formal enactment of such public events—which highlighted both the distinctive features and the points of convergence among the doctrines of Buddhism, Confucianism, and Daoism—was a potent symbol of China's embrace of a broad framework of religious pluralism. This kind of ecumenical stance stood in stark contrast to the interreligious strife and intolerance that at the time prevailed in Europe and elsewhere. A number of these debates were held at the imperial courts of various dynasties, including the Tang, often in front of the emperor and his senior officials, some of whom took part in the proceedings. Beside their religious and educational functions, at times the debating performances had certain entertainment value and were integrated into larger imperial celebrations.

Typically the official interreligious debates were carefully staged events, often set in convivial ambience and performed in accord with formulaic patterns of courtly ritual. Nonetheless, at times the stakes were real and the outcome of the debate had substantial repercussions for individual religions. That was especially the case with the Buddhists and the Daoists, who occupied conterminous social and religious spaces, and were often in direct competition for status and patronage. There was often a sycophantic undertone to the debates, as each tradition tried to score points by establishing its greater usefulness to the imperial state.

A major point of argument put forward by Daoist leaders in their intellectual duels with the Buddhists was a well-known theory that the emergence of Buddhism was outgrowth of a "conversion of the barbarians," undertaken by none other than Laozi. This notion was given canonical sanction by *Huahu jing* (Scripture on the Conversion of Barbarians), an apocryphal text initially composed around 300 CE and greatly expanded over the subsequent centuries. This spurious scripture was widely circulated in Daoist circles and often evoked in the debates with the Buddhists. According to *Huahu jing*, the Buddha was an incarnation of Laozi, who traveled to India in order to edify the ignorant foreigners. This idea was based on the well-known legend about Laozi's final journey to the West. It essentially insinuated that Buddhism is little more than a diluted form of Daoism, devised for the benefit of culturally inferior people.

The formulation of this kind of religious and pseudo-historical lines of argument, presented in *Huahu jing* and other similar polemical tracts, seems to have been initially animated by a spirit of inclusiveness. They also reflected a concern for accounting the seeming similarities between the teachings and practices of the two religions. Before long, however, the tone of the arguments, as evidenced in later versions of *Huahu jing* and other texts with similar message, became more combative and defamatory. In effect, the original contention about the putative relatedness of Buddhism and Daoism deteriorated into scratchy polemical assertions about the inferiority of Buddhism and triumphant declarations of the superiority of Daoism, tinged with xenophobic sentiments about innate Chinese superiority. That annoyed many Buddhists, who vehemently objected to what they perceived to be slanderous remarks about their religion's founder and open affront to his teachings.

The choice of the conversion of the barbarians theme as a debating point turned out to be a losing proposition and a source of considerable grief for the Daoists. The Buddhists were repeatedly successful in discrediting *Huahu jing* as a ludicrous forgery, even if in the process of doing that they themselves used far-fetched sources and dubious arguments about the greater age of the Buddha and the like. Some fringe Buddhist texts even put forward a curious theory that Laozi was a disciple of the Buddha, as was Confucius. The string of debates lost by the Daoists—a number of which incorporated the *Huahu jing* and its tenets, but also covered other areas of difference or disagreement—started during the early sixth century, although it is worth noting that at times the Daoists were successful in making their case and gaining an upper hand.

The last series of formal debates took place at the Mongol court of Kubilai Khan (r. 1271–1294) during the Yuan dynasty. The Daoists were primarily represented by the Complete Perfection school (see below). According to traditional accounts, they were defeated at the last debate of 1281 and suffered disastrous consequences. Not only was there an imperial decree that all copies of *Huahu jing* must be destroyed, but the same fate was to befall all other Daoist texts, with the sole exception of *Laozi*. At the same time, severe restrictions were placed on the Daoist clergy, although it is unclear how strictly the imperial decree was actually enforced on the ground.

Monastic orders and institutions

Even before the emergence of Daoism as organized religion, various forms of reclusion—withdrawal from society that usually involved (temporary) renunciation of social status and worldly pleasures—were familiar features of the Chinese religious landscape. Examples of religiously-inspired abandonment of conventional norms and adoption of alternative lifestyles during the Han era, often linked with eremitic ideals, are evident among the *fangshi* practitioners of magical arts and the seekers of immortality. Nonetheless, the fully developed ideals and institutions of monasticism were essentially unknown in China before the advent of Buddhism. Although the Celestial Masters instituted comprehensive communal structures and formal rules that governed the behavior of their followers, their movement did not adopt a monastic orientation. Their priests were married householders with distinct ranks and ritual functions, unlike the Chinese followers of Buddhism, the most fervent among whom adopted a monastic ethos imported from abroad; however, during later periods some of the Daoist clergy choose to lead a celibate life.

The monastic vocation involves observance of celibacy as part of a distinctive religious way of life, ideally oriented towards the pursuit of spiritual perfection. Entry into a monastic order is effectively an expression of individual commitment, but it usually takes place within a structured communal setting, meant to provide optimal conditions for a religious quest, ostensibly directed towards the pursuit of ultimate truth and self-realization. The emergence and codification of Daoist variants of the monastic vocation was a gradual process that unfolded over several centuries. The evolution of Daoist monasticism involved extensive borrowings from the Buddhist monastic order, which brought to China longstanding models of monastic institutions with evolved organizational structures, systems of communal rules, and established patterns of interaction with the surrounding society and the state.

The Buddhist monastic models were selectively adapted in accord with Daoist ideas and practices. Gradually they coalesced with the communal ethos of the Celestial Masters and the previously-mentioned eremitic ideals. By the fifth century we already encounter quasi-monastic communities led by noted Daoist leaders such as Kou Qianzhi and Lu Xiujing, whose members practiced celibacy and embraced reclusive lifestyles. A similar trend is observable in the Daoist community on Maoshan that was led by Tao Hongjing during the early sixth century, paving the way for the emergence of two parallel—though not necessarily radically disjoined—vocational patterns for the Daoist clergy that continue to the present day: as celibate monastics (male and female) or married priests (typically male).

The flourishing of fairly developed monastic tradition was a prominent feature of Daoism during the Tang period. This was an integral part of the overall consolidation of Daoism during its heyday, which went along with its mature assimilation of elements from Buddhism. During this period we find a large number of monastic establishments situated across the Tang empire, from large and imposing abbeys in the two capitals to small temples and hermitages scattered across scenic mountains. In these establishments thousands of Daoist monks and nuns pursued their religious vocations, which in addition to various forms of spiritual discipline also included the performance of liturgies for their patrons and the imperial state. The abbeys and convents developed elaborate institutional structures, with extensive administrative offices, comprehensive sets of regulations, and evolved liturgical programs. They served as important centers of Daoist practice and learning, but they also performed important cultural roles and were frequented by commoners and literati alike.

Daoist monasticism underwent further development and formalization after the Tang era. A prime example of monastic Daoism from the late imperial period is the Complete Perfection (Quanzhen) school, which initially emerged in the twelfth century and by the thirteen century became the dominant tradition of Daoism in northern China. The clergy of the Complete Perfection school were celibate, followed vegetarian diet, and lived in well-ordered communities. They practiced mendicancy and led austere lifestyles; a focal point of their spiritual regiment were contemplative practices aimed at realizing one's true nature (see last section). The school's founder Wang Zhe (1113–1170) was a scion of a wealthy family who entered religious life

Figure 4.5   Daoist monks and laypeople in front of a shrine room, Baxian (Eight Immortals) Abbey, Xi'an

as a middle-aged person; prior to his conversion he was an eccentric figure prone to heavy drinking. After a series of visionary experiences, during which he purportedly established communion with distinguished immortals and celestial beings, Wang came to prominence as the charismatic leader of a band of dedicated and talented disciples, some of whom became notable figures celebrated in popular Daoist lore.

The Complete Perfection school is sometimes described as the first fully-developed monastic order within Daoism, within evolved structures and distinctive communal way of life that paralleled those of the Buddhist monastic order. Especially noticeable are the similarities with the Chan school, the predominant tradition of elite Buddhism, evident across the areas of monastic discipline, doctrine, and practice. Notwithstanding the movement's monastic orientation, its leaders also cultivated a close relationship with numerous lay supporters. The laity was organized in associations that provided support for the monastic communities.

Wang is also notable for his syncretic tendencies and ecumenical attitudes, including his advocacy of the unity of the three teachings. He advised his disciples to recite popular Confucian and Buddhist texts, especially the *Classic of Filial Piety* and the *Heart Scripture*. Wang and his disciples were prolific writers, leaving behind a large body of Daoist literature that included poetry and essays. They also composed manuals of spiritual cultivation, transcripts of oral teachings, hagiographical collections, and exegetical works.

A key event marking the Complete Perfection school's rise to great prominence was the meeting in 1222 between Wang's most prominent disciple Qiu Chuji (1143–1227) and the great Mongol conqueror Chinggis Khan (d. 1227). The meeting took place at the Mongol court in Central Asia, and before long Qiu's epic journey became celebrated as a seminal event in the Daoist tradition's history. The Mongol ruler was duly impressed by the Daoist master and his teachings. Consequently, Chinggis Khan issued a decree that all Daoist monks and nuns should be given tax-exempt status and placed under the control of the Complete Perfection patriarch. Subsequently the Complete Perfection school became the most powerful religious movement in northern China.

Although it subsequently lost some of its initial vigor and influence, to this day the Complete Perfection school remains the main representative of monastic Daoism, even though the majority of its clergy are in fact married. The gradual decline from its peak, achieved during the thirteenth century under the Mongol Yuan dynasty (1271–1367), parallels the overall weakening of Daoism during the late imperial period, although recent scholarship has shown that on the whole Daoism flourished during the Ming era. The religion's gradual decline is especially evident during the Qing dynasty (1644–1911). Together with the Celestial Masters—who by the fourteenth century resurfaced in the South as a major Daoist tradition—the Complete Perfection school remains one of the two main schools of Daoism. Its strongest presence is in northern China, while Celestial Masters Daoism is more prevalent in the South.

Female role models and adepts

Generally speaking, throughout history the pursuit of religious vocation within a Daoist milieu has been open to both sexes. For example, women were welcomed as full-fledged members in the early communities of the Celestial Masters, and they could also serve as libationers. Later women could join the ranks of the religious and enter Daoist convents. There they could lead pious lives, presumably oriented towards plumbing the mysteries of the Dao, in ways that mostly paralleled the vocational patterns of their male brethren. On the whole, Daoist methods of spiritual cultivation are gender-neutral and realization of the ultimate goals of practice is open to both men and women. Although it is true that some of the early stages in the practice of internal alchemy differ somewhat between men and women, that is primarily due to the need to take into account the physiological differences between the two genders.

There were of course exceptions to the prevalent egalitarian attitudes of female acceptance and participation. For instance, in certain sexual practices male adepts used multiple female consorts as sources of vital energy that bolstered the circulation of their sexual essence, often without being overly concerned with the wellbeing of the women in question. There are also indications that Daoists were not always immune to various forms of prejudice directed towards women, which were rampant within the patriarchal social order of imperial China—as well as in virtually all other societies at the time—especially if we judge from the vantage-point of modern Western ideas about gender equity. Nonetheless, on balance it is fair to say that Daoism was especially welcoming to women, giving them unique opportunities to act as individual agents and pursue alternative avenues of personal growth and expression. That included exceptional opportunities to get away from the dominating relationships with men, which governed the lives of females in the Confucian-oriented society of traditional China.

Women attracted to Daoist life and practice had a number of positive female role models to follow. The Daoist pantheon includes many female divinities and immortals, such as the Queen Mother of the West and the female deities and perfected that inhabit the Shangqing heaven. There were also famous female adepts and priestesses, some of whom became apotheosized and turned into objects of cultic worship (see

Figure 4.6   Female devotees reading scriptures, Xingtian Temple, Taipei

Notable female divinities and practitioners

- Queen Mother of the West (Xiwangmu), the supreme Daoist goddess, believed to rule over a western paradise from her majestic palace at mythical Mt. Kunlun.
- Wei Huacun (252–334, also known as Lady Wei), noted adept in the Celestial Masters tradition and deity that revealed the Shangqing scriptures.
- He Xiangu (Immortal Maiden He, also known as He Qiong), the sole female member of the renowned group of Eight Immortals, said to originally have been a girl that lived during the Tang era.
- Sun Buer (1119–1182), one of the seven major masters of the early Complete Perfection tradition.

box). As a result of the veneration of notable female figures and the hospitable attitudes towards female participation, Daoist convents attracted a broad range of women into their ranks, from girls coming from peasant families to imperial princesses.

The prominent women who entered Daoist convents included the daughter of Empress Wu (r. 684–705), the only female monarch in Chinese history. Although renowned for her outstanding support of Buddhism, the empress was also a patron of Daoism. She had a Daoist convent built for her only daughter, who was installed as its abbess. Nuns also remained a prominent fixture in the Daoist orders that thrived in late imperial China, especially those of the Complete Perfection tradition. One of Wang Zhe's most prominent disciples—hailed as the "seven perfected ones"—was the female adept Sun Buer, and there were many other prominent nuns and female adepts. The tradition of Daoist nuns continues to this day.

Internal alchemy and meditation

One of the prominent features of the Complete Perfection school's soteriological orientation is the integration of internal alchemy (*neidan*, lit. "inner cinnabar") into its comprehensive program of spiritual cultivation. Internal alchemy stands in contrast to external or laboratory alchemy, which seeks to procure the elixir of immortality by means of chemical procedures performed in the alchemist's furnace (see previous chapter). While internal alchemy adopted much of the chemical vocabulary of external alchemy, it used it in a metaphorical manner to indicate inner essences and processes that occurred within the individual practitioner. In effect, the body and mind of the Daoist adept became the primary foci and tools of spiritual transformation, replacing the mineral substances and laboratory instruments of external alchemy.

In the context of Complete Perfection praxis, the earlier goal of transmuting the body and achieving physical immortality is largely beside the point. Instead, the primary focus within its soteriological paradigm is on bringing about inner transformation that ultimately involves transcendence of the mundane realm, in which the adept's mind/heart (*xin*) harmonizes with the primordial and ineffable Dao. While spiritual cultivation incorporates corporal aspects and physiological elements, it is essentially a meditative process guided by and centered on the mind/heart that culminates with the experience of enlightenment. At the end of the spiritual journey, the adept uncovered his or her true mind or original nature, which is unborn and is never destroyed.

The shift from external to internal alchemy developed gradually, over a number of centuries. Early precursors of the tenets and procedures of internal alchemy are evident in the contemplative visualizations and inwardly-oriented practices of the Shangqing school. An example of that is the meditative formula of "guarding the One" (*shouyi*), earlier versions of which circulated before the Shangqing revelations. The practice is based on the notion of correspondence between the macrocosm and the microcosm—a central idea featured in many Daoist texts—which implies close linkage of the individual with the cosmos. An important facet of that correlation is the inherence of the gods that populate the cosmos within the human body.

Like the bureaucratic pantheon of their celestial counterparts, the gods of the body have discrete areas of oversight, ensuring the proper working of bodily organs and physical processes. The contemplative practice of "guarding the One" consists of visualizing and concentrating on the One, a supreme deity that represents a divinized presence of the primordial void and controls the other gods in the body, who in turn are responsible for the proper operation of different bodily organs and functions. By means of this form of meditation, the adept is supposedly able to safeguard the bodily gods and thus ensure his or her health and longevity, while also harmonizing with larger cosmic forces and attuning to the Dao.

A major turning point in the development of internal alchemy took place during the Tang era. At the time external alchemy reached its highpoint of influence, but

Realization of the true nature in Complete Perfection Daoism

If you want to nurture your vital energy and complete your spirit, you must completely get rid of your myriad attachments. Be pure and still on the surface and within. If you remain dedicated and devoted for a long, long time, your spirit will be stable, and your vital energy will be harmonious .... Only those who study the Dao will reach the stage where their spirit will reside together with the Dao and thereby be indestructible forever, and also have the power to raise nine generations of ancestors to the [realm of] Supreme Purity.

From the recorded sayings of Complete Perfection patriarch Ma Yu (1123–1184); translation adapted from Eskildsen 2004: 90–91.

we also witness the first development of identifiable strands of internal alchemy. The two types of alchemy were sometimes cultivated together and had overlapping imagery and vocabulary. Another trend observable during the Tang period was the development of discursive types of meditation, which were connected with the formulation of new doctrinal schemes influenced by Buddhist philosophies. This kind of meditation corresponds to the Buddhist practice of insight (*guan*), which together with calmness (*zhi*) is one of the two basic types of Buddhist meditation. A representative example of these tendencies comes from the writings of the Double Mystery (Chongxuan) school, which flourished during the first half of the Tang era and was heavily influenced by the Middle Way or Madhyamaka philosophy of Buddhism.

The notion of "twofold mystery" denotes dual repudiation of one-sided beliefs in existence and nonexistence (or nonbeing). The first mystery entails transcendence of existence and nonexistence, while the second mystery involves obliteration of attachment to the first mystery. At the stage of the first mystery, the Daoist adept cultivates detachment from dualistic conceptions of reality that revolve around the notions of existence and nonexistence. Then, at the second stage the adept becomes disengaged from the state of detachment itself. That implies complete elimination of all desires and attachments, including the attachment to tranquil abiding in a state of absence of desires.

The process of self-cultivation followed by practitioners of mature forms of inner alchemy in late imperial China, including those of the Complete Perfection school, implies gradual ascent from coarser to more refined levels of reality or states of existence. Looked at from a different perspective, it represents a procedure of reversal or inversion of natural processes that leads back to a primordial state of perfection and wholeness, return to an original oneness that purportedly existed "before Heaven." That involves gradual move from the everyday existence of ordinary people towards the increasingly subtle and pure states of being that are ascribed to the sages. At the preliminary stage, the adept's self-cultivation mostly takes place at the level of the physical body, which is fortified and balanced by various forms of calisthenics, psychosomatic exercises, diets, and massages. Then the practice unfolds at three basic levels, represented by essence (*jing*), vital energy (*qi*), and spirit (*shen*). Often referred to as the "three treasures" (*sanbao*), these three function as basic components in the inner process of alchemical transmutation.

At the initial stage of the inner alchemical process, special attention is paid to physiological functions, especially the circulation of sexual essence—the conventional or coarse form of essence—whose leakage must be prevented at all cost. The essence is gathered and refined, and its circulation becomes regulated. This stage culminates with the transmutation of essence into vital energy. At the next stage, the adept's practice focuses on the purification and refinement of vital energy, which is enabled to circulate unobstructed inside the body. The most subtle and pure mode of vital energy is caused to rise up to the highest of the three "cinnabar fields" (*dantian*)—key points in the body that control physiological functions and where alchemical transmutations take place—located in the head and associated with thoughts and consciousness. This stage is perfected when the highly purified vital energy is transmuted into spirit.

At the third stage, the spirit is gradually refined, as the adept's mind disengages from dualistic thoughts and reverts to a state of emptiness. The purified spirit constitutes an embryo of immortality that, after being properly nurtured over a period of gestation, leaves the body by way of the top of the head (see Figure 4.7). The whole process of spiritual transformation purportedly culminates in transcendence of the foregoing domains and stages, as the primeval spirit leaves the body and returns to the point of origin, merging with the primordial state of absolute nothingness and becoming absorbed into the timeless and all-pervading Dao.

Figure 4.7 The embryo of immortality leaves the body of a Daoist practitioner

Key points

- The Shangqing scriptures were originally revealed and disseminated within a southern aristocratic milieu, where they were accepted as divine revelations communicated by perfected beings. While the Shangqing tradition incorporated elements from the various strands of medieval Daoism, it placed special emphasis on exploration of the inner world and the contemplative aspects of spiritual cultivation.

- Within the Lingbao scriptures, which appeared soon after the Shangqing revelations, there is a move away from solitary forms of interior exploration and towards ritual forms of worship that are communally oriented. This is also the first time that we find a substantial infusion of Buddhist concepts and ideas into Daoism.

- Lingbao rites were central in the codification of Daoist ritual, which incorporates two main categories: rituals of purification and rituals of renewal. In their classical form, Daoist rituals are multidimensional and incorporate a variety of elements, including the chanting of scriptures, making of petitions and prayers, performance of dance movements, and playing of musical instruments; these are often followed by communal feasts.

- The various Daoist scriptures were by the fifth century organized into a coherent canon, which in its classical form was divided into three parts, the so-called "three caverns," to which additional supplements were added later. The Daoist canon was an open collection of sacred texts, which meant that over the centuries many new texts, composed in different genres, were added to it.

- During both the medieval and the late imperial periods the Daoist church was for the most part closely aligned with the imperial state. The state was an important source of patronage for the Daoist clergy and its temples; the state also asserted its authority over the religion and used it for its own purposes.

- Under the influence of Buddhism, Daoism developed its own monastic orders and institution, which came to play central roles in the religion's historical growth. A prime example of monastic Daoism is the Complete Perfection school, which was formed in the twelfth century and continues to exist to this day as one of the two main traditions of Daoism.

- Daoism was open to female participation, either as a layperson or a nun. Daoist women had numerous positive role models to follow, from various goddesses and females perfected to exemplary nuns and famous female practitioners.

• From the Tang era onward there was a shift from external to internal alchemy. In internal alchemy the focus is on an inner process of alchemical transmutation that takes place with the body and mind of the Daoist adept. The whole process culminates when the purified primeval spirit separates from the body and returns to the point of origin, becoming absorbed into the eternal Dao.

Discussion questions

1. What were the main roles of sacred texts in medieval Daoism, and what were the prevalent beliefs about the origins of the Daoist scriptures?
2. Trace the growing impact of Buddhism on medieval Daoism, as it is played out in the doctrines and practices of the three main Daoist traditions: Celestial Masters, Shangqing, and Lingbao.
3. What was/is the status of women in Daoism and how does it compare with the general status of women in traditional Chinese society?

Further reading

See also the reading suggestions for Chapter 3.

Bokenkamp, Stephen R. *1997. Early Daoist Scriptures. Berkeley, CA:* University of California Press.

Bokenkamp, Stephen R. 2007. *Ancestors and Anxiety: Daoism and the Birth of Rebirth in China.* Berkeley, CA: University of California Press.

Cahill, Suzanne Elizabeth. 1993. *Transcendence and Divine Passion: The Queen Mother of the West in Medieval China.* Stanford, CA: Stanford University Press.

Despeux, Cathrine and Livia Kohn, eds. 2003. *Women in Daoism.* Cambridge, MA: Three Pines Press.

Eskildsen, Stephen. 2004. *The Teachings and Practices of the Early Quanzhen Taoist Masters.* Albany, NY: State University of New York Press.

Girardot, N. J., James Miller, and Xiaogan Liu. 2001. *Daoism and Ecology: Ways within a Cosmic Landscape.* Cambridge, MA: Center for the Study of World Religions, Harvard Divinity School.

Goossaert, Vincent. 2007. *The Taoists of Peking, 1800-1949: A Social History of Urban Clerics.* Cambridge, CA: Harvard University Asia Center.

Kohn, Livia. 2003. *Monastic Life in Medieval Daoism: A Cross-Cultural Perspective.* Honolulu, HI: University of Hawai'i Press.

Kohn, Livia. 2008. *Introducing Daoism.* London and New York: Routledge.

Little, Stephen, and Shawn Eichman. 2000. *Taoism and the Arts of China.* Chicago, IL: Art Institute of Chicago.

Mollier, Christine. 2008. *Buddhism and Taoism Face to Face: Scripture, Ritual, and Iconographic Exchange in Medieval China*. Honolulu, HI: University of Hawai'i Press.

Robinet, Isabelle. 1993. *Taoist Meditation: The Mao-Shan Tradition of Great Purity*. Albany, NY: State University of New York Press.

Schipper, Kristofer. 1993. *The Taoist Body*. Berkeley, CA: University of California Press.

Schipper, Kristofer Marinus, and Franciscus Verellen. 2004. *The Taoist Canon: A Historical Companion to the Daozang*. Chicago, IL: University of Chicago Press.

Wong, Eva, trans. 2004. *Seven Taoist Masters: A Folk Novel of China*. Boston, MA: Shambala Publications.

5 Spread and flourishing of Buddhism in China

In this chapter

Within the broad sweep of Chinese history, Buddhism was undoubtedly the most significant and influential among the religious traditions that originated outside of China. This chapter—the first of two that deal with Buddhism—provides an overview of the history of Buddhism in China. It covers the main events and issues that shaped the initial spread and subsequent flourishing of Chinese Buddhism, from the early beginnings in the first century of the Common Era until the demise of imperial China at the start of the twentieth century. While covering the general historical trajectory of the Chinese encounter with Buddhism, the chapter also discusses in some detail key developments that marked the Sinification of Buddhist doctrines, practices, and institutions, such as the formation of Chinese Buddhist canon and the formulation of taxonomies of teachings.

Main topics

- Early development of Buddhism in India and its growth into an important pan-Asian religion.
- Initial entry of Buddhism into China during the later Han dynasty.
- Barriers that Buddhism had to overcome in the course of its growth in China.
- Reasons for the successful growth and enthusiastic acceptance of Buddhism in medieval China.
- Translation of Buddhist scriptures into Chinese and the creation of a Chinese Buddhist canon.
- Survey of popular scriptures and other notable texts.
- Chinese appropriations of Mahāyāna philosophies and formulations of doctrinal taxonomies.
- Emergence of Buddhism as the major religious tradition in medieval China and its golden age during the Tang dynasty.

- Status and positioning of Buddhism vis-à-vis the imperial state.
- Buddhism in late imperial China.

Buddhism as a pan-Asian religion

Tracing its origins back to the teachings of Siddhartha Gautama, who lived and taught in what is now Northern India some twenty-five centuries ago and came to be popularly known as the Buddha (the Awakened One), over the centuries Buddhism developed into a major pan-Asian religious tradition. After the initial consolidation of its doctrines, development of the monastic order and codification of its rules, and broadening of its institutional presence in the land of its birth, Buddhism gradually spread throughout much of Asia, including China. In the process of its historical growth and evolution in India and elsewhere, Buddhism underwent profound changes as it adapted to local cultural norms and responded to changing sociopolitical predicaments, developing an astounding variety of teachings and traditions. With its lack of central authority and decentralized ecclesiastical structures, Buddhism came to encompass diverse and at times seemingly conflicting theoretical templates, rich arrays of ritual expressions, comprehensive ethical systems and monastic institutions, innumerable texts written in a variety of languages and genres, and a lush tapestry of popular beliefs and practices.

Figure 5.1   Entrance of Famen monastery, Shaanxi

During its long and prominent history in China, Buddhism developed interlinked assemblages of doctrines, practices, traditions, and artistic expressions, and exerted far-reaching influence on various aspects of Chinese society and culture. The transmission of Buddhism into China involved extensive introduction and diffusion of initially alien systems of ideas and institutions that in their scope and impact were unrivaled in Chinese history, at least until the modern period. The Chinese adoption of Buddhism opened up new intellectual horizons, distinct avenues of spiritual engagement, and novel esthetic sensibilities that enriched Chinese civilization and substantially expanded its contours.

In the course of their mutual encounters and multifarious interactions, which were not without occasional tensions and conflicts, Buddhism and Chinese traditions were each challenged and transformed. Buddhism added new features to Chinese civilization and contributed to the ongoing evolution of native cultural norms and expressions. On the other hand, in the process of its Sinification, which entailed adaptation to China's social ethos and cultural milieu, Buddhism underwent significant changes that reflected distinctively Chinese worldviews and spiritual predilections. That made it into a multifaceted tradition that was perceived as both foreign and domestic, incorporating complex mixtures of alien and native elements and practices, which over the last two millennia has been a prominent and integral part of China's multifaceted religious landscape.

Initial entry of Buddhism into China

Buddhism initially entered Chinese territory during the early part of the Eastern Han dynasty (25–220 CE), approximately at the beginning of the Common Era. The first Buddhist followers and missionaries arrived in the land of the Han people through the empire's northwestern frontier, accompanying merchant caravans. They came along the so-called Silk Road, the famous network of trade routes that linked China with Central Asia and Persia, with auxiliary roads that branched into South Asia and further west leading all the way to the Mediterranean world. By that time Buddhism already had a well-established presence in Central Asia, which contained a number of smaller kingdoms whose merchants, some of whom were Buddhists, controlled much of the trade along the Silk Road.

Early literary evidence of Buddhism's entry into China comes from the official Chinese histories, which link the foreign religion's initial arrival into the Middle Kingdom with the Han monarchy and the ruling elites. Such connection is explicit in the well-known story about Emperor Ming's (r. 58–75 CE) dream about a golden deity coming to his palace from the West, which afterwards his court advisors identified as the Buddha. That supposedly precipitated the emperor's sending of a western-bound expedition that brought back to China the first Buddhist text. According to later embellished versions of the story, the imperial expedition also

Figure 5.2   Main entry gate of White Horse Monastery, Luoyang

brought back two distinguished monks, the first known missionaries to enter China. According to legend, the foreign monks took up residence in a monastery that was built in the imperial capital Luoyang, White Horse monastery (Baimasi), which is still a major Buddhist establishment in the area (see Figure 5.2).

When we take into consideration the court-oriented perspective of official Chinese historiography, the stated focus on the emperor's role in the arrival of Buddhism evidenced in Emperor Ming's story should come as no surprise. However, in light of the prevalent patterns of trade and cultural exchanges between China and the lands beyond its northwestern frontier during this period, it seems probable that Buddhism had already entered China by the time of Emperor Ming's reign. The first Buddhists to come into China were probably anonymous merchants and travelers who left no records of their presence or activities. Moreover, there are other historical records that indicate there were already established Buddhist communities in other parts of China around the time of Emperor Ming's reign. That suggests that there was some Buddhist presence in China around the middle part of the first century at the latest, possibly even earlier.

The foreign missionaries who transmitted Buddhism into China were predominantly members of the monastic order (*saṅgha*). For the most part, they did not come straight from India. Reflecting the influence of geography, as well as the prevalent patterns of trade and movements of people, a majority of the Buddhist missionaries were Khotanese, Kushans, Sogdians, and other Central Asians. Accordingly, more often than not the transmission of Buddhism did not involve the forging of a direct link between India and China. Instead, the teachings, rituals, and practices brought into China were often mediated or influenced by Central Asian varieties of Buddhism. The early Buddhist missionaries entered a somewhat weakened but still powerful empire with an entrenched sense of cultural superiority, which perceived itself as the center of the world. Han China had highly evolved and fairly stable social customs and political institutions, in conjunction with established intellectual and religious traditions. Accordingly, Buddhism was not readily welcomed as a vehicle for the importation of key aspects of a superior foreign culture, as have happened in other places throughout Buddhist history. However, in an important respect the timing was opportune, as the gradual weakening and eventual collapse of the Han order made the Chinese elites more reflective about their cultural traditions and receptive to new ideas and worldviews.

Most of the Buddhist monks who entered China were associated with the Mahāyāna (Great Vehicle) tradition—a self-styled designation invented in order to distinguish it from the earlier Buddhist schools, which were pejoratively labeled as Hīnayāna (Small Vehicle)—and that became the predominant orientation of Chinese Buddhism. As it gradually developed a few centuries after the Buddha's lifetime, the Mahāyāna tradition highlighted the bodhisattva ideal, at the core of which were compassionate concern for the wellbeing of all beings and single-minded pursuit of the path to Buddhahood. It is worth mentioning that as Mahāyāna beliefs and practices were being transmitted into China and increasing in popularity, the Indian tradition was still undergoing creative doctrinal and textual developments.

Over the early centuries of the Common Era, major paradigm shifts in Indian Buddhism resulted in the formulation of novel doctrines, which were explicated and popularized by the introduction of new scriptures and treatises. The early growth of Chinese Buddhism thus ran parallel with the evolution of Mahāyāna and its growth as a major tradition of Indian Buddhism. The steady stream of new doctrinal systems and canonical texts—which at times seemed incompatible with each other—occasionally caused confusion and consternation among the Chinese. Nonetheless, that was also a great source of vitality, as well as a harbinger for new developments that became hallmarks of Chinese Buddhist thought and praxis.

Incisive critiques and cultural barriers

In the course of its initial entry and subsequent growth in China, Buddhism elicited a variety of responses, which ranged from enthusiastic acceptance to benign indifference to outright rejection and trenchant criticism. The earliest Buddhists were predominantly found among the immigrant communities from Central Asia and elsewhere, and during the first century or two Buddhism had limited impact on Chinese life and values. The situation changed with the growing popularity of Buddhism, as increasing numbers of Chinese became followers of the religion. That translated into increased support for the monastic order, which was open to both genders and incorporated separate communities of monks and nuns.

The shift towards increased acceptance of Buddhism coincided with the protracted collapse of the Han order and the ensuing period of social instability and political fragmentation. With the passage of time the monastic order came to include an ever-increasing number of native Chinese. Eventually foreign-born monks became a distinct minority, which marked a successful process of domestication and assimilation of Buddhism into the social fabric of medieval China. The situation was similar among the lay followers and supporters, who were much more numerous than the monks. The laity came from varied backgrounds, covering the whole spectrum of medieval Chinese society, from peasants to emperors.

With the greater visibility and importance of Buddhism, segments of the Chinese elites began to voice negative reactions and opinions. Some of them argued that the foreign religion was at odds with cherished cultural attitudes and prevalent social norms. A major sticking point and cause of consternation was the institution of monasticism. Monks and monasteries were central to Buddhism and were an integral part of the Indian religious landscape. However, they were without religious and intuitional analogies in the Chinese context, and because of this they were seen as something alien and unusual. The monastic order's stress on ascetic renunciation, deliberate distancing from societal norms, and adherence to its own code of discipline went against the grain and were foreign to the Chinese. Key aspects of monastic mores and practices, such as the monks' observance of celibacy and mendicancy, were perceived as an oddity that clashed with Confucian-inspired customs that infused Chinese culture and were safeguarded by the imperial state and the aristocratic elites.

In response to the gradual spread of the alien religion, some among the Chinese officials and literati articulated a set of explicit critiques of Buddhism that drew attention to supposed areas of conflict between it and the prevalent Confucian-based ideology. Many of their criticisms centered on the monastic order, which had a visible institutional presence and was widely perceived as a symbol of the Buddhist religion. Buddhist monks were accused of not being filial—a major transgression from a Confucian or Chinese point of view—because their celibate vocation meant they did not produce heirs and thus failed to secure the continuation of their families' ancestral lineages. Other criticisms against the monastic order were based on economic and political foundations. Monasteries and convents, along with individual monks and nuns, were accused of being economically unproductive, thereby placing unwarranted financial burden on the imperial state and the general populace.

In the political sphere, the traditional monastic emphasis on religious freedom and independence from secular authorities clashed with basic tenets of Chinese imperial ideology, according to which nothing and nobody was outside of the purview and direct control of the emperor, whose power (in theory at least) was deemed absolute. Buddhist notions about the independent status of the monastic order were thus perceived as undermining the traditional authority of the emperor, which led to charges that Buddhism subverted the established sociopolitical order. In addition, some Chinese intellectuals critiqued Buddhist teachings and practices for being primarily concerned with individual salvation and transcendence of the world of everyday affairs, at the expense of an ingrained Confucian emphasis on human interactions and the fulfillment of social obligations. The quest for otherworldly salvation, while as we have seen was not without parallels in other Chinese traditions, went counter to the pragmatic trust of prevalent Confucian norms and teachings, with their emphasis on the maintenance of rigid social order and political stability.

Buddhism was also dismissed by some of its detractors as being unsuitable for the Chinese on account of its foreign (or "barbarian," in traditional Chinese parlance) origin. Since China already had great sages such as the Duke of Zhou and Confucius, they argued, why is there any need to worship a strange foreign deity? According to this xenophobic point of view, with their rich history and superior culture the Chinese did not need to bother with a religious system that was developed by culturally inferior people, especially if that meant going astray from their native traditions. All of these critiques were articulated relatively early and were brought up throughout the subsequent history of Chinese Buddhism. They were repeated time and again even long after the religion had became thoroughly acculturated, all the way up to the present.

In addition to these misgivings, foreign missionaries and native adherents alike had to contend with formidable linguistic and cultural barriers that influenced their ability to understand and communicate the teachings of Buddhism. There was a formidable language gap that impeded verbal communication between the two groups, which was exasperated by the great differences between Chinese and the Indic languages in which Buddhist scriptures were written, with Sanskrit, the classical language of India, functioning as the principal canonical language. Two languages could be hardly more different than Chinese and Sanskrit. Chinese uses logographs and is monosyllabic, terse, uninflected, and has relatively simple grammar. In contrast, Sanskrit is written in a variety of alphabets and is polysyllabic, verbose, highly inflected, and has complex grammar as well as rich grammatical tradition. Consequently, the linguistic gap necessitated experimentation with ingenious translation strategies and necessitated the gradual formation of highly technical Chinese Buddhist vocabulary.

The language barrier was compounded by the substantive divergences between Chinese and Indian cultures and worldviews, especially as they related to religion.

The humanistic, this-worldly, and family-focused character of traditional Chinese culture, especially as expressed in its Confucian form, was fundamentally at odds with the exuberant flights of religious imagination emblematic of Indian ways of thinking. This was especially the case with the Buddhist variants of Indic religiosity that set transcendence of the everyday world as the final goal of spiritual life, which also featured expansive depictions of supernatural realms populated by arrays of celestial beings.

As we have already seen, there was of course more to traditional Chinese culture than Confucian-inspired ethical humanism and this-worldly pragmatism. Nonetheless, Indian notions about a quest for personal liberation that culminates in transcendence of a cycle of births and deaths, which also involves rejection of established social norms and familiar cultural frames of reference, called for extensive intercultural translation and negotiation. Accordingly, it took the Chinese an extended period of ingenious interpretation and selective appropriation before they could claim mastery of the full range of Buddhist beliefs, doctrines, and practices. Nevertheless, when that was eventually accomplished, the stage was set for the establishment of uniquely Chinese forms of Buddhism.

Enthusiastic responses and broad acceptance

Notwithstanding the qualms and impediments surveyed above, by the fall of the Han dynasty in 220 CE Buddhism managed to obtain a footing among the Chinese, and its growth accelerated during the subsequent period of disunion (311–589). That was an age of social dislocation and political fragmentation, as non-Chinese tribes established empires that ruled the northern parts of the former Han empire, while the south was governed by a series of native Chinese dynasties. Although the social changes and political upheavals led to occasional warfare and had negative impact on the aristocrats and common people alike, the fluid and unsettled circumstances actually encouraged the growth of Buddhism. In the eyes of many members of the Chinese elites, the collapse of the Han imperial order brought about a crisis of cultural confidence and stimulated a more reflective mood. That led many of them to question the tenability of old values and institutions, especially those linked with the prevailing Confucian ideology. With the intellectual vacuum brought about by such uncertain and open-ended predicament, there was a sense of receptiveness to new ideas, including innovative religious paradigm and foreign traditions such as Buddhism.

During the period of disunion Buddhism was attractive to the non-Chinese rulers in the north, who were eager to use its universalistic teachings to fortify their authority and successfully rule over mixed populations. Buddhism thus became a potent tool in their quest for political legitimacy, although undoubtedly the official support for Buddhism, which became increasingly prominent as time went on in both the north and the south, was also influenced by the personal faith of individual emperors. Another contributing factor that facilitated the spread of Buddhism was the growing interest in religious and philosophical Daoism, which was also undergoing a period of significant growth and development. Many upper-class Chinese familiar with Daoist texts and teachings were drawn to Buddhism's sophisticated texts and doctrines, as well as to its colorful rituals and arrays of practices, including meditation.

Buddhist doctrines evoked comparison with aspects of Daoist philosophy, while Buddhist practices bore reassuring (if often superficial) resemblance to some of the spiritual disciplines of religious Daoism. In elite and popular circles alike those similarities facilitated the appreciation and acceptance of Buddhist teachings, as they could be related to native intellectual templates and understood as exotic variations of familiar religious themes and practices. On the other hand, as the Chinese achieved better understanding of Buddhism, gradually the lines of demarcation and the finer points of distinction between the foreign and native traditions became less blurred. With the increased familiarity with Buddhism, the Chinese became better equipped to interpret and approach the imported religion on its own terms, albeit within the delimiting context of their culture. As they became actively engaged with Buddhist teachings and practices in ways that were personally meaningful and culturally agreeable, many Chinese turned to them as sources of religious truths and values, eventually making Buddhism the main form of organized religion throughout much of China.

While historical exigencies and utilitarian considerations aided the growth of Buddhism, its great success in becoming a major Chinese tradition—which some scholars called the Buddhist conquest of China—was principally based on the appeal of its teachings and its ability to meet deeply felt religious needs. Buddhism brought new elements to Chinese religious life and culture, including unique intellectual perspectives, imaginative approaches to spiritual growth and personal transformation, and engaging answers to questions about ultimate values. It also engendered creative avenues for artistic expression, along with instituting a plethora of cultic practices and other techniques of spiritual cultivation.

The historic growth of Buddhism was further enhanced by the openness and adaptability of the Mahāyāna traditions that were imported into China. The favorable reception of Buddhism into China was helped by its ability to avoid rigid dogmatism and be responsive to native cultural norms, sociopolitical realities, and spiritual predilections. Buddhist monks and lay followers effectively negotiated the necessity to adapt their traditions and practices to native Chinese cultural norms and social situations on one hand, with the need to retain fidelity to the basic principles of their religion on the other hand. As they established Buddhism as a major presence and force in Chinese religious life, they also expanded and enriched the contours of Chinese civilization.

Translation of scriptures and canon formation

During the early stages of the transmission of Buddhism into China a principal concern for the foreign missionaries and their native collaborators was the production of dependable and readable translations of the Buddhist scriptures and other related texts. The task of translating the Buddhist canon was monumental because of its sheer size, being one of the largest collections of sacred texts ever compiled. Moreover, the Mahāyāna canon was open and was constantly expanding, so steady streams of new texts composed in India and elsewhere were in due course brought into China. The aforementioned linguistic differences between Sanskrit and Chinese also posed serious challenges, along with the frequent lack of bilingual expertise among the foreign missionaries and the native clergy, exacerbated by the Chinese difficulty and reluctance to learn foreign languages. Due to these circumstances, the translation of the Buddhist canon into Chinese was a vast and complex undertaking that spanned the first millennium of Chinese Buddhist history.

During the early period many of the translations of Buddhist texts were small collaborative undertakings, typically led by a foreign monk who recited the scriptures—often from memory—and was aided by native assistants in rendering them into classical Chinese. At times the selection of texts to be translated by the early missionaries reflected a tendency to render into Chinese the kinds of texts that would appeal to native audiences, even if they were somewhat peripheral within the Buddhist tradition and did not deal directly with the essential elements of Buddhist doctrine. Cases in point were texts concerned with respiratory exercises, which reflected popular Chinese interest in these kinds of yogic exercises, especially in certain Daoist-influenced milieus.

Many of the early translations also exhibit a tendency to render Buddhist concepts and ideas by recourse to terminology derived from native Chinese thought, especially from Daoist sources. Such translation strategy was a mixed blessing. On one hand, it facilitated broad diffusion and more ready comprehension of Buddhist texts and teachings among the educated Chinese, at a time when most Chinese were ill equipped to deal with the nuances of Buddhist concepts and struggled to grasp doctrinal complexities. On the other hand, the recourse to Chinese philosophical and religious vocabulary—which had multivalent connotations and was imbedded in native conceptual grids and worldviews—obscured the precise meanings of central Buddhist ideas and easily led to doctrinal misunderstandings.

For instance, some Chinese translators used the well-known Daoist phrase *wuwei* (lit. no action) to render Buddhist technical terms such as Nirvana and the unconditioned (*asamskrta*). That inevitably confounded the situation, as it led to mixing-up of the different senses these terms had in their original contexts and respective traditions. In a similar vein, the Daoist term for immortals (*xianren*) was used to refer to Indian saints, both in the Vedic and Buddhist traditions, including various Buddhas. Such usage glossed over the fact that the Daoist and Buddhist conception of religious life and its ultimate goal diverged in significant respects, and that the pursuit of immortality was not part of the Buddhist soteriological system.

This method of pairing technical Buddhist terms with select Chinese expressions, customarily labeled as "matching the meaning" (*geyi*), was criticized by eminent Chinese monks such as Dao'an (312–385) as an impediment to the proper understanding of Buddhist doctrine. This reflected a growing awareness that Buddhism had to be understood and approached on its own terms, rather than via native systems of values and templates of meaning. The situation with the translation of sacred texts changed considerably during the early fifth century, in large part because of the coming of Kumārajīva (344–409/413). Although there were other influential translators before him who produced high quality works, Kumārajīva became the most famous and influential translator in the history of Chinese Buddhism. Born in Kucha, Kumārajīva arrived in Chang'an in 401 at an invitation of the imperial court, after a lengthy journey that included an extended period of captivity. He was warmly welcomed by the imperial family, which offered him extensive support and facilitated the creation of a large translation bureau to help his translation work.

Kumārajīva's fame attracted many brilliant Chinese monks, who came to study with him and serve as his assistants. With the help of his aides, Kumārajīva produced a large number of readable translations of key Mahāyāna scriptures and treatises. His prodigious efforts were celebrated as a huge success and his renditions of canonical texts came to be considered as benchmarks for subsequent translators. Because of their readability and superior styling, most of the texts he translated remained standard versions throughout the history of Buddhism in East Asia, even after later translators produced alternative versions that in some cases were more philologically exact. Kumārajīva also taught a number of talented disciples about the fine points of Mahāyāna doctrines, especially the Madhyamaka (Middle Way) philosophy of Nāgārjuna, of which he was a leading exponent.

A number of influential translators followed in Kumārajīva's footsteps, including Paramārtha (499–569), whose translations of Yogācāra texts served as a catalyst for the considerable Chinese interest in the doctrines of this Indian school of Mahāyāna philosophy (see below). One of the last great translators was the famous Tang monk and pilgrim Xuanzang (ca. 600–664). His celebrated pilgrimage to India began in 629, when as a young monk he illegally sneaked out of China, intent on making a dangerous pilgrimage to the birthplace of Buddhism. His primary motivation was to seek answers to queries he faced in his early study of Buddhist doctrines, especially those of the Yogācāra tradition with which he came to be associated. After a treacherous overland journey, he finally reached India and for many years studied at prominent centers of Buddhist learning. Xuanzang returned home triumphantly in 645, becoming a widely admired cultural hero (see Figure 5.3). He

Figure 5.3   Statue of Xuanzang in front of the Great Wild Goose Pagoda, Xi'an

was enthusiastically welcomed by the emperor and his court in Chang'an, which offered him generous support and facilitated his translation work.

Xuanzang spent the last two decades of his life translating the numerous manuscripts he brought back to China. He also wrote exegetical treatises and a travelogue of his study-pilgrimage in India, which remains a major source of information about ancient Indian and Central Asian religion, culture, and history. His work was undertaken under imperial auspices, with the help of numerous assistants that included leading Buddhist scholars. Despite their superior styling and greater philological accuracy, Xuanzang's translation did not achieve the same widespread acceptance and popularity as Kumārajīva's earlier translations, in part because they were more technical and difficult to read.

Xuanzang was the most famous in a series of monks who made the arduous journey to India in search of Buddhist texts and teachings. His predecessors and contemporaries included illustrious pilgrim monks such as Faxian (ca. 337–418) and Yijing (635–713). Faxian was the first Chinese monk to leave a record of his travels abroad. He left Chang'an in 399 in order to procure texts about monastic discipline (Vinaya), which at the time were not yet available in China. He traveled via land to India; after visiting various holy sights and studying there, he moved to Sri Lanka. He eventually returned to China via a sea route after an arduous journey, and went on to translate the texts he brought with him, as well as write an account of his journey.

Xuanzang's younger contemporary Yijing left China in 671. In contrast to the land routes taken by most of his predecessors, he decided to travel by boat. His first stop was at the island of Sumatra (now in Indonesia), then a stronghold of Buddhism. He then proceeded to travel in India, where he studied at Nalanda, the famous monastic university. After returning to China in 695 he had a productive career as a scholar and translator. He translated a variety of canonical texts, including scriptures and texts on monastic discipline; he also wrote exegetical treatises and reference works, and compiled a record of his travels that contains depictions of the Buddhist practices he observed overseas.

Popular scriptures and other texts

The canonical texts translated by the foreign missionaries and the Chinese pilgrims included many popular Mahāyāna scriptures that left an indelible imprint on Chinese religious life. Arguably the most popular canonical text in China and the rest of East Asia is the *Lotus Scripture*, which proclaims to contain the ultimate teaching of the Buddha. The scripture's main ideas and its potent imagery served as foundations for philosophical systems, ritual and cultic practices, and wide-ranging forms of artistic expression. The texts asserted the superiority and universality of its teachings under the rubric of One Vehicle of perfect Buddhahood, which supposedly was the supreme expression of the Buddha's wisdom that subsumed all other Buddhist teachings (see quote box on facing page).

Within the *Lotus Scripture's* conceptual scheme all other teachings were relegated to the category of "expedient means"—a central concept in the text that became immensely influential in Chinese Buddhism—introduced by the Buddha in response to the diverse spiritual capacities and predilections of his audiences. The text unequivocally proclaimed the universality of Buddhahood as the final religious goal to be realized by all. It also asserted that the Buddha is eternal, not subject to becoming and constantly preaching the truth, told a number of stories that captured the popular imagination, and served as foundation for cultic beliefs and practices, especially the Guanyin cult (see next chapter).

Another significant canonical text that elicited a wide range of philosophical and devotional responses was the *Huayan (Flower Adornment) Scripture* (see quote box, on facing page). A composite text of encyclopedic proportions that is replete with potent symbolisms and evokes striking visual images, the scripture communicates a cosmic vision of boundless realm of reality, which functions as an illimitable causal

The One Vehicle of the *Lotus Scripture*

All the Buddhas, honored by the world, appear in this world because they wish to enable all living beings to open up to the knowledge and vision of the Buddha, to cause them to attain purity. ... The Buddhas preach the [true] doctrine only by means of the one Buddha vehicle; there are no other vehicles, neither two nor three.

From the "Expedient Means" chapter, *Lotus Scripture*; cf. Watson 1993: 33.

The Buddha wisdom according to the *Huayan Scripture*

There is not a place where the wisdom of the Buddha does not reach. Why? There is not a single living being that is not in full possession of the wisdom of the Buddha. It is only due to their false thinking, fallacies, and attachments that beings fail to realize this. If they could only abandon their false thoughts, then the all-encompassing wisdom, the spontaneous wisdom, and the unobstructed wisdom [of the Buddha] will clearly manifest themselves.

From the "Manifestation of the Tathāgata" chapter, *Huayan Scripture*; trans. adapted from Poceski 1993: 105.

matrix that incorporates infinite number of perfectly interfused worlds. The scripture's unobstructed realm of reality, in which each thing is causally related to everything else in the universe, is symbolically presided over by Vairocana, its central Buddha, who is presented as the cosmic embodiment of the Buddha's body of truth and symbol of ultimate reality. The scripture also provides detailed explanations of the practices and stages of the bodhisattva path. Besides being seen as a rich repository of abstruse doctrines, the text achieved broad appeal and inspired various pious acts and cultic practices, such as purification rituals, vegetarian feasts, chanting, and copying by hand. The scripture also stimulated rich artistic traditions, evident for instance in the numerous statues and painting of its central deity Vairocana Buddha (see Figure 5.4).

Other immensely popular scriptures included the *Amitābha Scripture* and the *Vimalakīrti Scripture*. The first depicts the paradise of Amitābha Buddha and offers the prospect of being reborn there, which became focal points of popular devotion and cultic practice. The *Vimalakīrti Scripture* was also named after its main hero, a rich layman with wisdom and preaching skill superior to those of the other disciples of the Buddha, who became an inspirational role model for Chinese lay Buddhists. The text also contains a number of memorable passages that explicate important Buddhist doctrines and tenets.

Figure 5.4   Giant statue of Vairocana, the cosmic Buddha of the *Huayan Scripture*. Longmen, Henan

Besides the translations of canonical texts from Sanskrit and other languages, there was a large body of apocryphal texts composed in China. The native origins of the Chinese apocrypha were concealed by presenting them as translations of Indian canonical texts. They incorporated a wide range of topics and orientations, from sophisticated explorations of doctrinal themes to popular recasting of prevalent beliefs or practices. Commonly used apocryphal scriptures reflected native Chinese concerns and sentiments, covering diverse areas such as ethical norms and moral principles, eschatological and messianic beliefs, ritual procedures and cultic practices, and depictions of celestial realms and supernatural powers.

The apocryphal scriptures sometimes crossed the ambiguous lines of demarcation that separated Buddhism from popular religious beliefs, which made some of them an occasional subject of critique by members of the monastic elite. On the other end of the spectrum were apocryphal texts concerned with doctrinal issues and subjects, which exemplified native appropriations of Mahāyāna teachings that were shaped by Chinese intellectual concerns and spiritual predilections. The problematic provenance of the apocryphal scriptures and treatises was occasionally noted by medieval cataloguers, but still a number of them attained broad acclaim and became integral parts of the Buddhist canon.

In addition to texts translated from Indian languages, the Buddhist canon also came to contain a large number of texts written or compiled by Chinese authors. Composed in different genres and adopting a broad range of perspectives, these texts provide a wealth of information about diverse beliefs, doctrines, practices, historical developments, and institutional structures central to Chinese Buddhism. They include exegetical works, especially commentaries on important scriptures, and systematic expositions of doctrinal systems such as those articulated by the Huayan and Tiantai traditions (see the next chapter). Buddhist authors also composed collections of biographies of eminent monks, texts dealing with monastic regulations and practices, meditation and ritual manuals, encyclopedias and other reference works, and historical works.

The voluminous Buddhist literature composed in China also includes many popular tracts and other non-canonical works that reflected prevalent Buddhist beliefs and practices. Examples of such texts are the various collections of miracle tales and the "transformation texts" (*bianwen*) discovered among the Dunhuang manuscripts, which contain popular stories that were told in the context of elaborate public performances. The transformation texts are the earliest models of vernacular writing in China and exerted considerable impact on the subsequent development of the performing arts and vernacular fiction. Buddhist themes and ideas can also be found in secular literary works, especially the poems and other writings of major Chinese poets and writers. Notable cases in point from the Tang era are the poetry of Wang Wei (701–761) and Bo Juyi (772–846), while comparable examples of the infusion of Buddhist themes and imagery from the Song period can be found in the writings of Su Shi (1037–1101).

Philosophical systems and doctrinal taxonomies

In the course of its historical development Chinese Buddhism absorbed the range of Buddhist doctrines explicated in the scriptures and treatises of the Mahāyāna tradition. The first doctrinal system of Indian Mahāyāna appropriated by Chinese monk-scholars was that of the Madhyamaka or Middle Way tradition. The central Madhyamaka teaching was the doctrine of emptiness (*śūnyatā*), which explicated the absence of substantive self in both person and things. Also important were the related doctrines of the conditioned origination (*pratītyasamutpāda*) of phenomena, according to which the temporal existence of all things depends on the coming together of diverse causes and conditions, and the two levels of truth, absolute and relative. These concepts became popular in China in large part through the influence of the famous translator Kumārajīva and his disciples.

During the sixth century there was a shift in interest towards the teachings of the Yogācāra (Practice of Yoga) school. Yogācāra texts imported into China provided sophisticated analyses of different types of consciousness and explored the mind's role in the construction of phenomenal reality. They also contained elaborate explanations of the stages of meditative practice and the process of actualizing enlightenment. Before long they attracted the attention of leading Buddhist scholars in China, whose creative intellectual and religious responses led to the production of a large volume of learned treatises and elaborate exegetical works.

Chinese appropriations of Yogācāra thought were accompanied with growing interest in the related doctrine of Buddha-nature, along with the closely related notion of the tathāgatagarbha (variously explained as the womb or embryo of Buddhahood). The tathāgatagarbha and Buddha-nature theories occupied relatively minor positions in Indian Buddhism and never achieved status compatible to the Madhyamaka and Yogācāra traditions, but they became prime doctrinal tenets and key articles of faith within Chinese Buddhism. The Buddha-nature doctrine stressed the mind's essential purity, the immanence of enlightenment, and the universality of Buddhahood (see the "Buddha wisdom" box, p. 125). It postulated that everybody is endowed with a luminous, true mind, which is primordially enlightened and pure. Although the pure mind is originally present in each person, due to accumulated karma and ingrained misapprehension of reality it is covered with defilements such as greed and anger. Accordingly, ordinary people are ignorant of their true nature and are unable to experience spiritual freedom and liberation, although through the practice of Buddhism they can redress their regrettable predicament and gradually go beyond their self-imposed limitations.

The assimilation of these ideas into the basic doctrinal and soteriological frameworks of Chinese Buddhism had profound ramifications for the subsequent history of Buddhism throughout East Asia. The Buddha-nature doctrine's overly optimistic outlook on human perfectibility resonated with entrenched Chinese notions about the basic goodness of human nature, including those articulated by Mencius some centuries earlier. In it Chinese Buddhists found a compelling theory that validated the everyday world as the arena where spiritual practice and realization took place. Accordingly, its popularity signaled the growth of Buddhist perspectives that were distinctly Chinese. On the other hand, popular Chinese interpretations that reified the Buddha-nature and ascribed to it some sort of substantive existence also signaled a move away from established Buddhist orthodoxies, as they conflicted with the basic Buddhist creed of no-self. This highlighted a perennial problem of interpreting diverse Buddhist doctrines and relating them to each other. When different doctrines were linked together into a coherent whole, it necessitated the coming to terms with a host of seeming conceptual or theoretical incongruities.

Chinese Buddhists believed that the numerous scriptures and the systems of doctrine articulated in them all went back to the Buddha. But how could the Buddha teach so many doctrines, especially considering the fact that often they appeared to be mutually contradictory? Faced with the vast body of texts contained in the canon and the disparate teachings they received from India, Chinese Buddhist scholars developed strategies for organizing the huge body of Buddhist literature and doctrine into coherent classificatory schemes known as doctrinal taxonomies (*panjiao*), which were carefully constructed in accord with preset hermeneutical principles.

The creation of doctrinal classificatory schemes exemplified a prevalent concern for order and conceptual clarity that was typical of the worldview of medieval Chinese intellectuals. The various doctrinal taxonomies presumed organic relationships among disparate doctrines, based on the premise that all Buddhist teachings are integral parts of an all-inclusive whole. However, they also had polemical character and functioned as control apparatuses. By instituting preset hierarchies of meaning and validity that supported specific truth-claims, the taxonomies ascribed fixed ranks of authenticity and legitimacy to the various doctrines included in them. In that sense, they advocated specific points of view and promoted distinctive proto-sectarian agendas.

The authors of various doctrinal taxonomies typically relegated competing teachings to lower levels, and placed at the top those advocated by them or by the school of Buddhism they were affiliated with. That is evident in the influential hierarchical nomenclature developed by the Tiantai school, which can be traced back to the writings of its founder Zhiyi (538–597). Zhiyi approached the problem of ordering and classifying the teachings of Buddhism from a variety of perspectives. He came up with three separate taxonomic schemes, each of them based on different classificatory principles. The basic premise underlying them all is that the various Buddhist teachings are all expressions of ultimate truth—that in the final analysis is ineffable and beyond conceptualization—adapted to the spiritual aptitudes and intellectual abilities of the Buddha's audiences, and in tune with the specific circumstances under which they were preached.

Known as the "eight teachings and five periods," the three taxonomic schemes developed by the Tiantai tradition organized the texts and teachings of Buddhism into: (1) four teachings according to their doctrinal content, (2) four teachings according to the means of instruction employed by the Buddha, and (3) five periods of the Buddha's public ministry and preaching (see box). By instituting this complex taxonomic model, Zhiyi was able to avoid narrow dogmatism and adopt an

Five periods of the Buddha's preaching according to the Tiantai school

- Preaching of the Huayan Scripture just after the Buddha's enlightenment
- Twelve years of preaching Hīnayāna doctrines
- Eight years of preaching mixed Mahāyāna and Hīnayāna doctrines
- Twenty-two years of preaching the perfection of wisdom scriptures
- Eight years of preaching the Lotus Scripture, followed by the final preaching of the Nirvana Scripture

Fazang's classification of Buddhism in terms of Five Teachings

- Hīnayāna teaching
- Elementary Mahāyāna—Madhyamaka and early Yogācāra teachings
- Advanced Mahāyāna—tathāgatagarbha doctrine
- Sudden teaching (that abandons words and concepts)
- Perfect teaching of the One Vehicle—the Huayan tradition

ecumenical stance by incorporating all Buddhist teachings—albeit in an ahistorical fashion that glossed over the problematic provenance of various Mahāyāna texts and doctrines—while also highlighting the superiority of the *Lotus Scripture* and its teachings, and by extension of the Tiantai school that based its doctrines on it.

In contrast to Tiantai's valorization of the *Lotus Scripture*, the Huayan tradition placed its principal canonical text, the *Huayan Scripture*, at the top of the fivefold taxonomic scheme developed by its famous philosopher Fazang (643–712). In this prominent doctrinal taxonomy the lowest level is represented by the Hīnayāna teaching, while the tathāgatagarbha doctrine is placed above the two primary systems of Indian Mahāyāna doctrine, those of the Yogācāra and Madhyamaka traditions. At the apex of the taxonomy is the "perfect teaching" that reveals the whole truth in all of its respelled glory and is solely contained in the *Huayan Scripture* (see box).

Emergence of Buddhism as a major religious tradition

During the period of division, namely from the early fourth until the late sixth century, political and cultural fragmentation contributed to the emergence of different characters and growth trajectories for Buddhism in the northern and southern parts of China. Buddhism in northern China was characterized by close connections between the clergy and the state, which was controlled by ethnically non-Chinese rulers who adopted Chinese political institutions and culture. Other salient features of Buddhism in the North were interests in thaumaturgy, asceticism, devotional practice, and meditation. Buddhism during this period was also marked by remarkable artistic creativity, as inspired expressions of fervent faith were cast in striking material forms, such as those of the statues and reliefs found in the expansive complexes of cave art at Longmen and Yun'gang, which are among the greatest artistic achievements of Chinese civilizations.

In contrast, in the southern kingdoms during this period there was an emergence of so-called "gentry" Buddhism, which was infused with a sense of intellectualism and elitism. Members of the southern upper classes with interest in metaphysical speculations were attracted to the Buddhist doctrine of emptiness, as presented in the perfection of wisdom scriptures, which they often conflated with Daoist concepts and ideas about reality. There was also deeply ingrained fascination with Buddhist rituals, such as the complex repentance rituals formulated at the court of Emperor Wu of the Liang Dynasty (r. 502–549), who is known as one of the most fervent supporters of Buddhism among all Chinese emperors. During this period the socioreligious milieu in the South was characterized by close connections between literati and Buddhist monks, many of whom shared the same cultural upbringing and gentry background.

During the era of disunion Buddhism suffered temporary setbacks in the form of two persecutions, during the 446–454 and 574–577 periods, which covered only parts of China. Despite those stumbling blocks, by the sixth century Buddhism had extensive presence and strong roots throughout the whole territory of China, permeating the societies and cultures of the northern and the southern dynasties. During this era Buddhism was also exported to other parts of East Asia that were under China's cultural influence, first to Korea in the fourth century and then to Japan in the sixth century. Before long Buddhism became the predominant religious tradition in both Korea and Japan, and during the subsequent centuries continued to serve as a potent vehicle for the importation of varied elements of Chinese culture into the two neighboring countries. Over the centuries numerous Korean and Japanese monks went to study in China, and Buddhism played an important role in the flow of people and ideas between China and its neighbors. This resulted in the creation of a pan-East Asian religious network, with Chinese Buddhism at its center, that predated the present-day globalization of religion by many centuries.

Golden age under the Tang dynasty

The reunification of the Chinese empire under the Sui dynasty (589–618) initiated a new phase in the historical growth of Chinese Buddhism. Under the pro-Buddhist Sui regime, Chinese Buddhism reached great heights of intellectual creativity, religious vitality, and institutional vigor. The two Sui emperors were both pious Buddhists and they were keen to use Buddhism as a unifying force in their efforts to recreate a consolidated empire after centuries of deep divisions. The pattern of remarkable flourishing and ingenious development continued during the succeeding Tang dynasty (618–907), a prosperous period marked by unprecedented dynastic power and extraordinary cultural effervescence that is widely considered the golden age of Chinese civilization. Throughout the Sui-Tang period, Buddhism was widely accepted throughout the vast empire and was practiced by members of all social classes, from poor peasant to aristocrats and the royal family.

During the Sui-Tang period Buddhism was undoubtedly the most powerful and influential religious and intellectual tradition in the Chinese empire. To a large degree

Buddhism eclipsed Confucianism and Daoism, although the other two traditions also flourished during this period, which was marked by cultural openness and imaginative embrace of religious pluralism. The main schools of Chinese Buddhism surveyed in the next chapter were also formed during this era, representing the formation of uniquely Chinese systems of Buddhist philosophy and methods of spiritual praxis, which were accompanied by new forms of literature and art. These developments represent the culmination of the Sinification of Buddhism, which involved the formulation and wide diffusion of Buddhist beliefs, doctrines, practices, and institutions that were uniquely Chinese. In light of these developments, the Sui-Tang period is often recognized as the apogee of Buddhism in China, which coincided with the most glorious epoch of China's long history.

The influence of Buddhism and the resilience of its institutions were put to a harsh test during the reign of Emperor Wuzong (r. 842–845), who initiated the most devastating anti-Buddhist persecution in the history of imperial China. The emperor decreed wholesale destruction of virtually all monasteries in the empire, appropriation of their lands and other property by the government, as well as mass and forcible laicization of the clergy. The onset of the persecutions was shaped by several factors, including the influence of the emperor's Daoist officials and confidants, along with economic considerations. The emperor and his advisors were also able to tap into feelings of dismay over monastic corruption and dormant anti-Buddhist sentiments among some Confucian officials. The persecution was short-lived and Buddhism quickly rebounded, as the next emperor rescinded the anti-Buddhist policies and offered generous support to the religion. However, many scholars see the persecution as a turning point in the history of Buddhism and a beginning of its protracted decline.

Relationship with the state

As Buddhism gradually increased in popularity and became a major religious tradition, Buddhist monasteries and the monastic order grew in size and influence. By the early sixth century the capitals of the various northern and southern dynasties were filled with numerous monasteries, temples, and chapels; many Buddhist establishments, large and small, also mushroomed all over the rest of China, in urban centers and in mountainsides. Many Chinese emperors offered lavish patronage to Buddhism, as expression of personal piety as well as out of political expediency. The aristocracy and the general populace also extended their generous support, donating land and making openhanded contributions to the buildup and upkeep of monasteries and shrines.

As a result of such circumstances, Buddhist monasteries became an important part of the Chinese economy. In addition to the regular donations from the faithful, for whom religiously-inspired giving was a key way of securing spiritual merit, the monasteries also had extensive lands, which were farmed by servants or tenant farmers. Certain monasteries also operated various commercial enterprises, such as mills, oil presses, and pawnshops (for details, see Gernet 1995). Some of the funds obtained from donations and commercial activity were diverted to charitable undertaking, such as providing aid to the poor and the ill, by means of which Buddhism provided valuable social services.

In addition to providing operating funds for certain officially-designated monasteries, the imperial state extended limited privileges to legitimately ordained monks and nuns, who were exempt from taxes, corvée, and military service. That made the monastic vocation attractive to many who were not influenced by genuine piety. The clergy compensated by bolstering the reigning regime and offering a veneer of religious legitimacy to imperial rule and ideology. With their prayers and rituals, the clergy also accrued merit and secured supernatural protection for the reigning dynasty. In light of these circumstances, it is not surprising that the number of Buddhist establishments grew into the thousands (or even tens of thousands, according to some sources), while the numbers of monks and nuns by the sixth and seventh centuries reached into the hundreds of thousands (see Gernet 1995).

The support extended to Buddhism by the imperial state was accompanied by efforts to control the religion. Various emperors and government officials were eager to harness the power and prestige of Buddhism to bolster their authority and achieve specific political ends. From early on there was an underlying tension between the state and the monastic order, as the government made concerted efforts to assert its control over Buddhism, while the monastic order struggled to safeguard its independence. These frictions were often expressed in symbolic terms, like in the case of the long-lasting debates about whether monks should be required to bow to the emperor and their parents, as was deemed proper by Chinese custom and Confucian ideology.

In the long run, the efforts of prominent Buddhist figures such as Huiyuan (334–416), the famous monastic leader and proponent of seeking rebirth in the pure land of Buddha Amitābha, to secure a semblance of independence for the monastic community were largely a losing proposition. Huiyuan's courageous stand, along with the influence of his personal charisma, scored symbolic victories for Buddhism. At the time, the emperor backpedaled and rescinded his earlier decrees, which aimed to limit the size of the monastic order and force monks to bow to the ruler (see Ch'en 1964). However, in the long run the Chinese state was able to wrestle extensive control over Buddhism.

The manner in which Buddhism provided Chinese rulers with a valuable source of legitimacy, which bolstered their political authority, is aptly illustrated by the case of Empress Wu Zetian (r. 684–705), the only female monarch in Chinese history and one of the greatest patrons of Buddhism. The rise to power by the empress was unprecedented in the annals of Chinese history. In her machinations to secure absolute governmental control, she had to contend with a prevalent Confucian-based ideology that was unabashedly patriarchal and precluded the possibility of a female ruler. She went around that by turning to Buddhism, the most prevalent religious tradition among her subjects, as a key source of political legitimacy (although she also did not shy away from using Daoism and popular religion for the same purpose, when opportunities presented themselves). The pious yet shrewd empress publicly proclaimed herself an incarnation of Maitreya, the Buddha of the future. She also widely publicized a prophecy about the imminent coming of a righteous female monarch, which was presented in an obscure apocryphal scripture that was conveniently brought to her attention by some of her close cronies.

Notwithstanding the latent tensions noted above, the early rapprochements between Buddhism and the imperial state evolved into a close and stable relationship between the two. As Buddhism became firmly integrated into the social fabric, the economy, and the political system of late medieval China, its fortunes became increasingly tied to the changing attitudes of individual emperors and dynasties, as well as the prevalent patterns of patronage among the socioeconomic elites. The state asserted its right to control key aspects of religious life, including the bestowal of monastic ordinations, the building of monasteries, and the allocation of abbacies. Overall control of the religion was assigned to one of the governmental bureaus; while some prominent monks were given nominal official titles, on the whole the overarching administrative authority was in the hands of civil officials (or eunuchs during certain periods). The governmental control went even so far as to extend to the selection of new texts to enter into the Buddhist canon. On the other hand, the state was not overly concerned with micromanaging everyday life in the religious communities, as long as it did not directly impinge on its interests. Consequently, for the most part Buddhist monks and the laity had relative freedom to practice their religion.

Buddhism in late imperial China

Late imperial China—the period from the Song (960–1279) era until the end of the Qing dynasty (1644–1911)—can be seen as a distinct late phase in the history of Chinese Buddhism. This period was marked by the consolidation of mainstream doctrines and practices, amidst a prevalent sense of religious and institutional conservatism. The history of Buddhism during this era, especially from the late Song period onward, is usually told as a narrative of protracted decline devoid of significant changes, punctuated by sporadic attempts at reform and efforts to revive the tradition's ancient glories. During this long period there was little in terms of radical changes or major paradigm shifts that resulted in new schools of Buddhist doctrine or innovative paradigm of practice. There was also a slow decline in the status of Buddhism and its influence on Chinese society and culture, especially when compared with the grandeur of bygone eras. Even so, throughout this period Buddhism remained a permanent fixture and major presence in the Chinese religious landscape.

Lately some scholars (mostly in North America) have argued that the negative characterization of post-Tang Buddhism does no justice to the religious and institutional vitality of Buddhism during subsequent eras, especially the Song period. It is unquestionable that under the Song Buddhism remained influential and attracted large followings among the members of all social classes. The religion continued to enjoy state patronage and the monastic vocation attracted many individuals. Many of the basic features that still characterize Chinese Buddhism—including specific patterns of monastic life and systems of meditative practice—were fully formulated during the Song era. Buddhist influence on Chinese culture during this period was also pervasive, as can be observed in the literature and visual arts of the period. At the same time, there were signs of creeping decline, especially in terms of intellectual creativity, notwithstanding innovative developments in Tiantai scholasticism or Chan literature and praxis.

The intellectual decline of Buddhism was manifest in the lack of compelling and effective responses to the formidable challenge brought about by the Neo-Confucian revival, which started with the Song era. The gradual shift of interest away from Buddhism and towards Confucianism among the Chinese elites was given a major boost when Neo-Confucianism was officially instituted as state orthodoxy during the fourteenth century (see Chapter 8). For the rest of the imperial period Buddhism continued to exist as a notable religious presence, but in diminished capacity when compared to the glories of the Tang and Song eras, often finding itself on the margins. A noteworthy development during this period was the growing presence of Tibetan forms of tantric Buddhism in China, which were patronized by the Mongol rulers of the Yuan dynasty (1271–1367) and the Manchu rulers of the Qing dynasty (1644–1911). But these alien traditions exerted little impact on Chinese Buddhists, who for the most part assumed a conservative stance and were disinclined to adopt new influences or initiate significant paradigm shifts.

Key points

- Prior to its entry into China Buddhism already had half a century of development, during which it branched into a number of traditions and emerged as a major religion that was on the way to becoming pan-Asian in scope.
- Initial records about the transmission of Buddhism into China take us back to the first century CE, when the earliest Buddhist missionaries arrived in China via the merchant routes popularly known as the Silk Road.
- In the course of its growth in China, Buddhism had to contend with criticisms, typically voiced by Confucian literati, that its teachings and institutions were at odds with Chinese norms and mores, and that it was not suitable for the Chinese on account of its foreign origin.
- During the period of disunion Buddhism attracted many followers across China and emerged as an influential religious tradition, with its doctrines, beliefs, rituals, and practices stirring the imagination and devotion of people from all walks of life, from peasants to emperors.
- The spread and acculturation of Buddhism were closely related to the translation of the Buddhist canon, which was undertaken on a large scale and was led by preeminent monks such as Kumārajīva and Xuanzang.
- A number of influential Mahāyāna texts such as the *Lotus Scripture* became immensely influential in China, and they were complemented by numerous texts composed by Chinese monks.
- Chinese Buddhist intellectuals mastered a wide range of doctrinal systems of Indian provenance, which they correlated with philosophical models developed in China and organized into doctrinal taxonomies.
- During the period of disunion Buddhism developed different features and growth trajectories in the northern and southern parts of China, as it gradually emerged as a major religious tradition.
- Chinese Buddhism reached the peak of its growth and influence during the Tang era, which is often cited as the golden age of both Buddhism and Chinese civilization.
- Although during the early period Buddhist monks strived to establish the independence of the monastic order from secular authorities, the Chinese state was able to bring Buddhism under its control; by the late medieval period Buddhism was securely integrated into the established sociopolitical order and the cultural mainstream.
- The history of Buddhism during the late imperial period is often described in terms of a gradual decline, especially when compared with the glories of the Tang (and even Song) eras, although there were occasional reform movements and other noteworthy developments.

Discussion questions

1. What were the barriers and criticism that Buddhism had to overcome in the course of its growth in medieval China, and what were the critiques directed towards the monastic order tells us about the nature of Chinese society at the time?
2. What was the scope and significance of the translation of the Buddhist canon into Chinese, and what were the key issues faced by the translators?
3. At what time did Buddhism assume the status of the main religious tradition in China and what were the key factors that contributed to its rise to preeminence?

Further reading

See also the reading suggestions for Chapter 6.

Buswell, Robert E., ed. 1990. *Chinese Buddhist Apocrypha*. Honolulu, HI: University of Hawai'i Press.

Ch'en, Kenneth. 1964. *Buddhism in China: A Historical Survey*. Princeton, NJ: Princeton University Press.

Ch'en, Kenneth. 1973. *The Chinese Transformation of Buddhism*. Princeton, NJ: Princeton University Press.

Gernet, Jacques. 1995. *Buddhism in Chinese Society: An Economic History from the Fifth to the Tenth Centuries*. Trans. by Franciscus Verellen. New York: Columbia University Press.

Liu, Ming-Wood. 1994. *Madhyamaka Thought in China*. Leiden: E. J. Brill.

Poceski, Mario (Cheng Chien Bhikshu), trans. 1993. *Manifestation of the Tathāgata: Buddhahood According to the Avatamsaka Sūtra*. Boston, MA: Wisdom Publications.

Teiser, Stephen F. 1994. *The Scripture of the Ten Kings and the Making of Purgatory in Medieval Chinese Buddhism*. Honolulu, HI: University of Hawai'i Press.

Watson, Burton, trans. 1993. *The Lotus Sutra*. New York: Columbia University Press.

Watson, Burton, trans. 1997. *The Vimalakīrti Sūtra*. New York: Columbia University Press.

Weinstein, Stanley. 1987. *Buddhism under the T'ang*. Cambridge: Cambridge University Press.

Wright, Arthur F. 1959. *Buddhism in Chinese History*. Stanford, CA: Stanford University Press.

Zürcher, E. 2007. *The Buddhist Conquest of China: The Spread and Adaptation of Buddhism in Early Medieval China*, 3rd edn. Leiden: E. J. Brill.

6 Traditions and practices of Chinese Buddhism

In this chapter

Following the survey of the broad historical trajectory and pattern of growth of Buddhism in China presented in the previous chapter, here we will discuss the main religious ideas, practices, and traditions that characterize Chinese Buddhism. We will learn about monastic and lay mores and ideals, discuss popular beliefs and cultic practices, and cover the four major traditions of Chinese Buddhism. While the chapter adopts a historical mode of narration and for the most part uses past tense, most of the attitudes and practices described in it are still part and parcel of Chinese Buddhism.

Main topics

- Monastic ideals and lay modes of engagement with Buddhism.
- Focus on merit making and elevation of compassion as prime virtue.
- Cultic worship of various Buddhas and bodhisattvas.
- Formation of various schools or traditions within Chinese Buddhism.
- Integration of doctrine and practice by the Tiantai school.
- Huayan school's conceptualization of the realm of reality.
- Growth of Chan as the main tradition of elite Buddhism.
- Belief in Amitābha Buddha within the Pure Land tradition.

Monastic and lay paradigms

Monasticism was the central institution of Buddhism ever since the Buddha ordained his first disciples in ancient India, shaping virtually all aspects of historical growth and the evolution of Buddhism as an organized religion. The monastic character of Indian Buddhism was transplanted into China, where monastic mores and institutions were adapted to suit local conditions and predilections. The monastic order was open to both males and females, who lived in separate establishments but followed similar observances and lifestyles. Entering a nunnery was a viable vocation for women with spiritual inclinations in traditional Chinese society, allowing them a measure of freedom and respect that were often lacking in a patriarchal society where women were relegated to second-class status. The social backgrounds of monks and nuns were varied: most of the monastic elites came from privileged backgrounds, but the majority of monastics, especially those who ministered to the religious needs of the common people, came from peasant stock.

The monastic vocation encompassed a variety of activities and could be approached in a number of ways. Many monks specialized in certain aspect of Buddhism, while others professed worldly expertise such as knowledge of healing techniques. From the collections of monastic biographies—which admittedly cover only the clerical elites—along with other historical records, we learn of a number of specializations that were traditionally valued within the Buddhist community: translators, exegetes, proselytizers, chanters, ritual specialists, thaumaturges, meditators, specialists in monastic discipline, and those who perform virtuous acts that benefit the religion. In pre-modern China the monastic order lacked strong and centralized ecclesiastical structures, and the circulation of power and authority within it was broadly diffused. As a rule, the official monasteries approved by the state were public, which meant that they were open to all properly ordained monks and the allocation of the abbacy was (in theory at least) based on merit and qualification, although secular authorities often had a say in the selection process. The majority of local temples, on the other hand, were hereditary in a sense that the abbacy was held by the monastic "family" and was passed on from the abbot to his most senior disciple.

Nominally the monastic order was regulated by the Vinaya (*lü*), the monastic code of discipline, initially compiled in India and available in Chinese in a few different versions. The level of adherence to the monastic rules varied depending on different individuals, communities, and time periods. In the version of the Vinaya most popular in China, known as the Dharmagupta Vinaya, the rules for fully ordained monks number two hundred and fifty (while the nuns also have additional rules). While throughout history many Chinese monks took the Vinaya seriously, a good number of its rules were seen as culturally alien and unsuitable for local conditions. Moreover, given the lack of opportunities for social advancement in traditional Chinese society and the relative comfort and security of monastic life, the monastic order attracted a range of individuals, including some who joined for reasons other than heartfelt religious piety. Consequently, critiques of clerical dereliction and corruption were (and still remain) a constant theme in perceptions and discussions of the state of Buddhism, both within and outside of the Buddhist community.

In the course of the growth and transformation of Buddhism in China, gradually some monastic rules and observance came to be quietly ignored by the majority of monks and nuns, for instance those that prohibited them to eat after noon or use money. Nevertheless, up to the present day all Chinese monastics continue to be ordained according to the Vinaya and technically they are bound by its regulations. A number of monastic codes were also written by Chinese monks, the best known among them being the Chan school's "rules of purity" (*qinggui*), although their function was to supplement rather than replace the Vinaya regulations. As part of their ordination Chinese monks and nuns also accept the separate "bodhisattva precepts," deemed to reflect the compassionate spirit of the Mahāyāna tradition, but based on an apocryphal scripture that many scholars believe was composed in China.

While the monastic order was sizable, often including hundreds of thousands of monks and nuns, the lay followers of Buddhism were always much more numerous. The monastic versus lay distinction is important in Chinese Buddhism, although occasionally there is blurring of the lines of demarcation between the two. In theory, the Buddhist path is equally open to all: even though monastic life is traditionally deemed more conducive to serious spiritual cultivation, lay people can also engage in an array of Buddhist practices. The laity can even aim at realizing the ultimate goal of final liberation from the circle of birth and death, although the vast majority of them are concerned with more tangible and immediate objectives.

During extended historical periods—for instance during the Northern Wei, Sui, Tang, and Sung dynasties—Buddhism was the main religious tradition in China. Accordingly, Buddhism was integrated in some way into the lives of most people, even if many of them did not claim exclusive allegiance to it in the manner we encounter in the contexts of other faiths such as Islam and Christianity. In the course of Chinese history various capitals and other towns had numerous monasteries and convents, which were centers of diverse religious functions, festivals, and other cultural activities. People from all walks of life, from emperors and powerful officials to ordinary townsfolk, frequented the monasteries, some of which housed hundreds of monks in splendorous settings that rivaled those of the imperial palaces. Even during periods when Buddhism was less thriving, Buddhist temples were still important fixtures in the urban and rural landscapes, where fervent devotees and casual visitors alike came to worship, socialize, or enjoy the quiet surroundings.

The level of commitment and the attitudes towards Buddhism among the laity have always varied considerably. In many instances fervent worship at Buddhist temples went alongside occasional prayers to the gods of other traditions (and the other way around). Many laypeople did little more than occasionally visit temples to pray to the Buddhas and bodhisattvas for mundane benefits, but others took the faith more seriously and engaged in a variety of formal practices and observances. Typically the most committed among them tried to emulate a lay paradigm of exemplary Buddhist life that in important respects resonated with the monastic calling. While the degree and nature of one's involvement with Buddhism was a matter of personal choice, there were certain formal acts that marked individual commitment to the Buddhist path. Among them especially important were (and still are) the taking of the three refuges—in the Buddha, his teachings, and the community of holy disciples—the receiving of the five precepts (see box), and the adoption of vegetarianism (*sushi*).

The laity often joined various Buddhist societies or associations. These were usually led by a respected monk, although in late imperial Chinese and during the modern period there has been a trend towards forming associations with a clearly articulated lay ethos. Customarily many lay societies were organized for specific purposes, such as the making of Buddhist statues, building or renovating of shrines, or printing of religious texts for free distribution. There were also various charitable organizations that tended to the sick or provided help to those in need. These activities were perceived as active manifestations of the cardinal Buddhist virtue of compassion, as well as potent vehicles for the accumulation of communal and personal merit. All of these elements are still very much parts of contemporary Chinese Buddhism.

Universal compassion and merit making

For the laity—and for most monastics, for that matter—the performance of pious acts and the cultivation of Buddhist virtues were above all ways for the accumulation of merit, which brought blessings in this life and secured favorable rebirth in the next. This outlook was based on widespread belief and acceptance of the law of karma that went beyond the confines of the Buddhism community. According to it, every action brings about corresponding recompense, either in this or in a future life. While virtuous acts produce good results, the opposite is true of unwholesome deeds.

Though some lay people engaged in the kinds of practices usually associated with monks, such as meditation and scripture study, for most the main expressions of Buddhist faith took the form of public and private rituals that were infused with heartfelt devotional sentiments. Many of the rituals, including the elaborate repentance ceremonies and the services that marked key days in the liturgical calendar, were elaborate rites held in lavishly decorated temples that often lasted for hours, or even days (see Figure 6.1). Public rituals were normally officiated by monks who led the chants and prostrations, while also playing ritual instruments such as

The five lay precepts

- Abstention from killing
- Abstention from stealing
- Abstention from lying
- Abstention from sexual misconduct
- Abstention from consuming alcohol

Figure 6.1 Laity attending a festival at Linggu Monastery, Nanjing

various bells and drums, and were also attended by pious layman (or more often laywomen, especially in the contemporary context).

Within popular Buddhist circles the belief that religious merit accrued through the performance of pious acts or worship can be channeled into the attainment of specific goals—either spiritual or prosaic—was given concrete expression in particular rituals. There was also a related belief that merit can be transferred to another person (or to a few select individuals) for similar purposes. Consequently, the performance of certain rituals was primarily geared towards the fulfillment of utilitarian objectives such as the securing of good health or long life. Another popular form of ritual was performed on behalf of deceased relatives or ancestors. As services for the dead were tied up with traditional Chinese emphasis on filial piety and ancestral worship, that gave rise to a popular form of Buddhist ritual that aimed at affecting the wellbeing and salvation of the deceased. These rites are still popular and remain substantial sources of income for the monasteries and the monks who perform them on behalf of the faithful.

Even if utilitarian concerns often lurk underneath ritualized expressions of Buddhist piety, under the influence of the universalist ethos of the Mahāyāna tradition, all virtuous acts and spiritual practices are ultimately meant to be directed towards the wellbeing and salvation of all living beings in the universe. Compassionate concern and love for others was commonly construed as the central virtue of Chinese

Buddhism throughout its history, being (along with wisdom) one of the two pillars of the bodhisattva path. Genuine compassion was meant to be extended not only to one's fellow human beings but also to all other creatures, including animals and even insects. The primacy of compassion in Buddhism and the centrality of the ethical principle of non-injury to others were expressed in a number of explicit ways, including proscription or critique of the killing of animals and widespread practice of vegetarianism.

There is a wide range of attitudes toward vegetarianism among different Buddhist traditions, ranging from strict adherence to a vegetarian diet in China to conspicuous consumption of meat by the clergy and the laity in other countries such as Thailand or Burma. While the Vinaya allows meat eating under certain conditions, explicit critiques of meat eating appear in certain Mahāyāna scriptures, which argue that causing the killing of animals is incompatible with the bodhisattvas' compassionate stance and selfless salvific acts. From early on Chinese Buddhists took such injunctions to heart, and vegetarianism became a distinguishing feature of their tradition. Consequently, meat eating is prohibited in Buddhist monasteries, and Chinese monks and nuns uphold a vegetarian diet that also precludes the consumption of eggs, dairy products, and certain types of leeks. Vegetarianism is also practiced by lay Buddhists, either on a regular basis or on special occasions, for instance during festivals dedicated to popular Buddhas and bodhisattvas. Vegetarian feasts are common elements of Buddhist celebrations, and Buddhist-inspired vegetarianism also had influence on traditional Chinese society. For instance, in imperial China the government issued decrees that restricted or prohibited the slaughter of animals on certain dates, and vegetarianism was also adopted by Daoist monastic orders.

Another popular practice motivated by a desire to accrue merit and manifest compassion is the freeing of captive creatures destined for slaughter—such as birds, wild animals, or fish—which are released into their natural habitat. Domestic animals were also sometimes donated to monasteries, thereby saving them from the slaughterhouse and enabling them to live out their natural lifespan. Traditionally many monasteries have pools in which lay devotees can drop fish and turtles they have gotten from local fishermen or from the market, thereby generating good karma for themselves and their families (see Figure 6.2).

Sometimes elaborate rituals that feature the release of animals are performed for the realization of communal goals like protection from natural disasters such as drought. Buddhist associations also sometimes organize mass releases of animals, especially during popular holidays and festivals. The rituals performed at such occasions frequently feature the monks' or nuns' recitation of the Three Refuges and the Five Precepts on behalf of the released animals, with the hope of helping them to amass good karma and thus enhance their prospects for favorable rebirth.

Figure 6.2   Pool for the release of creatures, Xingshan monastery, Xi'an

Popular beliefs and cultic practices

The Mahāyāna tradition brought to China a rich and complex pantheon of Buddhas, bodhisattvas, and other divinities. While in many temples and shrines the historical Buddha—customarily referred to as Shijia mouni, the Chinese transliteration of Śākyamuni (lit. "sage of the Śākyas")—was the main object of worship, often he was superseded by other celestial Buddhas. According to Mahāyāna buddhology, all Buddhas share the same essence or nature, which is formless and identical with ultimate reality. The plethora of different Buddhas manifests in the universe in order to meet the varied spiritual needs and predilections of all beings. The most popular among the celestial Buddhas in China are Amitābha (or Emituo in Chinese), the Buddha who presides over the western pure land (see the last section of this chapter), Vairocana, the cosmic Buddha associated with the *Huayan Scripture* (see below),

Medicine Master Buddha (Yaoshi in Chinese or Bhaiṣajyaguru in Sanskrit), the Buddha of healing, and Maitreya (or Mile in Chinese), the Buddha of the future who is presently still a bodhisattva. A ubiquitous and uniquely Chinese form of Maitreya is the fat laughing Buddha, which is based on the image of monk Budai, who lived during the tenth century.

Often the main hall of worship in large monasteries houses a Buddha trinity, which might consist of imposing statues of Śākyamuni, Amitābha, and Medicine Master Buddha (or some similar combination of Buddhas), which are the central devotional objects worshiped by the devotees. Usually a monastery also houses other minor halls and shrines that are dedicated to various bodhisattvas and other deities. The devotees and casual visitors are thus faced with a wide choice of objects of worship, and on a single visit they typically venerate a number of shrines and images, often all of them. In the act of worship usually the faithful offer incense and bow down in front of the deities as a sign of respect, perhaps stopping briefly to pray for blessings, repent, or supplicate for divine intervention on their behalf.

While traditionally the various Buddhas were greatly esteemed as paradigmatic beings and pivotal sources of spiritual power and authority, they also exuded an aura of otherworldliness and inaccessibility. In contrast, the popular bodhisattvas were often perceived as being more approachable and readily responsive to the needs of the faithful. As potent religious symbols and exemplars of central Buddhist virtues, the bodhisattvas functioned at a few different levels. They were paradigmatic embodiments of religious perfection whose acts should be emulated by Buddhist practitioners, but they were also seen as celestial beings with supernatural powers that were objects of devotion and focus of cultic practices. Some of the major bodhisattvas also served as embodiments of key spiritual qualities such as compassion and wisdom.

Figure 6.3   Bodhisattva holding a lotus bud (early Song dynasty) (Arthur M. Sackler Gallery, Smithsonian Institution, Washington, D.C.: Gift of Arthur M. Sackler, S1987.223)

By tracing the prevalence of specific bodhisattva figures in large cave temple complexes, such as those at Longmen and Yun'gang, art historians have been able to document changing patterns of worship and popularity among the various Buddhas and bodhisattvas. Among the various bodhisattvas arguably the most important and popular was (and still is) Guanyin, the embodiment of compassion. Guanyin is a seemingly ubiquitous deity and a popular object of cultic worship not only in China but also throughout East Asia. In his Indian form, Guanyin (or Avalokiteśvara in Sanskrit) is featured in a number of canonical texts and he is frequently objectified in Buddhist art. There he is portrayed in a conventional fashion as a princely male figure, and that remained the main representational form during the early phases of the transmission of Buddhism into China.

From the tenth century onward, however, the Chinese representation of the bodhisattva underwent a process of feminization that involved the blurring of gendered characterizations. Eventually Guanyin came to be perceived as a female deity, although hypothetically the bodhisattva transcends all distinctions, including those of gender, and can appear in a number of different forms or guises as she performs her compassionate activity of universal salvation. Among the diverse

Figure 6.4   Statue of Dizang Bodhisattva, Xingshan monastery, Xi'an

female forms of Guanyin, especially popular is the bodhisattva's manifestation as Princess Miaoshan, the daughter of an evil king, who is celebrated as a paragon of chastity and filial piety (see Yü 2000). Other popular forms are those of a young woman in white robes holding a vase and a willow branch in her hands, or a deity with a thousand hands and eyes. Sometimes Guanyin is also depicted surrounded by children. Believing that she helps all those in need, the devotees pray for Guanyin's divine help and protection in a seemingly endless variety of circumstances and predicaments, for instance in situations when they face danger or when a woman is having trouble to become pregnant. Guanyin's enormous popularity also spilled over the boundaries of his/her original Buddhist milieu. The bodhisattva's image is worshiped in numerous Daoist and popular temples or shrines, as well as in individual homes.

Other popular bodhisattvas include Wenshu and Dizang (see Figure 6.4). Wenshu (or Mañjuśrī in Sanskrit) is the personification of wisdom, often portrayed riding a lion and holding the sword of wisdom with which he slays the forces or states of ignorance. Dizang (or Kṣitigarbha in Sankrit) is usually depicted as a monk holding a staff in his hand, who descends to the hells to save their suffering denizens. Along with the major Buddhas, popular bodhisattvas such as Guanyin and Wenshu are frequent objects of artistic representation. Serenely beautiful statues, reliefs, and painting of the bodhisattvas and other Buddhist figures, created in a variety of forms and styles, are among the most remarkable achievements of classical Chinese art. The ubiquity and quality of Buddhist art are important factors in establishing the central position of Buddhism in the cultural heritage of China. The bodhisattva cults also gave rise to distinctive literary traditions, which include collections of stories about their compassionate acts and efficacious responses to the sincere faith or fervent prayers of their devotees.

The worship of some of the prominent bodhisattva was also closely connected to the practice of pilgrimage, as the faithful made pious journeys to worship at sites associated with particular divinities. This was given clear localized expressions

The four Buddhist mountains and the Bodhisattvas associated with them

- Putuo shan (Zhejiang), the sanctuary of Guanyin (Avalokiteśvara), the bodhisattva of compassion
- Wutai shan (Shanxi), the sanctuary of Wenshu (Mañjuśrī), the bodhisattva of wisdom
- Jiuhua shan (Anhui), the sanctuary of Dizang (Kṣitigarbha), the bodhisattva who saves those who have fallen into the hells
- Emei shan (Sichuan), the sanctuary of Puxian (Samantabhadra), the bodhisattva of practice prominently featured in the *Huayan Scripture*

with the identification of four mountains in China as the principal dwelling sites or sanctuaries of four key bodhisattvas (see box, previous page). Located in areas of great natural beauty and dotted with numerous monasteries and hermitages, to this day the four Buddhist mountains are major centers of Buddhist practice and popular pilgrimage (and more recently tourist) destinations. There the faithful come to worship and meditate, frequently with hopes of catching a glimpse of the particular bodhisattva's sublime presence, which is believed to permeate the area.

Schools and traditions of Chinese Buddhism

Scholars habitually approach the study of Chinese Buddhism in terms of particular "schools" or traditions (*zong*). The Chinese term *zong* is somewhat ambiguous and has multivalent connotations. In the Buddhist context it can signify a particular doctrine, tradition of canonical exegesis, essential principle of a scripture, religious group that adheres to a set of principles or ideals, or a combination of some of these. But even when the expression is used in the sense of a distinct group or faction within Buddhism, in the Chinese context it does not designate separate sects, as the notion of "sect" is defined by sociologists of religion. In the sociological sense, the idea of a sect stands in contrast to that of "church," and implies an exclusive stance or character, which is accompanied with opposition to existing social and religious institutions. While such designation might be applicable in the contexts of other Buddhist traditions—in regard to Japanese or Tibetan Buddhism, for instance—it is not pertinent to any of the distinct schools of Chinese Buddhism, which lacked institutional independence or distinct ecclesiastical structures.

The Chinese schools of Buddhism were primarily doctrinal or exegetical traditions, or in some instances loosely-organized religious groups that were subsumed within the mainstream monastic order, rather than standing in opposition or outside of it. There was thus no way for an individual to be formally ordained as a "Chan monk," for instance, although it was possible to choose to be a follower of the Chan school, perhaps while also adhering to beliefs and practices associated with other Buddhist traditions. While there were occasional doctrinal disputes and squabbles over authority, sometimes permeated with quasi-sectarian sentiments, on the whole Buddhism in China tended to be ecumenical and accepting of diverse perspectives and approaches. Affinity or adherence to a particular school or tradition, or lack thereof, was essentially a matter of personal choice. It is also useful to keep in mind that in general, despite their great historical significance, the main schools of Buddhism involved only a limited segment of the monastic elite (with a possible exception of the Pure Land tradition), while local and popular manifestations of Buddhist piety among the general populace often had little to do with them directly.

As we saw in the previous chapter, during the early phases of the development of Buddhism in China the central intellectual and religious agendas were mainly set by canonical texts and doctrines that originated in India. During the fourth and fifth centuries the most influential doctrinal school of Mahāyāna was the Madhyamaka (Middle Way), whose teachings about emptiness were initially popularized by Kumārajīva. In China this tradition culminated with the formation of the Sanlun (Three Treatises) school—usually identified as a Chinese version of the Madhyamaka—whose best-known exponent was the erudite scholar-monk Jizang (549–623). From the sixth century onward, interest in Yogācāra teachings about the structure of consciousness, the nature of reality, and the stages of spiritual practice led to the development of new exegetical traditions, represented by the Shelun and the Dilun schools, both of which were based on scholastic treaties composed by famous Indian monks.

The tathāgatagarbha (*rulaizang*) and Buddha-nature (*foxing*) doctrines did not give rise to any new Chinese schools, although they became central articles of belief and key tenets in the new Buddhist traditions that were formed during the Sui-Tang period. The schools or traditions that came to dominate elite Buddhism during this period, such as Tiantai and Chan, were uniquely Chinese expressions of Buddhism with no direct counterparts in India or Central Asia. Because of that, the emergence of these traditions is usually viewed as culmination of the Sinification of Buddhist doctrines and practices. They exemplify how the protracted encounter with the initially foreign religion ultimately gave birth to traditions of Buddhism that were unmistakably Chinese. Before long, each of these traditions was also exported to Korea and Japan, where they exerted indelible impact on the growth of Buddhism in those countries (see Figure 6.5, p. 154).

Among the four main Buddhist schools or traditions covered in the subsequent sections, Tiantai and Huayan are traditionally acclaimed for their scriptural exegesis and the creation of sophisticated systems of Buddhist doctrine that represent the highest philosophical achievements of Chinese Buddhism. Conversely, Chan and Pure Land are renowned for their compelling soteriological frameworks and methods of spiritual cultivation. In the case of the Chan school, the main focus was on meditation and intuitive comprehension of reality, while the Pure Land tradition placed emphasis on faith and devotional practices.

The Chan and Pure Land traditions came to dominate the religious landscape from the late Tang era onwards, and still continue to be the two main streams or approaches within Chinese Buddhism. In general, Chan was popular among the monastic elite and their sophisticated supporters, who tended to be members of the social and political elites. Pure Land tradition enjoyed greater following among the common people, although to this day the lines of demarcation between the two traditions and the groups of practitioners that follow them are often ambiguous and easily crossed. Traditionally the two approaches are perceived as being complementary rather than antithetical. They are often employed in tandem, or seen as viable alternatives in a larger Buddhist scheme centered on perennial quests for spiritual solace or liberation.

The Tiantai school

Tiantai was the earliest of the so-called new Buddhist schools of the Sui-Tang era. Tracing its canonical foundation back to the popular *Lotus Scripture*, the school's name is derived from a mountain in southern China that was historically important and functioned as a major center of Tiantai studies. Tiantai school's balanced and sophisticated approach to the study and practice of Buddhism combined meticulous scriptural exegesis, creative metaphysical speculation, and comprehensive systematization of meditative practice. Tiantai school's founding figure and best known representative is Zhiyi (538–597), one of the most brilliant thinkers in the history of East Asian Buddhism. Zhiyi synthesized the prevalent strands of Buddhism at the time, bringing together the intellectually-oriented traditions of southern Buddhism with the contemplative practices characteristic of Buddhism in the North. By integrating these two main streams into a coherent whole, he produced a comprehensive system of theory and praxis that is widely acknowledged as one of the hallmarks of Chinese Buddhism.

During his life Zhiyi achieved great fame and was widely respected as a prominent monk who embodied some of the most significant and respectable monastic archetypes, including those of a captivating lecturer, meditation adept, and innovative thinker. He also received profuse honors and generous patronage from the first two emperors of the Sui dynasty, which reunited China in 589. However, the close ties with the Sui dynasty proved to be a somewhat double-sided blessing, as they negatively impacted the Tiantai school's fortunes after the succeeding Tang dynasty came to power in 618. The school survived in an organized fashion well into the Song era, experiencing periods of notable resurgence and creative development during the eighth and eleventh centuries.

A central philosophical framework formulated by Zhiyi was the doctrine of three truths, which expanded on the doctrine of two truths propounded by the Middle Way tradition of Indian Buddhism. The two truths postulated two levels or aspects of reality, conventional and absolute. Zhiyi presented an analysis of reality in terms of three integrated and interrelated aspects: (1) emptiness, (2) conventional existence, and (3) the mean (or "middle"), which incorporates the first two into a unitary reality. Ultimate reality itself is deemed to be inconceivable, its inestimable subtlety being beyond the human ability for conceptualization or verbal explanation. Within Zhiyi's interpretative scheme, the three truths point to the unitary nature of reality, which encompasses all modes of existence, from the denizens of hell all the way up to the fully enlightened Buddhas (for more on the three truths, see Swanson 1989). That led Zhiyi to formulate a peculiar understanding of reality that encompasses the existence of all things in the universe, succinctly expressed by a famous Tiantai maxim, according to which "the three thousand realms of existence are inherently present in each moment of thought."

Zhiyi also systemized the meditative traditions of medieval Buddhism, producing a comprehensive schematization of contemplative practice that brought together the two basic approaches to Buddhist meditation, calmness and insight. In this multifaceted scheme Zhiyi took into account the needs and dispositions of a wide range of practitioners. Framing his explications of contemplative praxis around the central Buddhist notion of expedient means and drawing on a variety of canonical sources, Zhiyi presented an array of contemplative practices that utilized sound and silence, movement and stillness, form and formlessness. The varied practices also combined a mixture of postures, ritual procedures, cultic activities, and other techniques of mental control and purification.

Within Zhiyi's inclusive scheme, some methods of meditation—the Guanyin repentance, for instance—were to be cultivated in a special sanctuary over a predetermined time period. They incorporated complex assemblages of ritual components and meditative techniques, such as invocation of the three refuges, offering of incense and flowers, seated meditation that incorporates mindfulness of the Buddha, recitation of verses, confession of sins, repentance, and making of vows. At the other end of the spectrum, the formless meditation of "being attentive at wherever one's mind is directed at a given moment" had no fixed procedure or time frame, and its object of meditation was no other than the mental processes that initiate and accompany actions. The profuse variety of contemplative practices propounded by Zhiyi was directed towards a broad audience of individuals with diverse abilities and backgrounds, but they were all structured according to common principles. At their core was intuitive discernment of the fundamental principle of Tiantai theory and praxis: the emptiness of mind and phenomena, which leads to the realization of ultimate reality.

The essentials of Tiantai meditation

The perfect and sudden practice of calmness and insight from the very beginning takes the true nature of reality as its object; being identical with the mean, within it there is nothing that is not true reality. When one's mind connects with the realm of reality and the realm of reality is present within a single thought, then there is no sight or smell that is not the middle way. The realm of self, the realm of Buddhas, and the realm of living creatures are all also like that…. There is only one unadulterated reality, and there is nothing outside of that reality. That the nature of all things is quiescent is called calmness; that things are quiescent and yet illuminated is called insight.

From Guanding's (561–632) preface to Zhiyi's *Great Calmness and Insight;*
cf. Donner and Stevenson 1993: 112–13.

Zhiyi also created influential doctrinal taxonomies (see Chapter 5), wrote scriptural commentaries, and compiled a code of monastic discipline. His ideas were interpreted and elaborated by later generations of Tiantai monks and scholars. Tiantai text and teachings continue to be studied in China and Japan—where the native variant of Tiantai, the Tendai sect, is one of the main Buddhist traditions—as significant part of the philosophical and historical legacies of Chinese Buddhism.

The Huayan school

The Huayan school is primarily known for its thorough and rarefied system of religious philosophy, which is usually perceived as a high point of doctrinal development in Chinese Buddhism. As suggested by its name, the Huayan school was based on or inspired by the *Huayan Scripture* (see Chapter 5). The central Huayan themes and concepts were derived from this voluminous scripture, but the tradition also used other canonical texts and was predisposed towards ingenious theoretical innovation. Even as Huayan thinkers integrated the major traditions of Mahāyāna scholasticism and cited a broad range of canonical text, their writings show a distinctly Chinese penchant for harmony and balance. Huayan texts display a tendency to focus attention on the phenomenal realm of everyday reality, even while adopting a cosmic perspective and engaging in rarefied metaphysical speculation. Key Huayan doctrines thus go beyond the parameters set by their canonical sources and templates. They entail innovative philosophical reflections on the nature of reality and the path of practice that leads to its realization.

The Huayan tradition combined erudite scriptural exegesis with a sophisticated system of religious philosophy. Its growth was largely due to the towering influence of a few exceptional monks who lived during the Tang era, five of whom came to be retroactively recognized as the tradition's founding patriarchs. Among them, Fazang (643–712) is widely acknowledged as the main architect of the Huayan system, and by extension the founder of the tradition. Born in Chang'an (present-day Xi'an) in a family that traced its ancestry to Sogdia in Central Asia, as a young man Fazang participated in Xuanzang's famous translation project, but left due to disagreements about some points of doctrine. As a prominent member of the monastic elite in the imperial capital, Fazang's multifarious activities placed him at the center of the Tang empire's religious, cultural, and political life. Renowned for his extraordinary scholarship, creative thinking, and prolific writing, Fazang achieved great fame and received extensive imperial support. Throughout his illustrious career one of his main supporters was Empress Wu Zetian. By means of his erudite lectures and prolific writings, Fazang was incredibly successful in popularizing the Huayan tradition and bringing it to the intellectual forefront of Chinese Buddhism.

At the core of the Huayan school's comprehensive doctrinal system is a holistic view of the cosmos as a dynamic web of causal relationships, in which each individual thing or phenomenon is related to everything else, and all phenomena are perfectly interfused and interpenetrate without any hindrance. This interpretation of reality represents an ingenious adaptation of the principal Buddhist teaching of dependent origination (*pratītyasamutpāda*), according to which all things are empty of self-nature and lack independent existence, but exist provisionally through the interaction and combination of assorted causal factors. In Huayan philosophy the focus of discussion moves away from the relationship between emptiness and material reality, as formulated in canonical texts belonging to the perfection of wisdom corpus. Instead, the focus shifts to the relationship between discrete phenomena or events (*shi*) and the basic principle of reality (*li*), which is predicated on the notion of emptiness and implies the mutual inclusion and identity of all phenomena. The basic modes of the relationship between individual phenomena and ultimate reality is elaborated in the doctrine of the four realms of reality (*dharmadhātu* in Sanskrit and *fajie* in Chinese), formulated by Chengguan (738–839), the fourth Huayan patriarch (see box).

According to Fazang's explanation of dependant origination, all things are ultimately based on the true nature of reality, which he equates with their emptiness or suchness. Therefore, the nature of reality is the ultimate source of all things, but it does not exist independently or outside of them. Huayan philosophy therefore does not hypothesize a dichotomy between the absolute and phenomenal realms. More exactly, it explicates the interdependent relationship between ultimate reality and the world of everyday things or phenomenal appearances.

Huayan theory also goes a step further, explaining the causal relationship that obtains among discrete phenomena. Since everything lacks self-nature and is dependently originated, each and every thing is determined by the totality of all phenomena, namely the whole cosmos, even as the totality is determined by each of the infinite things and events that comprise it. Therefore, all things are interdependent and interpenetrate with each other, even as each one retains its individual character and identity. According to this perspective, nothing exists by itself, but requires everything else to be what it really is, while the totality of all things is also causally dependent on each thing that is included in it.

The Huayan's idea of mutual interpenetration of things/phenomena is popularly represented by the metaphor of Indra's net of jewels, which can be traced back to the *Huayan Scripture*. The scripture describes how in the heaven of the god Indra

Four realms of reality according to the Huayan school

- Realm of (discrete) phenomena
- Realm of principle
- Realm of non-obstruction between principle and phenomena
- Realm of non-obstruction among all phenomena

Figure 6.5   The main hall of Tōdaiji, Nara, Japan

there is a limitless net that extends in all directions. In each knot of the net there is a lustrous jewel, and there are countless jewels in the vast cosmic net. As the many-sided surface of each jewel reflects all other jewels in the net, each of the reflected jewels also contains the reflections of all other jewels. As a result, there is a never-ending web of infinite reflections that symbolize the mutual interpenetration of all things in the universe.

By means of that kind of captivating imagery and because of the allure of its recondite doctrines, the basic principles of Huayan philosophy found receptive audiences in China and the rest of the Buddhist world in East Asia. Its teachings became broadly diffused and influenced the theoretical frameworks of other Buddhist traditions throughout East Asia. They continued to resonate within diverse religious and cultural milieus long after the Huayan school ceased to exist as a living tradition. The Huayan system of religious philosophy is still widely perceived as remaining relevant to fundamental human concerns and to issues of supreme import. Lately Huayan doctrines have inspired noteworthy cross-fertilizations of ideas with other philosophical and humanistic traditions, while the image of Indra's net and the notion of causal interrelatedness of all things are often evoked by modern proponents of environmentalism.

The Chan school

The Chan school is commonly associated with the practice of meditation, as suggested by its name, which is based on a Chinese transliteration of the Sanskrit term *dhyāna*, which denotes meditation. It is the best-known—although also the most misunderstood—school of Chinese or more broadly East Asian Buddhism. This is especially the case in the West, where it is usually referred to as Zen, from the Japanese pronunciation of its name. The early Chan movement originated within the context of the meditative traditions of medieval Chinese Buddhism, as loosely connected groups of contemplative monks gradually forged a common identity as members of a distinct tradition. At the core of that identity were the interlinked notions of dharma transmission and patriarchal lineage. In their fully developed form, they entail the idea that the spiritual ancestry of the Chan school goes back to the historical Buddha via a lineage of patriarchs. In contrast to the doctrinal schools that traced their teachings and legitimacy back to the Buddhist canon, the Chan school came to assert that it transmitted the essence of the Buddha's enlightenment, directly passed on from a teacher to a disciple via its lineage of patriarchs.

A key figure in the patriarchal transmission was Bodhidharma, an itinerant Indian monk whose life story became the stuff of legend and a central motif in Chan lore. According to tradition, Bodhidharma brought Chan teachings into China sometime during the early sixth century. Modern scholarship, however, has revealed the mythical origins of the Chan school's normative narratives about its early

Figure 6.6   The main Buddha hall of Guangxiao monastery, Guangzhou

transmission and has debunked the idea of an Indian Chan tradition transmitted by Bodhidharma. Notwithstanding its historically questionable origins, once the notion of patriarchal lineage was established, it came to serve as a central article of faith and linchpin of Chan ideology. This enabled Chan writers and adherents to claim uniqueness for their tradition and proclaim its superiority in relation to the other schools of Chinese Buddhism.

The Chan school's initial emergence and rise to prominence occurred during the Tang era, when a large number of charismatic Chan teachers such as Huineng (638–713), the renowned "sixth patriarch," and Mazu Daoyi (709–788), the leader of the Hongzhou school that by the early ninth century came to dominate the Chan movement, achieved wide acclaim and attracted numerous disciples. A prominent feature of the early Chan school's character and a major reason for its popularity were the personal charisma of its prominent teachers and the appeal of their teachings, which contained creative reconfigurations of essential Buddhist themes and concepts, recast in a distinctive Chan idiom (see box). For the Chan school, the Tang era was a period of nascent growth marked by great intellectual creativity and religious vitality, often considered to be the tradition's golden age. Subsequently memories (along with creative imaginings) of the glories of Tang Chan came to dominate traditional narratives of Chan history, even if those narratives were constructed in ways that reflected the beliefs and ideologies of later traditions.

Tang-era Chan is typically represented as a revolutionary movement, led by a host of enigmatic Chan teachers who supposedly rejected mainstream mores and institutions. It paved the way for the formation of a unique tradition that, we often are told, represented a major paradigm shift in the history of Chinese Buddhism. The central motifs of that characterization are based on numerous stories that convey

Chan teacher Mazu on ordinary mind

The Way (Dao) needs no cultivation; just prevent defilement. What is defilement? When with a mind of birth and death one acts in a contrived manner, then everything is defilement. If one wants to know the Way directly: ordinary mind is the Way! What do I mean by "ordinary mind?" It is a mind that is devoid of contrived activity, and is without notions of right and wrong, grasping and rejecting, terminable and permanent, worldly and holy. The [*Vimalakīrti*] scripture says, "Neither the practice of ordinary people, nor the practice of sages, that is the bodhisattvas' practice." Right now, whether walking, standing, sitting, or reclining, responding to situations and dealing with people as they come: everything is the Way.

From the *Recorded Saying of Mazu*;
trans. adapted from Poceski 2007: 183.

striking images of an inimitable and radical religious movement, led by dynamic Chan teachers who come across as iconoclasts par excellence. As these stories became principal components of Chan literature and the foundations of Chan ideology, they helped establish an image of the Chan teacher as an indomitable religious figure that subverts established norms and employs an array of unconventional pedagogical techniques—including beating, shouting, and inscrutable verbal ramblings—that supposedly are meant to lead his often perplexed disciples to a state of spiritual enlightenment. Modern scholarship has shown the problematic provenance of these stories, which for the most part are apocryphal and tell us little about the actual lives and teachings of their main protagonist. Nonetheless, they still remain the central element of traditional Chan lore, and continue to shape the tradition's public image and its self-understanding.

The provenance of popular perceptions of Tang-era Chan teachers as bearers of a new iconoclast ethos goes back to classical Chan literature, as codified from the tenth century onward. Later generations of Chan writers and editors developed distinctive literary genres, including the well-known *gong'an* (or *kōan* in Japanese) collections, in which the focus shifted away from discussions of the teachings and practices of canonical Buddhism, and towards the recounting of pithy and spirited exchanges between Chan teachers and their students. Ironically, the manufacture of such pseudo-historical records, which feature radical styles of Chan rhetoric and pedagogy, occurred while the Chan school was adopting an increasingly conservative stance as foremost representative of the religious mainstream and linchpin of Buddhist orthodoxy. Notwithstanding the radical rhetorical posturing, in actual reality the Chan school was far from being iconoclastic, and on the whole it was not as separate or different from the rest of Chinese Buddhism as is often assumed.

The compilation and codification of texts that popularized iconoclastic images of famous Chan teachers largely took place during the Song period (i.e. from the late tenth through the late twelfth century). That was part of far-reaching changes that the Chan school underwent during the Tang-Song transition, as the ongoing reconfiguring of the parameters of orthodoxy helped solidify the Chan school's position as the main tradition of elite Chinese Buddhism. By the Song era, most of the major public monasteries, which received recognition and support from the imperial state, were officially designated as Chan monasteries. At the time, influential Chan teachers enjoyed great renown and authority, while their tradition occupied a dominant position within Buddhist circles and exerted notable impact on elite culture, particularly in the intellectual and artistic spheres.

In conjunction with the aforementioned formulation of new narrative formats and literary genres, which often adopted rarefied and flowery language that appealed to the tastes of the literati, a major development during the Song period was the development of distinctive methods of Chan meditation. Especially noteworthy in that regard was the style of meditation practice called "investigating the critical phrase," which involved meditation on famous *gong'ans*, condensed accounts of putative exchanges between famous Chan teachers and their students that often employ ambiguity and paradox. This style of Chan practice remained dominant during the subsequent epochs, and with some adaptations it is still the main method of Chan meditation. The same style of meditation was also exported to other parts of East Asia, where it became incorporated into the dominant strains of native Chan/ Zen traditions, such as the Rinzai sect in Japan or the Chogye (Jogye) order in Korea.

The Pure Land tradition

Classical Mahāyāna expositions on the state of Buddhahood include the notion of pure lands, which are paradise-like worlds that have been made beautiful and pure by the virtues and presence of particular Buddhas. Among the innumerable worlds depicted in Buddhist cosmology, especially important within the context of Chinese Buddhism is the pure land of Buddha Amitābha. Located very far away from this world in the western direction, Amitābha's "land of bliss" (Sukhāvatī) was supposedly made pure by his fulfillment of past vows to attain enlightenment in order to establish an immaculate realm where those who have faith in him can be reborn. Described as a place of utmost splendor and flawlessness, devoid of all the suffering and imperfection that characterize everyday life in this world, the western pure land purportedly offers its inhabitants blissful existence, graced by the presence of Amitābha and his retinue of bodhisattvas, which includes Guanyin.

While depictions of Amitābha's pure land appear in some Mahāyāna scriptures, the rise of a full-blown Pure Land (or Jingtu in Chinese) tradition centered on the worship of Amitābha and the quest for rebirth in his land was a distinct Chinese

The Pure Land of Amitābha Buddha

At that time, the Buddha told Sariputra, the elder: "From here in the western direction, after passing through hundreds of thousands of millions of Buddha lands, there is a world that is called Utmost Bliss. In that land there is a Buddha called Amitābha, who presently preaches the Dharma. Sariputra, why is that land named Utmost Bliss? The living beings of that realm never suffer, but enjoy all kinds of bliss; for that reason it is named Utmost Bliss.... Furthermore, Sariputra, in that Buddha land there is always the sound of celestial music, while the ground is made out of pure gold. During the six periods of day and night there is a rain of celestial flowers. In the clarity of dawn the living beings of that land, each of them holding a multitude of splendid coral tree flowers in the robes, make offerings to billions of Buddhas who reside in other regions.

From the *Amitābha Buddha Scripture* (*Emituo fo jing*).

development. The Pure Land movement did not become a separate school of Buddhism in the same sense as the other three traditions surveyed above, notwithstanding efforts to create such identity by forging a discrete patriarchal lineage. Nonetheless, it was successful in instituting popular beliefs and practices that became widely diffused throughout Chinese Buddhism. The popularity of Pure Land teachings and practices remained very high all the way into the modern period—their followers generally outnumbering those of other traditions—although in the ecumenical milieu of Chinese Buddhism they were often mixed with elements and perspectives of other Buddhist schools. As a result of such popularity, the tangible prospect of rebirth in the western land of bliss frequently replaced the somewhat abstruse and impersonal notion of Nirvana as the desired goal of Buddhist devotion and practice.

In contrast to Western notions about paradise, technically speaking the pure lands of Amitābha and other celestial Buddhas do not correspond to a paradisiacal realm that serves as the ultimate destination or permanent abode of beatific repose. A Buddhist pure land such as that of Amitābha is supposed to serve more in the manner of a way station, being a beautiful and pleasant place that is conducive to Buddhist practice, where even the birds and the plants preach Buddhist doctrine. Theoretically speaking, being reborn there simply makes it easier for the devotee to advance towards the final goal of Nirvana, although in actual practice such distinctions are often glossed over. The pure land is also sometimes interpreted in metaphorical terms as a state of mind, as expressed by the famous adage "if the mind is pure, then the Buddha land is also pure." In the same vein, Amitābha is explained as a symbolic embodiment of the essence of Buddhahood, which is beyond all forms and attributes. Traditionally this kind of exegetical move is put forward by teachers who adopt a Chan perspective, which at times includes critique of literal interpretations of the pure land. Furthermore, the two explanations of the pure land, literal and metaphorical, are often juxtaposed and used in tandem.

Such fine distinctions and alternative interpretative schemes, however, are more often than not overlooked by the faithful. Above all, Pure Land believers are attracted to a promise of perfect world that is readily reachable in the afterlife, where they can escape from the tribulations and miseries encountered in this world. Accordingly, the Pure Land tradition is conventionally perceived as an easy path of practice. Within the Pure Land scheme, cultivation of the bodhisattva path and reliance on individual effort are replaced by simple faith in the salvific agency of an external Buddha. In the early history of the Pure Land movement this also tied up with popular Buddhist prophesies of decline, according to which Buddhism gradually underwent distinct phases of irreversible deterioration, which made it difficult to fully practice its profound teachings and realize the ultimate goal of liberation. This set up a dichotomy between the Pure Land tradition as an easy path, in which one relies on the "other power" of Amitābha, and the Chan school as a difficult path, in which the individual practitioner relies on his or her "self power."

At the core of Pure Land devotionalism is belief in the salvific power and boundless grace of Amitābha, which is expressed in various cultic practices. Since the goal of rebirth in the pure land is realized only upon one's death, from the late medieval period onward symbols and rituals associated with the Pure Land tradition became central elements of dying practices and funeral rites, although they are also widely practiced outside of those contexts. While faith is the basic condition for rebirth in the pure land of Amitābha, devotees are also advised to observe basic moral injunctions, perform meritorious deeds, and engage in other forms of spiritual cultivation. Within the early Pure Land movement especially popular were contemplative exercises that entailed mindful recollection or visualization of Amitābha, his attendant bodhisattvas, and his land of bliss.

Most often, however, the recollection of Amitābha (*nianfo*) takes the form of invoking or chanting his name, either vocally or silently. Customarily that is done by using the formula "Namo Emituo fo" (Homage to Amitābha Buddha!), which remains one of the most popular practices in Chinese Buddhism. Invocation of the Buddha's name and related devotional practices can be cultivated solitarily, but most often they are done in communal settings. Historically that contributed to the rise of numerous Pure Land associations. Moreover, Pure Land-related chants and invocations were also integrated into the daily liturgies of virtually all Chinese Buddhist temples, and they remain essential parts of the liturgical repertoire of contemporary Chinese Buddhism. Pure Land beliefs and practices continue to be prominent elements of Chinese Buddhism, and the same also applies to Korea and Japan.

Key points

- Monastic ideals and institutions were successfully transmitted into China, where they underwent further adaptation and growth. There was a parallel process of acculturation among the laity that included the development of distinctive mores and modes of practice, while there was also significant overlap between the monastic and lay paradigms.
- Most popular manifestations of Buddhist devotion and piety revolve around the quest for making merit, and are embedded in a distinctive religious ethos that highlights the virtue of universal compassion.
- One of the most conspicuous features of Buddhism in China is the widespread worship of various Buddhas, such as Śākyamuni, Amitābha, and Vairocana, and popular bodhisattvas such as Guanyin and Mañjuśrī.
- A number of distinctive schools or traditions developed in the course of Buddhism's growth and its Sinification, although all of them did not turn into independent sects and they were all subsumed within the mainstream monastic order.

- Zhiyi and other leading thinkers of the Tiantai school engaged in a disciplined yet creative philosophical reflection on the core truths of Buddhism. A central element of their recasting of Buddhist doctrine was the theory of three truths, which they carefully integrated with their comprehensive systematization of contemplative praxis.
- The Huayan school created a rarefied system of Buddhist philosophy, in which the whole cosmos is conceived as a dynamic and organic web of causal relationships; in it all things interpenetrate and are causally related to each other and to the totality of everything.
- The Chan school established its religious authority in large part by claiming to transmit the essence of the Buddha's enlightenment, which it tried to communicate by means of innovative teachings and meditative techniques, elaborated in a large body of texts composed in distinctive Chan genres.
- At the core of the Pure Land tradition is belief in the salvific power of Buddha Amitābha and quest for rebirth in his "land of bliss," which is said to be achieved by the development of unshakable faith and the perfection of various devotional practices.

Discussion questions

1. Which popular bodhisattva underwent a gender transformation in China and what are the possible explanations for that?
2. Explain the use of the symbolism of Indra's net in the texts of the Huayan school and elucidate its doctrinal background.
3. What are the main beliefs and primary modes of practices in the Pure Land tradition, and how do they contrast with those of the Chan school?

Further reading

See also the reading suggestions for Chapter 5.

Cleary, Thomas F. 1983. *Entry into the Inconceivable: An Introduction to Hua-yen Buddhism.* Honolulu, HI: University of Hawaii Press.

Donner, Neal Arvid and Daniel B. Stevenson, trans. 1993. *The Great Calming and Contemplation: A Study and Annotated Translation of the First Chapter of Chih-I's Mo-Ho Chih-Kuan.* Honolulu, HI: University of Hawaii Press.

Gregory, Peter N., ed. 1986. *Traditions of Meditation in Chinese Buddhism.* Honolulu, HI: University of Hawai'i Press.

Gregory, Peter N. and Daniel A. Getz, Jr., eds. 1999. *Buddhism in the Sung.* Honolulu, HI: University of Hawai'i Press.

Halperin, Mark. 2006. *Out of the Cloister: Literati Perspectives on Buddhism in Sung China, 960–1279*. Cambridge, MA: Harvard University Asia Center.

Heine, Steven and Dale S. Wright, eds. 2004. *The Zen Canon: Understanding the Classic Texts*. Oxford and New York: Oxford University Press.

Kieschnick, John. 1997. *The Eminent Monk: Buddhist Ideals in Medieval Chinese Hagiography*. Honolulu, HI: University of Hawai'i Press.

McRae, John R. 2003. *Seeing Through Zen: Encounter, Genealogy, and Transformation in Chinese Chan Buddhism*. Berkeley, CA: University of California Press.

Poceski, Mario. 2007. *Ordinary Mind as the Way: The Hongzhou School and the Growth of Chan Buddhism*. Oxford and New York: Oxford University Press.

Swanson, Paul L. *Foundations of T'ien-t'ai Philosophy: The Flowering of the Two Truths Theory in Chinese Buddhism*. Berkeley, CA: Asian Humanities Press, 1989.

Welter, Albert. 2006. *Monks, Rulers, and Literati: The Political Ascendancy of Chan Buddhism*. Oxford and New York: Oxford University Press.

Yampolsky, Philip B., trans. 1967. *The Platform Sūtra of the Sixth Patriarch*. New York: Columbia University Press.

Yifa. 2002. *The Origins of Buddhist Monastic Codes in China: An Annotated Translation and Study of the* Chanyuan Qinggui. Honolulu, HI: University of Hawai'i Press.

Yü, Chün-fang. 2000. *Kuan-yin: The Chinese Transformation of Avalokiteśvara*. New York: Columbia University Press.

Zhiru. 2007. *The Making of a Savior Bodhisattva: Dizang in Medieval China*. Honolulu, HI: University of Hawai'i Press.

7   *Popular religion*

In this chapter

This chapter surveys the rich plethora of beliefs and practices that are subsumed within the broad category of Chinese popular religion. While sometimes denigrated by proponents of the great religious traditions such as Confucianism and Christianity, or summarily dismissed by disbelieving secularists as old-fashioned superstitions, these often local manifestations of popular piety have over the centuries constituted a vibrant, widely diffused, and immensely significant part of Chinese religious life.

Main topics

- General contours and basic character of popular religion.
- Prevalence of syncretic tendencies.
- Teachings and movements that highlight the unity of the three teachings.
- The supernatural realm and the various beings that populate it.
- Worship of local gods.
- Organization of the celestial pantheon.
- Worship of Guandi and Mazu.
- Utilitarian character of popular religion.
- Proliferation of messianic movements, heterodox sects, and secret societies.

Contours and character of popular religion

We already noted some of the problems linked with attempts to narrowly define Chinese traditions such as Confucianism and Daoism, or to clearly delineate their boundaries. We also observed the Chinese tendency to often blur the lines of demarcation that separate the three teachings, which for most of Chinese history were each fairly open to interreligious interaction and syncretic adaptation. Throughout Chinese religious history there has also been a pervasive predisposition to construct multifaceted and open-ended religious identities, which allow individuals and communities to engage in a range of spiritual practices or worship deities linked with more than one religion. Such flexible attitudes towards religious categorization, affiliation, and identity formation contrast with the exclusivist identification with single religion—typically narrowly defined in terms of particular scripture(s), creeds, and institutions—that is characteristic of monotheistic religions such as Judaism, Christianity, and Islam.

Within the broad context of Chinese religious culture, these kinds of ecumenical and syncretic predispositions are further brought into focus when we look at the constellations of beliefs and practices that are grouped together under the category of popular religion. The category itself is largely a scholarly creation, introduced heuristically as a way of classifying a broad range of prevalent ideas, beliefs, and practices that are not officially part of any of the orthodox traditions, primarily represented by the three teachings (which in more recent eras can be further expanded to include Christianity and Islam). Because of its vagueness and broadness, the utility of popular religion as a distinct category is sometimes questioned or disputed by some scholars. Nonetheless, it is an important and useful category, as the beliefs and practices subsumed into it were/are widely diffused among the Chinese people and must be taken into account in order to arrive at a balanced and comprehensive understanding of Chinese religious and social life, in all its complexity and diversity. Accordingly, pre-modern Chinese religion is increasingly discussed in terms of four main traditions, namely popular religion and the three institutionalized religions of Buddhism, Confucianism, and Daoism.

Popular religion is notoriously difficult to pigeonhole or circumscribe, as it evades scholarly efforts to define it with great precision and certitude. To a large extent, that is due to it diffused character and the lack of fixed doctrinal and institutional cores. Unlike the large institutionalized religions, traditionally popular religion did not have any canon, although there are certain "scriptures" that can be ascribed to the category of popular religion. It also did not have an integrated collection of beliefs or a coherent system of tenets, nor a church that safeguards doctrinal orthodoxy. There is no way one could formally join or become an adherent of popular religion, so naturally the notion of conformity to dogma and the threat of excommunication do not play any part in it.

Being largely grounded in local religious and social practice, popular religion does not have ecclesiastical hierarchies or professional clergy, even though there are certain types of ritual specialists who officiate at particular rites or observances. That makes popular religious beliefs and practices highly adaptable and responsive to local conditions, which accounts for the fact that there are many modulations and inconsistencies in terms of how they are applied on the ground. Accordingly, popular religion is characterized by abundant variety and preponderance of local or regional variations. There is thus no single model that can be used to understand the whole range of popular Chinese conceptions and engagements with the supernatural realm and the divine beings that populate it. As an integral part of Chinese culture, popular religion provides a multifaceted system of models and symbolic resources that individuals or groups can use for a variety of purposes and situation, as they navigate the ebbs and flows of their lives. On the other hand, notwithstanding its grounding in the family and the local community, popular religion also encompasses key values and outlooks that are characteristic of Chinese civilization in general.

The beliefs and practices included within the category of popular religion are frequently interpreted primarily in terms of the roles they play in ordering and animating the religious and social lives of the common people. However, it is historically inaccurate to deny or gloss over the elites' involvement in popular religion, as has been done by scholars who emphasize rigid (and often imaginary) lines of demarcation between the supposedly rational worldviews and sensible ritual observances of the literati on one side, and the vile superstitions of the unenlightened masses on another (for an example, see Chan 1963). Most of the sources of information about popular religion during the pre-modern period were written by literati, so they reflect elite concerns and perspectives. While some members of the literati elites criticized aspects of popular beliefs and practices—and at times campaigned to change or abolish them—throughout Chinese history people from all backgrounds and walks of life, from peasants to emperors, participated in the rituals and observances of popular religion.

The broad range of understandings and attitudes towards popular beliefs and practices reflect different variables, including class, status, education, and gender; there is also always room for expressions of individual idiosyncrasies and predilections. The constellations of symbols, myths, and rituals included into popular religion are malleable to varied interpretations and modifications, as they are all parts of a common religious culture. Therefore, popular religion constitutes a rich substratum of religiosity that is shared by most Chinese people and reflects prevalent norms, values, and worldviews. Throughout history two of its key functions have been the preservation of normative values and validation of a hegemonic sociopolitical order. However, as we will see, at the time popular religion also performed destabilizing roles and was used by various historical actors to challenge the status quo. In light of that and given China's established political culture, it should not come as a great surprise to learn that in traditional China some of the gods of popular religion were granted ritual titles and were incorporated into the official pantheon, or that the state was frequently involved in issues related to popular cultic worship.

Syncretism

One of the enduring features of popular religion is its tendency towards syncretism. Syncretism refers to processes of borrowing, combining, or adapting elements derived from diverse sources. The notion of syncretism often caries negative connotations, especially when the study of religion is undertaken on the basis of limited Western perspectives. In such usage, the label of syncretism denotes prejudiced characterization of the religion of some (usually non-Westerner and traditional) society or group as a befuddling and superficial mélange of disparate elements that lack theological integrity. That is obviously not the way the concept of syncretism is used here. Overall, its usage is less problematic when applied to the Chinese context, given the predominant tendency to look at religions as not being mutually exclusive or antithetical. Syncretism is a basic component of interreligious interaction and to some degree it is found in all religions, notwithstanding the ahistorical claims of individual religious traditions that they are pure and unique, representing god-given dispensations free from external accretions or influences.

Within the Chinese framework, elements of syncretism are evident in each of the three teachings, especially in their popular manifestations. The tendency towards syncretism increases as the focus of attention moves towards the margins of each tradition, away from the orthodox formulations of the priestly and intellectual elites. Nonetheless, the Chinese openness or penchant for syncretic blending of diverse beliefs and practices is most readily discernable in popular religion. While the syncretism of popular religion has elicited recurring criticisms, voiced by native intellectuals and foreign missionaries and scholars alike, a more positive approach might be to look at it as a mark of religious creativity and cultural open-mindedness, influenced by a healthy aversion to dogmatism and rejection of exclusivism. While throughout Chinese history proponents of syncretism often functioned as agents of religious tolerance, it should also be noted that at times some of them adopted rigid attitudes and sectarian agendas.

Most of the elements that were adapted and absorbed into popular religion can be traced to one of the three teachings. For instance, much of popular morality reflects the pervasive influence of Confucian ethical norms and principles. That includes the virtue of filial piety, as well as a general moral ethos that promotes good traits such as honesty and fairness. Copious elements of Buddhist influence are observable in popular beliefs about hells and the afterlife (which are modulated by the insertion of Daoist elements), as well as in prevalent ideas about merit and karmic recompense. That goes together with the inclusion of Buddhist deities as objects of worship in popular religion. It is not uncommon for popular Chinese temples to have special areas set aside for Buddhist deities—which typically include popular Buddhas, bodhisattvas such as Guanyin, and sages such as Bodhidharma—with their shrines arranged in a manner similar to what one finds in Buddhist monasteries or temples.

The influences or correlations between Daoism and popular religion are even more extensive than those of Buddhism and Confucianism. They cover most aspects of popular religion, from the arrangement of the pantheon to the structure of key rites and other prevalent modes of worship. Even at the institutional level, Daoist priests

Yuan Huang's (1533–1606) articles of merit and demerit

Count as hundred merits: (1) rescuing a person from death; (2) preserving a woman's chastity; and (3) preventing someone from drowning a child or having an abortion. Count as fifty merits: (1) arranging for the adoption of a heir; (2) raising an orphan; (3) burying someone who has no one to take care of his or her remains; (4) and preventing a person from becoming a vagabond. Count as ten demerits: (1) ostracizing a virtuous person; (2) recommending a bad person for employment; (3) having contact with a woman who has lost her chastity; (4) keeping a deadly weapon.

Excerpts adapted from Cynthia Brokaw's translation, in Lopez 1996: 432, 434.

are often employed to officiate at rites performed at popular temples, especially in Taiwan and other parts of South China. This makes the lines of demarcation between popular religion and Daoism especially blurred. Consequently, at times the two are lumped together into a single category, as is evident in the official demographic data concerning religious affiliation compiled in contemporary Taiwan and Singapore.

Often elements of each of the three teachings are seamlessly interwoven into specific paradigms of popular belief or practice. A case in point are the notions about conventional morality and supernatural retribution integrated into the various ledgers of merit and demerit that proliferated in late imperial China (see box). The ledgers were meant to provide concrete guidance on how to lead virtuous life and accumulate merit, which led to tangible rewards in this or future lives. They provided templates for keeping score of one's virtuous and evil deeds, with the final balance pointing to the nature of karmic recompense or supernatural retribution that awaited the individual. The eclectic mixing of disparate elements, evident in the individual articles of merit and demerit included in the ledgers, illustrates how values and ideas derived from Buddhist, Confucian, and Daoist sources were integrated together into popular conceptions of morality.

The syncretic tendencies of popular religion are on visual display when one enters local Chinese temples, such as Thian Hock Keng Temple in Singapore or Tin Hau Temple in Hong Kong, which, at some level, can be described as spiritual supermarkets of sorts. In places such as these, besides worshiping or praying to popular deities such as Mazu (see p. 177), the devotees also have the option of doing the same in front of the statues of Buddhist deities such as Guanyin, Daoist immortals such as Lü Dongbin, or even the great sage Confucius himself.

Unity of the three teachings

Deliberate or conscious forms of syncretism, observable at different junctures in Chinese religious history, are especially well represented in the various attempts to highlight the unity or convergence of the three teachings. Within such interpretative schemes, the three main religious systems of China are deemed to be essentially alike, as conveyed by the popular notion of "unity of the three teachings" (*sanjiao heyi*) and its variations. The three teachings simply represent different modalities of an essential truth or reality, and in the final analysis they are subsumed into a larger organic unity. Sometimes these perspectives are elaborated from within the outlook of one of the three great teachings, and in such cases the clerics or writers in question tend to prioritize their own religion. A good example of that is the inclusion of Confucianism and Daoism in some of the Buddhist doctrinal taxonomies devised during the Tang era, in which they were allocated to the lowest categories, below the most basic Buddhist doctrines.

At times these kinds of syncretic themes and ideals were given concrete doctrinal and intuitional forms, as evident in the rise of religions movements based on the idea of the harmony and unity of Buddhism, Confucianism, and Daoism. A good example of that from the late imperial period—that continues into the present time—is the Three-in-one Teaching (Sanyi jiao). Initiated by Lin Zhaoen (1517–1598) in the sixteenth century, the Three-in-one Teaching became a distinct sectarian movement that claimed to unite the three teachings, albeit is a somewhat selective manner. Lin Zhaoen was born in a gentry family and received a classical education, but decided not to pursue an official career and instead dedicate himself to a quest for spiritual enlightenment. Initially he sought to revive and popularize Confucianism, which he felt has been reduced to a sterile intellectual discipline geared towards success in the official examinations. He promoted Confucian teachings that centered on the pursuit of sagehood, expressing them in a distinctly religious idiom and selectively combining them with elements derived from other traditions, namely Daoist internal alchemy and Buddhist teachings about mental cultivation, especially those of the Chan school. In a way, he amalgamated the theoretical scaffolding of Confucianism with the practical techniques of Buddhism and Daoism.

In their early form, the Three-in-one teachings emphasized the process of spiritual cultivation and had a distinctly contemplative orientation, although over time in its sectarian expressions the movement developed a range of popular cultic practices that operated at the level of local communities. As a sectarian movement, it developed a distinct organization, with its own sacred texts, initiations, moral precepts, and liturgies. While in the eighteenth century the Three-in-one Teaching was proclaimed heresy and was proscribed by the Qing government, it managed to survive and continues to flourish to this day, especially in Southeast China and among the Chinese diasporas in Southeast Asia. Over time, Lin Zhaoen became apotheosized and he is still widely worshiped by the followers of the sect he initiated.

> ## Lin Zhaoen on the unity of the three teachings and the brotherhood of their followers
>
> [Zhang Zai's] "Western Inscription" states: "All people are my brothers and sisters." Therefore, if one takes the actual birth parents as one's parents, then those born of the same parents are one's brothers. If one takes heaven and earth as one's parents, then all those born of heaven and earth are also one's brothers. As for Buddhists and Daoists, can any of them live outside of heaven and earth? If they cannot live outside of heaven and earth, what are they if not people born of the womb of the same mother, what are they if not our brothers.
>
> Translation adapted from Berling 1980: 217.

Other modern examples of popular religious movements or sects with manifest syncretic tendencies include Falun gong (Practice of the Dharma Wheel) and Yiguan dao (The Way of Unity, often transcribed as I-kuan tao). Falun gong gained notoriety after the Chinese government proscribed it in 1999, which was followed by the ongoing persecution of its followers that continues to this day (see Chapter 10). Its program of spiritual cultivation revolves around *qigong* exercises, although its texts also deal with ethical issues and other religious topics. While the teachings of Yiguan dao include a myth of origin that link it with mythical figures such as the Yellow Emperor and ancient sages such as Confucius and the Buddha, in its modern configuration the growth of this movement is essentially a twentieth century religious phenomenon. After the Communist takeover in 1949 the main locus of its activity moved to Taiwan, where recent surveys put the number of Yiguan dao followers to close to a million. There are also branch centers in other parts of the world, including the United States. The practices of Yiguan dao devotees include observance of moral precepts, largely derived from Confucianism, participation in initiation ceremonies, performance of daily liturgies, practice of vegetarianism, and chanting of scriptures.

Ancestors and ghosts

Much of popular religious practice in China revolves around the supplication and worship of various divine or supernatural beings. From early on, the Chinese have lived in a complex world populated by all sort of invisible and mysterious beings, some of them perceived as being kind and helpful, but others coming across as demonic and dangerous. Scholars often classify the numerous divinities and uncanny creatures that populate the spiritual realm of popular religion into three broad categories: gods (*shen*), ancestors (*zu*), and ghosts (*gui*). While the beings included into these categories possess different powers and attributes that separate them from ordinary people, they are all subject to uniform cosmic processes and partake of the same underlying reality.

Ontologically speaking, all beings, commonplace and supernatural, share the same substance. In the final analysis, they are different modulations of *qi*, the basic stuff or element out of which all beings and things are made. The concept of *qi* is intricate and multifaceted, encompassing mind and matter, spirit and energy. Accordingly, the supernatural and mundane worlds, as well as the realms of the dead and the living, are not radically disjoined. The living and the dead are believed to be connected and to influence each other, and the same principle applies to the human relationship with the gods.

Beliefs about the existence of supernatural or mysterious beings are based on the notion that, at some level, the soul or spirit of a person can survive the moment of physical death. Such conception of the soul and the afterlife is grounded in ancient cosmological schemes central to Chinese thought, which postulate fundamental order and unity in the universe. Customarily, Chinese believe in the existence of two kinds of soul: earthly soul (*po*), linked with the *yin* element, and heavenly soul (*hun*), linked with the *yang* element. Upon death the earthly soul—associated with darkness, sensuality, and corporality—moves downward towards the earth and can be transformed into a ghost. On the other hand, the heavenly soul—associated with brightness, intelligence, and spirituality—travels upwards and can be reborn as a god or an ancestor. Despite their apparent differences, there are therefore striking similarities between the ancestors and the gods, even though the gods are believed to be in possession of greater numinous power, and their influence purportedly extends beyond the confines of individual families. It is also possible for an ancestor to transform himself or herself into a god (but also into a demon). Accordingly, the two classes of supernatural beings, gods and ancestors, are usually worshiped in a similar manner.

At their core, the practices of popular religion center on the family (here understood in a broader sense than the nuclear family) and the local community. The veneration of ancestors, sometimes dubbed the "cult of the dead," reflects the pervasive influence of the kinship system on Chinese social and religious life. It has a very long history, going back all the way to the dawn of Chinese civilization (see Chapter 1). Ancestor worship is simply a ritualized extension of the virtue of filial piety that goes beyond one's immediate parents. By such ritual means, the living are able to convey their feelings of respect, as well as establish links and channels of communication with deceased members of the ancestral lineage, as they solicit their blessings or approval, and try to avoid their wrath or censure.

The spirits of the ancestors are traditionally symbolized and commemorated by means of ancestral tablets, on which their names are inscribed. Within individual homes the ancestral tablets are placed at special altars or shrines. In cases of wealthier households, there might be separate ancestral halls, or even whole ancestral temples (see Figure 7.1). Often ancestral tablets are also placed at a local temple, which might be a Buddhist or a Daoist establishment. Within the altar area the tablets are frequently accompanied with statues or paintings of popular deities such as Guandi, Mazu, or Guanyin. Offering incense and paying respects at the ancestral shrine are integral parts of the domestic routine of many Chinese households. On special occasions there are more elaborate rites and sacrifices, which usually involve the offering of food and incense.

Generally the ghosts do not receive the same reverence and devotion that is afforded to the gods and the ancestors. Ghosts are essentially the numinous spirits of dead people that roam around and infiltrate the world of the living. They are scary and haunting presences, which are best avoided or kept at bay. Many ghosts supposedly possess evil predispositions or are prone to mischief, while others are simply lonely or unhappy spirits that occupy marginal positions outside of established social frameworks. Sometimes they might assume alluring forms, such as those of beautiful women, but even in such instances they still harbor potential danger.

The best way to appease the ghosts and avoid being haunted or troubled by them, according to popular belief, is to make them offerings and show them respect. A popular class of ghosts is the hungry ghosts (*egui*), whose origins go back to Buddhist mythology and cosmology. These pitiful beings are depicted as being very ugly and utterly destitute, always troubled by unquenchable thirst and hunger. The popular ghost festival (*zhongyuan*), held in the seventh lunar month on the full moon day, is an occasion when offerings are made to these creatures—especially to ancestors who have been reborn as ghosts—in order to alleviate their suffering. There are also more explicitly Buddhist and Daoist variations on the same theme, and the same festival is also celebrated in Korea and Japan.

Figure 7.1　Entrance to the ancestral temple of the Chen family, Guangzhou

Worship of local gods

Some of the gods of popular religion have zoomorphic origins, while others trace their identity to archaic embodiments of natural forces and phenomena, such as wind or rain, mountains or rivers, stars or other celestial objects. However, overwhelmingly in China the gods assume anthropomorphic forms. Like people in many other cultures, the Chinese construed the gods in their own image. Many of the gods even have their own biographies and birthdays, while a number of them trace their origins to historical persons, who over the centuries became apotheosized and imparted with numinous powers. Moreover, occasionally the gods' personas and functions changed over time, while certain gods lost their popularity and quietly disappeared into the dustbin of history, having outlived their usefulness. Although many of the gods have local or regional influence, some of them enjoy wide acclaim and are revered throughout the Chinese world.

In popular religion the basic forms of relationship and patterns of interaction between humans and supernatural beings are based on the principle of reciprocity. That implies a system of mutual obligations: while human beings venerate and pray to the gods with the hope of receiving their help and harnessing some of their numinous power, the gods also rely on the offerings and sacrifices of the faithful. The gods' very status and authority as divine beings is dependent on the worship and respect they elicit from their devotees. That status must be continuously safeguarded and substantiated, primarily by the gods' ability to efficaciously respond to the supplications of the faithful, which among other things includes manifestations of miraculous events and divine grace. Such circumstances make the gods and other divinities eminently malleable to adaptation in response to changing socioreligious predicaments, which accounts for the astounding diversity and local variations within popular religion.

Different gods have disparate powers and spheres of authority, and they occupy different levels of distance from the people that worship them. There is typically an inverse relationship between an individual god's power and his or her remoteness from potential worshipers. The highest and most powerful gods are frequently perceived as being too remote or aloof to be approached directly. Conversely, the gods that possess more limited powers and spheres of influence are also the ones that are most accessible and responsive to felt religious needs, as they are situated closest to the main places where everyday worship takes place: the family and the local community. A prime example of a god that is closely linked with the family is the stove god (*zaoshen*, also referred to as the kitchen god).

As his name indicates, the stove gods is said to reside in the kitchen area of the home. He performs the function of a god of the whole household, and each family has its own stove god. The belief in this god is very ancient, probably going back to the time of Confucius. He is most prominent among the domestic gods that look over the home and the family. Other members of this group are the door gods, usually represented as a pair, whose images are posted on the outside doors to ward off evil and protect the home and its occupants (see Figure 7.2). The primary role of the stove god is to watch over all happenings in the household and keep detailed records of the deeds of all family members. Once a year, just before the lunar New Year, he ascends to heaven to give report on the meritorious activities and transgressions of each member of the family to the Jade Emperor, the supreme deity and the head of the celestial bureaucracy (see next section).

In the home the stove god is represented by a pictorial image (that sometimes also features his wife), which is placed above or near the stove. In recognition of its sanctity, the area around the god's likeness is expected to be kept neat and pure. In front of the god's image offerings are made and ritual observances are performed by members of the family, especially on the god's birthday and during the year-ending celebrations, when he makes his reporting trip to heaven. The rites performed before the god's ascent to heaven are especially important. They are meant to secure good fortune and ensure that his report does not contain any unfavorable accounts of family misbehavior, a hope symbolized by the smearing of sweet paste over the mouth of the god's image. The rites performed on such occasions include elements that are part and parcel of popular Chinese ritual: offerings of candles, incense, and

Figure 7.2   Image of door god, ancestral temple of the Chen family, Guangzhou

food, the performance of ceremonial bows, the making of supplications, and (at the end of the year) the burning of the god's paper image. A new paper image of the god is then installed on New Year's Day, when the god supposedly returns from his journey to heaven.

As we move away from the confines of the home and the family, we encounter other gods with different roles and realms of jurisdiction. At the level of the local community, they are best represented by the earth god (*tudi gong*). Every village or residential area has its own earth god, who is closely involved in the life of the community. Depicted in the guise of an elderly official, his abode is an unpretentious local shrine (see Figure 7.3). Small shrines dedicated to him are also installed in front of or inside individual homes and local business, often close to the ground, or in larger temples dedicated to other gods. From there the earth god allegedly oversees the affairs of the local community and is closely involved in the lives of its residents. He performs a protective function and the local people approach him with all sorts of entreaties and requests for blessings. Moreover, the earth god is integrated into the celestial bureaucracy, occupying a humble position at the bottom of the hierarchy, analogous to that of a village chieftain, who answers directly to the local magistrate.

Figure 7.3   Local shrine dedicated to the earth god, Singapore

Celestial bureaucracy

Besides the extended family, the bureaucratic system of government is one of the most enduring and important institutions in Chinese history. The influence of the imperial bureaucracy traditionally extended to virtually all aspects of everyday life, but also beyond that, since the supernatural world was also assumed to be populated and run by bureaucratic figures. One of the distinguishing aspects of popular religion, also observable in Daoism, is the influence of the bureaucratic metaphor on the constitution of its pantheon, in which the various gods corresponds to government officials. The impact of the bureaucratic model is evident throughout popular religion, including its iconography and architecture, as well as its rituals and festivals. Although the primary bureaucratic model is essential for understanding popular religion, we also have to be aware of its limitations, since not all popular divinities—the ubiquitous three stellar gods (see box), for instance—can be neatly fitted into it. Some gods occupy places outside the bureaucratic paradigm, with their own independent sources of power and authority. Consequently, individuals can approach such gods directly, instead of going via official bureaucratic channels.

Like its earthly counterpart, the celestial bureaucracy is structured hierarchically, with each of its members occupying a specific place and performing circumscribed functions. The whole bureaucratic structure is based on established rules and procedures, and written records are carefully kept by appropriate officials. At the apex of the celestial bureaucratic edifice is the Jade Emperor (Yuhuang or Yudi). His position corresponds to that of the Chinese emperor, who is perceived as the human son of heaven. Like the stove god noted above, the gods that fill the lower ranks of the bureaucracy all answer back to him, according to proper bureaucratic channels and procedures.

The Jade Emperor is said to preside over a sprawling bureaucratic apparatus that is divided into various sections and departments, each with distinct administrative function. For example, there are the officials that oversee the purgatories. These are located in the underworld and are places where the spirits of the dead are judged and undergo punishments for their earthly transgressions. The officials of the netherworld are said to be led by Yanluo (or Yanwang), the god of the death, who is also the chief judge that impartially dispenses justice to the deceased. This

---

The three stellar gods (*sanxing*)

- God of good fortune (*fu*)
- God of prosperity (*lu*)
- God of longevity (*shou*)

bureaucratic god is a Chinese variation of Yama, the Buddhist deity that presides over the hells, which are often depicted as being ten in number.

While the Jade Emperor is regarded as a supreme deity with great power, he is also seen as being aloof and far removed from people's everyday concerns, as is the case with the living emperor. Consequently, people direct their invocations and requests for help to his celestial officials, especially those with local jurisdiction, who are purportedly more in touch with the situation on the ground. Within these strictures, individual gods are able to grant favors and respond to prayers only within the confines of their power and authority, which are clearly defined. Since the gods are believed to resemble government officials, they are usually represented as such, as can be seen from the numerous paintings and images that depict them. By extension, they are treated in a manner similar to the ways in which the common people deal with their worldly counterparts in the imperial bureaucracy. This includes the making of formal requests and petitions, as well as the offering of gifts in exchange for favors, or put differently, the giving of bribes. Similarly, the temples that function as the gods' abodes are modeled on governmental offices and residences, while the structure of the rituals performed in them evoke formal governmental and courtly ceremonies.

A prime example of a celestial bureaucrat is the city god (*chenghuang shen*, lit. "god of walls and moats"). He occupies a higher position in the celestial bureaucracy than the earth god, who is under his authority. Each urban area has its own city god, housed in a temple dedicated to him, just as each jurisdiction has a local official—a county magistrate in pre-modern times—to administer it. The god assumes the appearance of a local official and is responsible for safeguarding peace, public safety, justice, and prosperity in his area. The symbolic persona of the city god embodies a range of outstanding qualities that are (publicly) admired by the Chinese literati and are associated with exemplary civil service, such as honesty, loyalty, and dedication to public duty.

On a special occasion the statue of the city god, accompanied with his celestial entourage, is taken on a public procession around the city. This event symbolizes the god's official circuit of his dominion, which corresponds to the formal inspection tours undertaken by local magistrates and other government officials. In addition to the performance of appropriate ritual observances, these processions are usually filled with pageantry and serve as important social occasions, bringing together the whole community in festive celebration. They also function as entertainment venues, featuring acrobatic and musical performances, firecrackers, and the like.

Customarily rituals and prayers for protection from baneful influences or procurement of mundane benefits are directed to the city god not only by the common townsfolk, but also by the local magistrate and other officials. In pre-modern times the city god was integrated into the official cult, serving as a visible symbol of the symbiotic relationship between the earthly and celestial bureaucracies.

Figure 7.4   Temple of the city god of Taipei

The parallel structuring of the two bureaucratic paradigms implies the bestowal of supernatural sanction onto existing social values and political institutions, exemplified by the bureaucratic system of imperial China. In light of that, it should not come as a surprise that the imperial state was involved in the structuring of the official pantheon. At various times imperial governments manipulated the status of particular gods, bestowing them different titles and rearranging their place in (and out) of the official pantheon. But the celestial bureaucracy proved more durable than the various Chinese governments, as it outlasted various dynasties. It even survived the collapse of the imperial system, as belief and veneration of its gods continues to shape the religious lives of millions of Chinese.

Two popular deities: Guandi and Mazu

While for reasons of space we cannot go over many more of the numerous gods that inhabit the popular pantheon, we might glean further insights into the processes that led to the exaltation of certain divinities and the functions they perform by looking at a couple of noteworthy examples. The two widely worshiped divinities described below, Guandi and Mazu, a male and a female, cover a range of attributes that popular religion ascribes to its gods and goddesses. They are also instructive in regard to the range of adulations and supplications the faithful direct towards the varied embodiments of divine power and authority.

Guandi is best known as the powerful god of war, who is widely worshiped across China and among the Chinese diasporas (see Figure 7.5). His origins go back to a famous historical person, Guan Yu (160–219 CE). A legendary general who lived during the late Han dynasty and the era of Three Kingdoms (220–265), Guan Yu was celebrated by posterity for his martial prowess and exemplary moral qualities, especially his bravery and loyalty. Gradually he was apotheosized into a martial deity, conventionally depicted as an imposing warrior figure with a red face, whose primary roles are the granting of protection and the safeguarding of righteousness. Because of those characteristics, he assumed the role of patron deity of soldiers and policeman.

Over the centuries different emperors bestowed imperial titles on Guandi and he became incorporated into the official pantheon. He also came to assume a number of different guises and functions, including those of a patron saint of commerce and protector of businessmen. Popular versions of the god were also incorporated into the Buddhist and Daoist pantheons. In the Buddhist contexts, he is depicted as a Bodhisattva and protector of the Buddhist teachings, while in Daoism he is known as a guardian deity and subduer of demons. There are numerous temples dedicated

Figure 7.5   Large statue of Guandi, Guanlin Temple, Henan

to Guandi, some built on a grand scale and under imperial auspices, which befits his official status of a "sagely emperor" (see Figure 7.6).

Originally Mazu was worshiped by fisherman and sailors along the southeast coast of China as goddess of the sea. According to popular legend, at first she was also a historical person, although in this case an obscure one: a woman known as Lin Moniang (Lin the Silent Girl), who lived during the tenth century. She was a sailor's daughter, born in a coastal town in Fujian province. The legend describes her as a pious girl that led a virtuous life, although she refused to marry, as required by custom. She died young, but before that she developed mystical powers that helped sailors in her area to weather storms and reach harbor safely. Consequently, the local people began to worship her and eventually she was transformed into a compassionate deity with broad appeal, often perceived as having a motherly character. She is often depicted as a feminine savior figure, somewhat reminiscent of Guanyin.

Besides her role as patron goddess of fisherman and sailors, Mazu is also revered as a local protector, extending her help to all those in danger or need. The people of Fujian also worship her as their ancestral goddess. Like Guandi, she was included in the official pantheon and given a number of imperial titles, the best-known of which is Tianhou (Heavenly Consort), which is often used as her primary appellation and appears in the names of temples dedicated to her. Mazu is widely worshiped in the southeastern provinces, especially Zhejiang, Fujian, Guangdong, and Taiwan, where

Figure 7.6 Entrance to Guanlin Temple, in the vicinity of Luoyang, Henan

Figure 7.7   Temple of Mazu, Tainan, Taiwan

there are many temples dedicated to her; there are also Mazu temples in other parts of China, including the Northeast (e.g. in Tianjin and Qingdao). She is also popular in much of Southeast Asia (esp. in Vietnam, Malaysia, and Singapore, but also in Thailand). More recently her worship has spread to other parts of the world where there are sizable communities of Chinese immigrants, including the United States, where we find Mazu temples in Los Angeles and San Francisco.

Ritual sacrifice, divination, and other utilitarian practices

One of the fundamental features of popular religious practices and observances is their utilitarian character. Generally speaking, popular religion is not principally concerned with profound insights into timeless metaphysical truths, realizations of subtle meditative states, or insightful reflections on recondite doctrines. Likewise, transcendence of the phenomenal realm and other issues that loom large in elite Buddhism and Daoism are not pressing concerns within the context of popular religion, if they enter the picture at all. Instead, the main objectives of the vast majority of worshipers are unabashedly pragmatic and geared towards the procurement of this-worldly benefits. The ritual sacrifices and supplications directed towards the various gods and other divinities, which constitute principal modes of pious behavior, aptly illustrate the utilitarian character and pragmatic orientation of popular religion.

In general, the reasons for worshiping different gods and offering them sacrifices are eminently pragmatic, even prosaic. The same pragmatism is evident in the content of the supplications directed towards the gods, which typically accompany various kinds of ritual acts. They are primarily concerned with avoiding the various misfortunes that befall human beings and with enhancing the quality of earthly life: procuring blessings, wealth, good health, long life, happiness, and worldly success. The invocations of supernatural beings and the efforts to tap into the unique powers ascribed to them are therefore primarily geared towards gaining greater control over human life, at the level of the individual, the family, or the local community.

The people's relationship with the gods implies mutual dependency, being primarily structured in terms of a system of quid pro quo exchanges between the two groups. The local people are responsible for building and maintaining the shrines and temples that serve as abodes of individual gods. The people are also expected to show respect and make sacrifices to the gods. Among other things, that involves the performance of various ritual acts such as bows, invocations, and chants, as well as the making of ceremonial offerings of incense, candles, fruits, and other food items. In return, the gods are expected to procure practical benefits for the individuals and the communities that worship them, and to be responsive to the supplications directed towards them. If any party violates the implicit terms of this contract, the other party is free to neglect its obligations. That means the gods can withdraw their blessings, or even show their displeasure by bringing misfortune to those who have slighted them. On the other hand, the worshipers can also stop paying respect and making offerings when a particular god is perceived to have lost his efficacy, or has failed to properly use his supernatural powers to bestow anticipated boons.

In China people are traditionally free to worship or pray at the local temple at any time, in accord with their individual needs and predilections. As previously noted in the discussion of the city god, there are also numerous festivals or birthday celebrations for the various gods, when the whole community gathers together for public rituals and celebrations. Typically these are festive affairs, although at times they also include dramatic acts of self-mutilation. Often popular rituals also incorporate symbolic burning of celestial money—available in dollar denominations in Chinese stores in the United States—and paper replicas of desirable items for the afterlife, including models of houses, which are disposed into special incinerators located in the temple precincts. The same pragmatic orientation also carries over into other practices associated with popular religion, such as divination, mediumship, exorcism, and geomancy.

Like in many other cultures, the Chinese practice of divination is concerned with the use of assorted techniques to determine the hidden meaning of specific happenings or ascertain causal relationships among disparate events. The practice of divination underscores basic human anxieties about making sense of present predicaments, deciphering the unfolding of future events, and gaining control over the unseen forces that affect human life. Much of it is based on a common desire to anticipate or foresee the future, which imparts a sense of security and control over one's life. There are many techniques used in China for divination purposes, including almanacs that give auspicious and inauspicious times for all kinds of activities (e.g. getting married or starting a journey), palmistry, dream interpretation, physiognomy, and other kinds of fortunetelling.

Perhaps the most common forms of divination practice in China are the uses of divination blocks and oracle sticks, which are widely performed not only at popular places of worship but also at Buddhist and Daoist temples. The divination blocks come as a pair, both of them shaped like crescent moons, flat on one side and round on the other. The oracle sticks are made out of bamboo and are placed together in a round container that is shaken, typically in front of a deity, until one of the sticks comes out. Often the two techniques are combined with the use of divination slips, each of them with a number that corresponds to one of the sticks. The divination slips relay terse and cryptic messages that supposedly shed light on the pertinent situation or appropriate course of action brought up by the supplicant. For instance, supplicants might pose questions about their relationships with other persons, job prospects, or dealings with sickness and other adversities.

The use of spirit mediums can also be regarded as a popular form of divination, through which the patrons seek guidance from various gods or ancestors. The spirit mediums are shamanic figures—that can be either male or female—that have mastered the arts of spirit possession or communication with the divine. They are supposedly able to enter trances by employing particular techniques, during which they communicate with certain divinities, or channel information from the spiritual realm by identifying with particular spirits, usually in response to specific questions posed by their clients or patrons. In effect, the medium is purportedly able to connect and become spokesperson for a particular deity. Often the medium speaks in tongues or resorts to spirit writing, in order to communicate the information imparted by the deity. Some mediums are also believed to be able to commune with the dead.

In contrast to the positive spiritual communication associated with mediumship, the priests or ritual specialists that perform exorcisms are concerned with neutralizing pestilences and banishing the baneful influences of bothersome ghosts or spirits. Typically the offending presence of demonic entities, which might infest either a person or a place, is brought to an end by carefully choreographed sequences of ritual acts, which include dancelike movements and incantations. The undesirable forces of disorder are thus banished away, via skilled ritual manipulation and engagement with the forces of order, primarily represented by various gods. Often exorcisms function as healing rituals, being meant to combat specific diseases, and they are also performed by Daoist priests.

The ancient technique of geomancy (*fengshui*, lit. "wind and water") is traditionally understood as a means for harnessing and balancing the unseen forces and energies that infuse specific spots or landscapes. Variously described as an ancient art or pseudoscience, geomancy is widely practiced as a method for selecting suitable sites for graveyards, family dwellings, temples, and public edifices. Geomantic principles—which take into account the manifestations of various *yin* and *yang* forces within the environment (graphically represented as a tiger and a dragon), along with the natural flows and circulations of *qi*—are also integrated in the architectural designs of specific sites and buildings, a procedure that is commonly applied to this day. Customarily the expert use of geomantic knowledge is utilized in order to bringing about harmony between humans, the natural environment, and the unseen powers, integrating them all together into a larger cosmic scheme.

Millenarian movements, heterodox sects, and secret societies

With its pantheon and the rest of the spiritual realm replicating the structures and institutions of the human world, throughout Chinese history two of the central roles of popular religion were reinforcement of conventional values and legitimization of the prevalent socioreligious order. On the other hand, frequently popular religious beliefs and practices also functioned as agents of change, especially when they were employed by groups or movements that sought to challenge or even demolish the status quo. Prime examples of that are the various millenarian or messianic movements and "heterodox sects" that flourished throughout Chinese history. Usually these kinds of movements recruited among commoners or members of marginal groups in Chinese society, but at times they forcefully erupted onto the sociopolitical scene and altered the course of history.

Even as they adopted diverse ideological orientations and social agendas, the various millenarian groups shared common anticipation of wide-ranging social and political transformation, initiated or supported by a supernatural agency. The impending transformation was understood in terms of the realization of particular socioreligious utopia that corresponded to a divinely sanctioned prototype. These processes of social and religious change—which were usually imbued with a larger cosmic sense of purpose—were linked with the destruction of decadent values and institutions associated with the old order. The remnants of the old order were to be replaced with the enlightened mores of a new dispensation. Often the followers of such movements felt the need to hasten the coming of a new age by a violent overthrow of established political authority. That is one of the prime reasons why successive Chinese governments, all the way to the present, have been highly wary and suspicious of religious groups or teachings that espouse millenarian or messianic ideas. Often such worries have led to the active pursuit of public policies aimed at control or repression of millenarian groups and heterodox sects, a recent example of which is the suppression of Falun gong.

We already encountered instances of Chinese millenarianism in the discursion of the early history of Daoism as an organized religion, exemplified by the Yellow Turbans movement and their utopian belief in the advent of a new age of great peace (see Chapter 3). Later we will also consider the Taiping movement in the nineteenth century, which drew inspiration from Christianity (see Chapter 9). There were also Buddhist-inspired forms of millenarianism, many of which revolved around belief in the imminent coming of Maitreya, the future Buddha, which was supposed to lead to a profound transformation of the established world order. These movements are related to the broad category of heretical sects (and teachings), whose deviation from established orthodoxies is based on their rejection of shared cultural premises and prevalent societal norms, which in the course of Chinese history often led them to collision courses with the government. Often these movements are linked with a particular religious tradition—thereby being labeled as Daoist, Buddhist, or Christian—but in general they exhibit syncretic tendencies and are rejected by the mainstream religious establishments.

Well-known examples of popular millenarian movements are the White Lotus Teaching (Bailian jiao) and its offshoots, which over the centuries were involved in several insurrections against the central government. The first emperor of the Ming dynasty started as member of a religious group with millenarian expectations centered on the Maitreya cult that rebelled against the Mongol Yuan dynasty. Moreover, an important White Lotus rebellion took place during the mid-Qing period (1796–1803) and was violently crushed by the Manchu government. The use of a prominent Buddhist symbol in the name of the White Lotus Teaching points to its origins as a popular movement that emerged within the context of lay Buddhism of the late Song and Yuan eras (namely the thirteenth century). The early followers of White Lotus teachings promoted vegetarianism, performed devotional practices (largely of the Pure Land variety), engaged in pious works, and believed in the advent of Buddha Maitreya. Later the White Lotus Teaching developed into a syncretic movement that encompassed a number of sectarian groups, some of them with seditious tendencies.

Generally the designation White Lotus Teaching is used in a loose sense—as a sweeping label, often with vague connotations—to refer to a range of groups, typically with millenarian or rebellious tendencies, even though such groups espoused a variety of beliefs and had disparate organizational structures. In the process of their development, religious groups subsumed with the movement absorbed a number of popular beliefs and practices, although in general millenarian ideas centered on the Maitreya myth remained an essential part of their worldview. An example of syncretic addition is the worship of a powerful female deity known as Eternal Mother (Wusheng Laomu), who assumes a central role in key mythical narratives produced by advocates of the White Lotus Teaching, included in sectarian scriptures collectively known as "previous volumes" (*baojuan*) (for more on the White Lotus movement, see Haar 1992).

Another noteworthy feature of popular religious life in China, often linked with the millenarian movements and heterodox sects, is the formation of various secret societies. While these are voluntary groups that initially grew out of mutual aid associations, typically they assume clandestine characters and have exclusive membership. In effect, they function as fraternal organizations that provide their members with a sense of identity and affiliation, outside of their normal kinship ties and the prevalent societal frameworks. New members are accepted after formal initiations, enjoined to keep oaths of secrecy, and expected to demonstrate unquestioning allegiance to the group. Consequently, the secret societies have clear lines of demarcation that separate insiders from outsiders, in contrast to the situation that usually obtains in Chinese religion.

The organizing principles and rituals of these groups are varied, and might incorporate a range of Buddhist, Daoist, or popular religious elements. In the course of Chinese history, often groups of this kind have manifested revolutionary or rebellious proclivities, and they have also been associated with illegal activities. For instance, during the seventeenth century the influential Triad Society (Sanhe hui)—originally known as the Heaven and Earth Society (Tiandi hui)—was involved in insurgent efforts to overthrow the newly-established Manchu regime of the Qing dynasty and restore the native Ming dynasty. The society was also involved in the Republican revolution and the overthrow of the Qing dynasty in 1911, but it gradually morphed into a notorious element of organized crime. Because of such history and association, secret societies are viewed with suspicion by governmental authorities, in China and elsewhere.

Key points

- The broad category of popular religion, while defying narrow definitions and clear-cut characterizations, covers a broad range of widely diffused beliefs and practices that are very important parts of Chinese religious and social life.
- The prevalent tendency towards syncretism, observable across the whole spectrum of beliefs and practices subsumed within the category of popular religion, typically involves incorporation of copious elements derived from each of the three teachings.
- On occasion the adoption of syncretism was a deliberate act and was given concrete theoretical or institutional forms by various proponents of the

notion of unity among the three teachings, as evidenced in the formation of the Three-in-one Teaching.

- Popular religion situates human beings into a multifaceted world that is also populated by various kinds of supernatural and mysterious beings, which are usually classified into three general categories: gods, ancestors, and ghosts.
- Obtaining supernatural protection and blessing for the family and the local community are central concerns in popular religion, as evidenced by the widespread worship of domestic and local gods, represented by the stove god and the earth god.
- One of the distinctive features of popular religion is the use of the bureaucratic metaphor in the construction of its pantheon, with the gods occupying specific places within a hierarchically structured celestial bureaucracy, all of them performing restricted functions that correspond to those of government officials.
- Popular gods such as Guandi and Mazu exemplify the ways in which historical persons were apotheosized and integrated into the official pantheon, and the varied roles and functions they assumed in the course of their divine existence.
- An essential feature of popular religious practices such as ritual sacrifice, divination, and exorcism is their utilitarian character or pragmatic orientation, with the vast majority of worshipers being concerned with procuring this-worldly benefits and gaining greater control over their lives.
- At times elements of popular religion functioned as agents of change, especially in the context of millenarian movements, heterodox sects, and secret societies that rejected mainstream values and challenged the sociopolitical status quo.

Discussion questions

1. Compare and contrast the attitudes towards the supernatural realm and the construction of religious identity in Chinese popular religion with those characteristic of monotheistic religions such as Christianity and Islam.
2. What earthly models were used in the fashioning of the divine pantheon, and what do such parallels tell us about the basic character of Chinese civilization?
3. What are the primary or typical governmental responses to the teachings and activities of millenarian groups or movements, and what are the historical examples and considerations that shape such responses?

Further reading

Berling, Judith A. 1980. *The Syncretic Religion of Lin Chao-En*. New York: Columbia University Press.

Brokaw, Cynthia Joanne. 1991. *The Ledgers of Merit and Demerit: Social Change and Moral Order in Late Imperial China*. Princeton, NJ: Princeton University Press.

Bruun, Ole. 2008. *An Introduction to Feng Shui*. Cambridge: Cambridge University Press.

Chau, Adam Yuet. 2006. *Miraculous Response: Doing Popular Religion in Contemporary China*. Stanford, CA: Stanford University Press.

Davis, Edward L. 2001. *Society and the Supernatural in Song China*. Honolulu, HI: University of Hawai'i Press.

Dean, Kenneth. 1998. *Lord of the Three in One: The Spread of a Cult in Southeast China*. Princeton, NJ: Princeton University Press.

Feuchtwang, Stephen. 2001. *Popular Religions in China: The Imperial Metaphor*. Richmond, Surrey: Curzon Press.

Haar, B. J. ter. 1992. *The White Lotus Teachings in Chinese Religious History*. Leiden: E.J. Brill.

Hansen, Valerie. 1990. *Changing Gods in Medieval China, 1127-1276*. Princeton, NJ: Princeton University Press.

Hymes, Robert P. 2002. *Way and Byway: Taoism, Local Religion, and Models of Divinity in Sung and Modern China*. Berkeley, CA: University of California Press.

Johnson, David, ed. 1995. *Ritual and Scripture in Chinese Popular Religion: Five Studies*. Berkeley, CA: Chinese Popular Culture Project.

Liu, Kwang-Ching and Richard Shek, eds. 2004. *Heterodoxy in Late Imperial China*. Honolulu, HI: University of Hawai'i Press.

Seiwert, Hubert Michael. 2003. *Popular Religious Movements and Heterodox Sects in Chinese History*. Leiden: E. J. Brill.

von Glahn, Richard. 2004. *The Sinister Way: The Divine and the Demonic in Chinese Religious Culture*. Berkeley, CA: University of California Press.

8 *Later transformations of Confucianism*

In this chapter

This chapter picks up at the end of the historical survey of early Confucianism presented in Chapter 2, telling the story of Confucianism in medieval and late imperial China (roughly a third through the nineteenth century). Its major focus is on a Confucian reform movement that emerged during the Song period (960–1279), which culminated in the grand Neo-Confucian synthesis formulated by Zhu Xi (1130–1200). This version of Confucianism became the official orthodoxy in late imperial China, a position it occupied until the early twentieth century, although there were other voices and alternative perspectives that challenged its preeminence.

Main topics

- Character and role of Confucianism during the medieval period.
- Reformation of the Confucian tradition by leading Neo-Confucian thinkers of the Song era.
- Zhu Xi's life and his creation of a comprehensive Neo-Confucian synthesis.
- Rewriting of earlier Confucian history.
- Formation of a new canon.
- Zhu Xi's articulation of a new program of Confucian learning and practice.
- The official examination system and its role in the perpetuation of Neo-Confucian dominance.
- Challenges to the hegemony of Zhu Xi's version of Neo-Confucianism.
- Impact of Confucian mores on the status of women in traditional Chinese society.

Confucianism during the medieval period

Conversional accounts of Confucian history typically gloss over the medieval period, largely dismissing it as a period of protracted decline, uncomfortably sandwiched between the purported glories of classical Confucianism—represented by Confucius and Mengzi—and the Neo-Confucian tradition that enjoyed centuries of institutional and intellectual dominance during the late imperial period. There is perhaps an element of truth in such summary evaluations, as there was a lessening or refocusing of Confucian influence on the various Chinese states and societies that rose and fell during the period of disunion (approx. third through sixth century). Traditional scholarship has argued that the usefulness and attractiveness of Confucianism as a state ideology noticeably declined during this era, amidst a lack of strong and stable imperial rule. That was especially the case in the North, which was predominantly ruled by non-Chinese dynasties that had fewer vested interests in upholding Confucian orthodoxy. The rulers of such dynasties were more prone to look elsewhere for the ideological underpinnings of their rule and were open to using alternative sources of political legitimacy, including Daoism and Buddhism. In reality, governments both in the North and the South continued to use Confucianism to justify their rule, and Confucianism was a core element of elite ideology and ritual practice. What was new during this period was that the various states and their elites became increasingly open to adopting other forms of legitimation as well.

Even though the medieval period was marked by the ascendancy of Buddhism and Daoism, Confucianism continued to play a vital role in Chinese life—especially during the Tang period—and its exclusion from the discussion of this important historical epoch is historically unwarranted. A summary disregard of Confucianism in the study of medieval culture and society negatively impacts our understanding of some of the most interesting patterns of intellectual syncretism and religious pluralism that were ever to take shape in China (or the rest of the world, for that matter). Furthermore, by denigrating medieval Confucianism we are basically buying into questionable historical stereotypes, especially the selective retelling of history promoted by the Neo-Confucian tradition. As we will see below, Neo-Confucians elevated the status of their tradition and bolstered its legitimacy by creating a quasi-historical narrative of Confucian decline after the time of Mengzi. From their perspective, there was a tragic loss of orthodox Confucian learning, a protracted period of doctrinal confusion and lack of clear moral vision, until the true way was rediscovered by the great Neo-Confucian thinkers of the Song era.

Pertinent examples of the continued influence of the Confucian classics and the ideas presented in them come from the well-known Recondite Learning (Xuanxue; sometimes also rendered as "mysterious learning," in the sense of "study of mysteries") movement, which was in vogue within elite intellectual and social circles, especially in the South, during the period of disunion. Although the Recondite Learning movement is usually characterized as Daoist in orientation—and it is therefore often referred to as Neo-Daoism—the study and reflection on the Confucian classics were major preoccupations among its leading figures. Within the ecumenical milieu prevalent at the time, thinkers such as the brilliant philosopher Wang Bi (226–249) creatively engaged Confucian as well as Daoist concepts and ideas, thereby establishing new philosophical paradigms and putting forward innovative ways of framing issues of ultimate purport. They introduced imaginative ways of looking at the Confucian heritage, thereby expanding its contours and bringing it into dialogue with other intellectual traditions, most notably Daoism.

Wang Bi and other thinkers associated with the Recondite Learning movement were also influential in the formulation or promotion of a distinctive philosophical vocabulary that had lasting influence on the subsequent development of theoretical discourses within Confucianism and Daoism. Examples of that include the concepts of "principle" (*li*) and "non-being" (*wu*), as well as the dichotomy of essence and function (*ti/yong*). This influence also extended to Buddhism, which by that time entered the intellectual scene and become an integral part of the constellation of philosophical systems and religious teachings that grew during the period of disunity. Such ecumenical framework fostered close interactions among diverse intellectual and religious traditions. Confucianism was very much a part of that multifaceted and ecumenical mix, even if that meant ceding some of the dominant position it came to enjoy during the Han era.

The importance of Confucianism grew markedly during the Tang dynasty, following the reunification of China and the establishment of a strong centralized state. The imperial state actively promoted classical scholarship and drew extensively on the ideological resources provided by the Confucian tradition, which legitimized its reign and helped consolidate the intricate structures of dynastic rule. The knowledge and skills of scholars trained in the Confucian canon proved to be indispensable to the Tang rulers in their organization of the government and the running of its institutions. Confucian teachings also provided key tools for the sanctioning of state power and royal prerogatives. Because of that, the imperial administration was a generous sponsor of canonical scholarship, most of which took place at official institutes and agencies in the capital.

One of the primary concerns of official Confucian scholarship was to provide authoritative and standardized editions of the canon, which were distributed throughout the empire. Confucian scholars also produced extensive commentaries on canonical texts, often accompanied with detailed sub-commentaries. While official scholarship tended to interpret the classics in terms of the perceived priorities and needs of the ruling dynasty, there was a tacit understanding that the canon was open to multiple interpretations that took into account changing historical predicaments. Accordingly, canonical exegesis was a cumulative scholastic enterprise that involved successive generations of academics and intellectuals.

Canonical scholarship was closely related to the codification of the imperial state's ritual program, which was largely based on precedents and models presented in the Confucian classics. The numerous ritual observances enacted at the royal court—some of which were monumental in scale and involved dazzling displays of imperial grandeur—were among the key foundations of dynastic power and prestige. They evoked a sense of cosmic unity by linking the ruling dynasty with Heaven and the unseen world. At the same time, they also reasserted existing stratified human relationships and fostered social harmony.

The Confucian canon also enjoyed a place of preeminence in the educational arena. Knowledge of the classics, along with related historical and philosophical texts, was taken as a given among the sociopolitical elites. The classics were a central part of the curriculum at the official schools instituted by the government. Moreover, these schools were instrumental in promoting the cult of Confucius, who was worshiped as the supreme sage. Not surprisingly, mastery of the classics was tested by the most prestigious of the state examinations. As we will see later, these examinations were key conduits for the procurement of bureaucratic positions in the central government, which in turn were the main sources of high status and wealth in Tang society. Confucian scholars were also largely responsible for two additional state-sponsored undertakings: the recording of history and the compilation of literary anthologies and bibliographies. Their role in the writing of official history is especially noteworthy, as it helps explain the pro-Confucian bias of most of Chinese historical writing, even during periods of Buddhist dominance such as the Tang era (for more on Tang Confucianism, see McMullen 1988).

On the whole, during the Tang era Confucianism was seen as being complementary to Buddhism and Daoism. The basic formula used to describe the harmonious relationship among the three teachings was "Confucianism for the external (world)," while "Buddhism and Daoism for the inner (world)," although of course this was a general schematization and there were exceptions to it. In practical terms, it meant that scholars concentrated their energies on traditional concerns and established areas of strength in Confucian learning. This implied focus on the needs of the imperial state, especially its governmental structures, the educational system, and the dynasty's ritual program, as well as involvement with public morality and literary activities. On the other hand, Buddhism and Daoism were perceived as being primarily concerned with the inner or spiritual world, providing comprehensive paradigms of self-cultivation and pointing towards rarefied realms of detachment and transcendence.

Neo-Confucian revival of the Song era

Not all literati agreed with the prevalent cosmopolitan attitudes and ecumenical sentiments noted above, nor was everybody at ease with the pluralistic culture of Tang China. One of the most forceful voices to take up the Confucian cause and rally against the perceived dominance of Buddhism was the famous official and writer Han Yu (768–824), who was among the leaders of a reform movement known as "ancient writing" (*guwen*, also referred to as "classical prose"). This movement called for return to the simple and unadorned writing forms evidenced in the early Confucian classics, which stood in contrast to the ostentatious and ornate literary style that was in vogue at the time. The reform of literary style was meant to go together with a return to the authentic contents and central messages of the classics, especially their moral injunctions and proscriptions for self-cultivation. For Han Yu the classics contained the orthodox teachings of the true way, which he felt had been neglected since the time of Mengzi, with great detriment to Chinese culture and society.

Han Yu's advocacy for return to the genuine Confucian way was tinged with exclusivist sentiments. While he also criticized the Daoists, in his eyes the main culprit for the social decline and cultural contamination that supposedly engulfed China during his time was Buddhism. In his famous "Memorial on the Buddha's Bone" (compiled in 819), he linked Confucianism with the glorious reigns of the ancient sage-kings, while he critiqued the Buddha as a crude barbarian, ignorant of proper (i.e. Chinese) social norms and relationships. Echoing the early critiques of Buddhism (see Chapter 5), Han Yu denounced it as a heterodox foreign faith that was unsuitable for the Chinese. He vehemently objected to the Buddha's relic entering the hallowed grounds of the imperial palace, which was the actual event that prompted him to compose his anti-Buddhist diatribe (see box). While some of Han's intolerant views and xenophobic sentiments were exceptional within the Tang context, his valiant stand in defense of the Confucian way won him many admirers among later generation of Confucians. Because of that, he is often

Han Yu's "Memorial on the Buddha's Bone"

Your humble servant submits that Buddhism is but one of the cultic practices of the barbarians, which filtered into China during the Later Han era. In ancient times there was no such thing here. The Buddha was of barbarian origin. He did not speak the Chinese language and wore clothes of a different style. His speech did not accord with the words of the ancient kings, while his garments did not conform to their prescriptions. He did not recognize the proper relationship between a ruler and his subject, nor did he understand the sentiments connecting fathers and sons.... Now that he has long been dead, how can it be fitting that his decayed and rotten bone, his ill-omened and filthy remains, should be allowed to enter into the hallowed precincts of the imperial palace? Confucius said, 'Respect ghosts and spirits, but keep away from them.' ... I beg Your Majesty to turn this bone over to the officials so that they can throw it into water or fire, thereby cutting off for all times the root of this evil. That will free the empire from grave error and prevent the confusion of later generations.

Translation adapted from Reischauer 1955: 221–24.

identified as a precursor of the Neo-Confucian revival that blossomed during the Song era.

When applied to the tradition's early historical development, Neo-Confucianism is a general designation that encompasses the thought and writings of a number of thinkers. The actual label is of a relatively recent Western origin. The traditional Chinese terms that from early on were used to designate what we call Neo-Confucianism are "Study of the Way" (Daoxue) and "Study of Principle" (Lixue). The leaders of the Neo-Confucian movement during its formative period—five of whom retroactively came to be celebrated as the five great masters of the Northern Song era (see box)—were creative and reform-minded scholars that engaged in far-reaching rethinking of the ancient Confucian heritage. On the whole, there was a palpable purist or fundamentalist streak in their basic intellectual orientations and religious attitudes, in the sense of an overarching concern with getting back to the inimitable truths and timeless insights of the Confucian tradition, which they believed to have been lost for many centuries.

The refashioning of Confucian norms and ideas at the hand of the Song-era reformers was accompanied with overt critiques of the doctrines and practices of Buddhism and Daoism. The critiques towards Buddhism, which in the eyes of the Neo-Confucian reformers had for a long time exerted undue influence on the minds and hearts of the Chinese literati, were particularly harsh. Some of the central critiques were directed towards principal Buddhist doctrines, especially the doctrine of emptiness, which was denounced as being nihilistic. Buddhists were also accused of being self-absorbed, other-worldly, and selfish, in contrast to the public-mindedness of the Confucians and their concern for the family and the good of the community.

While openly criticizing Buddhism and Daoism, the Neo-Confucian reformers were influenced by the ideas of the two competing religions, which most of them studied during their formative years. Much of their thinking and speculation about the nature of mind and reality, along with the manner in which they framed key philosophical issues, were shaped by their encounters with Buddhist—and to a smaller degree Daoist—teachings. In that sense, the rise of the Neo-Confucian movement must be placed in the context of its leaders' responses to the perceived dominance of Buddhism and their engagements with its teachings and practices.

Five masters of early Neo-Confucianism

- Zhou Dunyi (1017–1073)
- Shao Yong (1011–1077)
- Zhang Zai (1020–1077)
- Cheng Hao (1032–1085)
- Cheng Yi (1033–1107)

Nonetheless, while the influences of Buddhism (and Daoism) are readily observable in the teachings propounded by the major exponents of Neo-Confucianism, it is important to note that they ultimately went back to the Confucian classics as their main sources of inspiration and guidance. They produced a comprehensive system of thought that explained the whole of reality, in all of its multifacetedness and complexity. While retaining fidelity to traditional Confucian concerns with governmental structures, public morality, and political involvement, the Song-era reformers substantially expanded and enriched the contours of Confucian discourse. Most notably, they reoriented Confucian learning towards metaphysical speculation about the structure of the cosmos and the nature of reality. At the same time, they made concentrated efforts to focus attention on the processes of spiritual cultivation that culminated in the perfection of sagehood. They thus covered the two key areas—metaphysical reflection and spiritual cultivation—that previously were dominated by the Buddhists and the Daoists. The end result was a substantial broadening of the field of Confucian learning and the growth of new trends within it.

Initially the Neo-Confucian thinkers represented only one among several trends that participated in the revitalization of Confucianism that took place during the Song era. Ample examples of alternative perspectives on Confucian knowledge and values, some of them at great odds with the nascent Neo-Confucian notions about truth and orthodoxy, can be found in the writings of numerous influential officials and writers. For instance, the famous poet, intellectual, and official Su Shi (1037–1101) argued for the importance of artistic expression and opposed all form of dogmatic thinking. While arguing for the institution of benevolent government along traditional Confucian lines, Su Shi was also sympathetic to the doctrines and practices of Buddhism. Nonetheless, in the long run the Neo-Confucian reformers were successful in bringing about a gradual shift in intellectual interest away from Buddhism and towards Confucianism, with profound significance for the subsequent history of China. They influenced the protracted decline of Buddhism, as Buddhist leaders largely failed to provide compelling responses to the Neo-Confucian challenge. In the end, the eventual success of Neo-Confucianism was based on the appeal of its ideas among the literati, as well as on its ideological and institutional utility to the imperial state.

Each of the leading Neo-Confucian thinkers added unique perspectives and highlighted key philosophical concepts that came to be associated with the basic intellectual outlook of their movement. For instance, Zhou Dunyi made significant contributions to the formulation of Neo-Confucian cosmology, for which he drew extensively from the *Book of Change*. The central concept in his explanation of the origins and evolution of the universe was the Supreme Ultimate (*taiji*). Identified as the underlying origin of yin and yang, the five elements, and the myriad things, the Supreme Ultimate represents the unifying principle of reality. In contrast, Zhang Zai focused on the concept of *qi* (vital force or energy), which according to him is behind

Zhang Zai's "Western Inscription"

Heaven is my father and earth is my mother, and even such an insignificant being as myself finds an intimate place in their midst. Therefore, that which extends throughout the universe I regard as my body, and that which directs the universe I consider as my nature. All people are my brothers and sisters, and all things are my companions.

Translation adapted from de Bary and Bloom 2000: 683.

the origin of the universe and the endless changes that occur in it. According to him, all things in the world are constituted of *qi*, and thus share the same substance. But *qi* is also capable of assuming a variety of forms, which accounts for the individual characteristics of various things or phenomena. Within this overarching scheme of cosmic unity, human beings and all things in the universe partake of the same shared reality (see box).

Especially important contributions towards the development of Neo-Confucian philosophy were made by the two Cheng brothers, Cheng Hao and Cheng Yi. They established the notion of principle (*li*) as the central element of Neo-Confucian philosophy, in a manner that encompassed both the cosmological and the ethical spheres. While the Cheng brothers asserted the singularity and absolute nature of principle, they also allowed for its manifold manifestations. In their teachings principle was transformed into a crucial concept that brought together all other key concepts and ideas. For instance, at the level of the individual, they equated human nature (*xing*) with principle. Eventually, all these ideas were brought together into a synthesis that was fully articulated in the lectures and writings of Zhu Xi (1130–1200), the most famous of all Neo-Confucian thinkers. Under his wide-ranging vision and strong leadership, what was initially a loose and informal fellowship of like-minded thinkers was transformed into a coherent Confucian movement, with wide-ranging ramifications for later Chinese history.

Zhu Xi's grand synthesis

Zhu Xi was an exceptional person, with many talents and varied accomplishments. A remarkable classicist, philosopher, educator, administrator, and writer, he created the grand Neo-Confucian synthesis that dominated Chinese intellectual and social life until the early twentieth century. Zhu Xi popularized and clarified the writings of his predecessors in the Neo-Confucian movement, which greatly enhanced their stature. He readily acknowledged his debt to the early Song thinkers, as he wove together their central insights into a coherent system of thought that was noteworthy for its comprehensiveness and exactness. He was especially influenced by the ideas of Cheng Yi, particularly his doctrine of principle, which he further refined and integrated with the other key elements of Neo-Confucian philosophy. Because of that influence, the main stream of Neo-Confucian thought is also known as the Cheng-Zhu school, from the names of the two philosophers. During Zhu Xi's lifetime his version of Confucianism failed to receive official sanction, but subsequently he achieved such renown that for centuries he was regarded as one of the most important thinkers in the history of Confucianism, his stature approaching the exalted ranks of Confucius and Mengzi.

Born into a gentry family, the young Zhu Xi received classical education in preparation for the civil service examinations. During his formative years he was attracted to Buddhism and dabbled into the teachings of the Chan school. This gave him personal insight into the allure of Buddhism and its appeal to the literati, which he later perceived as a major threat to Confucian hegemony and tried hard to contest in his lectures and writings. He passed the highest of the official examinations, that of "presented scholar" (*jinshi*), at the extraordinarily young age of eighteen, after which he entered into governmental service. Most of his official appointments were

Figure 8.1   Portraits of Cheng Hao, Cheng Yi, and Zhu Xi, by Liu Minshu (Yuan dynasty) (Freer Gallery of Art, Smithsonian Institution, Washington, D.C.: Gift of Charles Lang Freer, F1916.584)

of relatively low rank and in local administration, and for many years he occupied sinecures (the position of temple warden, for example).

During his tours of duty Zhu Xi dealt with a number of practical issues, such as agricultural production, famine relief, and educational reform. In his work on educational policy and reform he advocated on behalf of both public (official) schools and private academies. He argued for expansion of the educational system, which he wanted to develop down to the village level. Especially noteworthy were his efforts to revive or establish local academies, which became important centers for the study and propagation of Neo-Confucian teachings. These endeavors were epitomized by his restoration of the famed White Deer Grotto Academy on Lu Mountain (in Jiangxi). Zhu Xi's concern with practical issues also extended to life-circle rituals. To that effect, he wrote a manual of family rituals, in which he codified rites concerned with the coming of age, marriage, funerals, and ancestral sacrifices. The manual was written in a straightforward manner and was easy to read, which contributed to it being widely used throughout East Asia.

Notwithstanding the importance of Zhu Xi's practical proscriptions on education and social issues, he is best known for his theoretical writings and his views on philosophical questions, which are widely regarded as the doctrinal culmination of Neo-Confucianism. According to him, the whole of reality is constituted by intricate combinations of principle and vital force. The two are interlinked and complementary, never separate and always intimately implicating each other. The coming together and continued existence of all distinct things and events in the universe implies the seamless amalgamation of principle and vital force. Accordingly, there is no vital force without principle, and vice versa. Principle constitutes the universal pattern or singular norm to which each thing or individual conforms, while particular configurations of vital force endow them with their distinct forms and peculiar qualities. Nonetheless, within this metaphysical scheme Zhu Xi stressed the primacy of principle, which he characterized as belonging to the realm beyond forms and material objects. The existence of vital force, which underlines the material appearances of all things, is predicated on the prior actuality of principle, even though principle always needs vital force to adhere to (see box overleaf).

For Zhu Xi, the existence of all things can be traced back to the pivotal actuality of principle, which is the essential source of all creation, in its infinite variety. Principle is the basic pattern or universal blueprint of reality. Underlying and inhering in all phenomena, principle constitutes the true nature of everything in the universe. It is the raison d'être for the existence of each thing and the ideal archetype to which it needs to conform. Fundamentally principle is one and indivisible, yet each thing, person, or affair has its own principle. To know the true natures of a butterfly or a bamboo, for instance, is to know their essential principles, which in turn can be linked to the one fundamental principle that underlies all of reality. In this way

Zhu Xi on principle and vital force

In the whole universe there has never been any vital force without principle, or principle without vital force.

Question: Which has prior existence, principle or vital force?

Answer: Principle is never separate from vital force. However, principle exists prior to the constitution of physical form, whereas vital force exists after the constitution of physical form. Accordingly, when speaking about being before or after physical form, is not there a difference in terms of priority and posteriority? Principle has no physical form, while vital force is coarse and contains impurities. Fundamentally, principle and vital force cannot be spoken of as being either prior or posterior. But if we want to trace their origin, we must say that principle is prior. Nonetheless, principle is not a separate entity. It exists precisely in conjunction with vital force. Without vital force, principle would have nothing to adhere to.

Translation adapted from Chan 1963: 634.

Zhu Xi was able to highlight the essential unity of all things and events, while also accounting for their diversity.

The Supreme Ultimate is basically the essential pattern of reality, the principle in its purest form or ultimate modality, which inheres in each of the myriad things as a kind of primordial archetype. Furthermore, Zhu Xi described principle as being real and substantial, in contrast to the nihilistic vacuity he (wrongly) imputed to a Buddhist view of reality based on the doctrine of emptiness. When this kind of analysis of the basic pattern(s) of reality is applied to individual human beings, in his writings Zhu Xi follows Cheng Yi by equating principle with human nature. As we will see in the discussion of spiritual cultivation presented below, to know the principle within oneself is to know one's essential and true nature, which is fundamentally good and contains within itself all prime virtues.

Constructing genealogy of the way

The Song era Neo-Confucians created a comprehensive system of thought that entailed innovative perspectives and new points of departure in the history of the Confucian tradition. They introduced novel concepts and theoretical outlooks, many of them shaped by their encounters with Buddhist teachings and practices. In the process they opened a new chapter in the evolution of Confucianism. Nonetheless, Zhu Xi and his fellow Neo-Confucians primarily saw themselves as recovering an ancient tradition that went back to Confucius and his disciples, not as radical reformers bent on creating a new-fangled movement primarily concerned with articulating a set of responses to specific issues that epitomized their era. They did not think of their teachings as one of many potentially valid interpretations of the Confucian way, but as upholders of the only true and orthodox way, which they wanted to restore to its ancient glory. Accordingly, they asserted their authority and legitimized their reform program by forging close links with the ancient Confucian tradition and representing themselves as its true heirs. To that end, they constructed a new genealogy of the way (Daotong)—a concept developed by Zhu Xi—and focused attention to a reconstituted version of the Confucian canon.

Zhu Xi and his followers situated themselves in the large sweep of Chinese history by reconstituting and reimagining the entire historical narrative of Confucianism up to their time. The central component in their new and quasi-historical account was the notion of a lineage of sage-philosophers who transmitted the essence of the Confucian way. The fashioning of this kind of spiritual genealogy, centered on an orthodox line of succession, represented an innovative development within the annals of Confucianism. This idea was not entirely new, however, as it evoked parallels with the concept of patriarchal lineage in Buddhism, which at the time was an especially important element of Chan ideology.

According to Zhu Xi, the true way flourished during the time of Confucius and was transmitted to Mengzi, the greatest of all sages after Confucius. Then the orthodox way was then lost and its transmission was broken off for over a millennium, during which the heterodox doctrines of Buddhism and Daoism came to prominence. During this extended period of decline and confusion, even foremost Confucians such as Dong Zhongshu of the Han dynasty and Han Yu of the Tang dynasty failed to grasp the true way in its genuine purity and ultimate profundity. It was only during the early Song era that the true way was supposedly rediscovered by the prominent Neo-Confucian philosophers, especially Zhou Dunyi and the Cheng brothers. They then reinstituted its proper transmission, which led to Zhu Xi and his followers.

Revising the canon

Another prominent part of the Neo-Confucian agenda was the revision and reinterpretation of the Confucian canon. Zhu Xi largely glossed over previous groupings of texts that constituted various versions of the canon, although he did study and comment on most of the ancient classics. This included the Five Classics of early Confucianism (see Chapter 2), which until the Tang era were the most authoritative sources of Confucian learning. Instead, he promoted a streamlined version of the canon, represented by the so-called Four Books (see box overleaf). This new selection of primary texts for study reflected the intellectual agendas and religious predilections of Zhu Xi and his fellow reformers. An important aspect of

The Four Books

- *Analects of Confucius*
- *Mengzi*
- *Great Learning*
- *Doctrine of the Mean*

that was the reorientation of canonical exegesis and philosophical discourse towards metaphysical speculation and moral cultivation.

The narrowing of the canon brought about the sharpening of doctrinal focus and greater exegetical control. Much of the Neo-Confucian program was framed in terms of expanded commentary on the new canon. Zhu Xi wrote important commentaries on each of the Four Books, which collectively assumed the status of fundamental statements of Neo-Confucian orthodoxy. During the late imperial period the Four Books, together with Zhu Xi's commentaries, were broadly disseminated and widely read, both within and beyond Neo-Confucian circles. They remained immensely influential until the early twentieth century, remaining the primary sources by which cultured Chinese approached and understood Confucianism.

Path to sagehood

Zhu Xi's penchant for abstract philosophizing and his passion for ritual observances notwithstanding, in many of his writings there is an unmistakable prioritization of the quest for becoming a sage. That echoes an overall shift in priorities and a change in tenor within Song Confucianism. In contrast to the public-mindedness and overriding concern with the requirements of the imperial state that were characteristic of medieval Confucianism, within Zhu Xi's corpus the pursuit of sagehood often takes the center stage. In some instances, that even comes at the expense of the pursuit of an official career, especially during periods of political corruption and moral turbidity. During such troubled times, when in Zhu Xi's estimation the Way does not prevail in the realm and there is a pervasive sense of spiritual malaise, it might be advisable to avoid governmental service altogether in order to preserve one's moral purity and integrity.

For Zhu Xi, the main goal of Confucian learning was the individual's moral improvement, not the acquisition of wealth and social status. Accordingly, his model of learning was primarily geared towards molding his disciples into committed students and preservers of the ancient way, rather than towards producing Confucian officials in a conventional mold. Echoing the salvific objectives of Buddhism and Daoism, Zhu Xi proclaimed that Confucian learning should first and foremost be concerned with moral cultivation and personal transformation, culminating in the attainment of sagehood. That kind of thinking was essentially religious in orientation, although he believed that individuals' realization of moral perfection would also lead to political stability and social harmony.

As was already noted, Zhu Xi equated human nature with principle, and he accepted Mengzi's dictum that human nature is fundamentally good (see Chapter 2). The proclivity for filial piety inheres in the human mind, and individuals are intrinsically endowed with all prime virtues, including benevolence, propriety, righteousness, and wisdom. On the other hand, the human mind is also filled with selfish desires and emotional attachments, which foster unwholesome tendencies and behaviors. Just as principle always comes together with vital force, which can be of various degrees of purity, the imperfect domain of human desires and emotions is linked and interfused with the immaculate actuality of the true nature. But at its core, the human mind is identical with the universal mind of the Dao; consequently, the mind has the inherent capacity of knowing the basic principle of reality. By consciously cultivating the innate potential for moral perfection, each individual has the potential to refine one's thoughts and purify the mind, thereby realizing the principle within oneself.

Figure 8.2   Statue of Confucius, Confucian Temple, Nanjing

Within Zhu Xi's philosophical scheme, the human mind is the locus or battlefield where a fundamental tension, between the true nature (principle) on one hand and self-centered emotions and desires on another, needs to be resolved. Accordingly, moral cultivation involves uncovering the essential goodness that inheres in the human mind/heart (*xin*). That necessitates gradual removal of all impurities and obstructions that prevent the true nature from becoming fully manifest in its resplendent perfection. Within the context of inner self-cultivation, for Zhu Xi that meant preserving the true mind or maintaining a reverential attitude towards the innermost nature. He also asserted that the process of spiritual cultivation can be enhanced by some forms of contemplation, in particular by the practice of "quiet sitting" (*jingzuo*).

While in his writings Zhu Xi addressed various issues related to the exploration of the mind and the inner world, overall he placed greater emphasis on the reflection and examination of the outer world of phenomenal appearances and concrete events. For him, principally the study of the Way consisted of "the investigation of things and the extension of knowledge" (*gewu zhizhi*). A concept that originally came from the *Great Learning*, the investigation of things became a focal doctrine closely associated with Zhu Xi's synthesis of Neo-Confucianism. For him the investigation of things—which included not only material objects but also human affairs and events—meant inquiry into their principles, leading to comprehension of the unitary principle that is manifest in all things. It was a process of extensive learning and reflection, primarily based on study and rumination on canonical formulations of timeless truths and essential principles.

The investigation of things was not an open-ended inquiry into empirical reality, certainly not as presently understood in the natural or physical sciences. It was primarily a study of the world of human affairs and social interactions, which were to be analyzed in terms of established conceptual templates and value systems. It meant apprehending the true principle of an ethical issue or a human predicament, for instance the proper pattern of interaction between parents and their children, or perhaps the intricate relationship between two spouses. By broadly investigating the principles of individual things and affairs, one gradually arrives at knowledge of the basic pattern that underlines them all. The extension of knowledge meant expansion of one's insight into principle, culminating in the realization of the universal pattern of reality, which is imprinted in the human mind. Since the principle inhering in external things and events is the same as the principle present within the individual, theoretically the apprehension of either of them should lead to the same self-realization, although Zhu Xi placed more emphasis on the first.

For Zhu Xi, textual learning and intellectual inquiry were the primary means for bringing about moral rectification and far-reaching personal transformation. While principle might be manifest in all things and events, it is fully embodied and best articulated in the timeless volumes and precious records bestowed to humanity by the great sages of the past. The sacred classics therefore serve as the main guides for the study of principle, which they encapsulate and convey in the clearest and most accessible way. They are indispensible tools in the pursuit of self-realization, and their assiduous study is a prime form of spiritual cultivation. This kind of cerebral orientation, with its emphasis on scholastic endeavors, marked Zhu Xi's approach to moral cultivation and gave it its distinctly intellectual character. This kind of scholastic focus on canonical learning and investigation of external things was perceived by some of Zhu Xi's critics as coming at the expense of inwardly-oriented reflection (see below). Nonetheless, this type of intellectualism was in tune with an established historical pattern, highlighting the importance of textually-oriented scholarship within the Confucian tradition. According to Zhu Xi and his followers, the intense study of principles, accompanied with conscious efforts at self-cultivation, was meant to lead to a state of moral perfection, in which one's actual conduct would accord with the basic principle(s) that constitute metaphysical and social reality.

Civil service examinations

Zhu Xi had a number of dedicated students and was successful in constructing a comprehensive Neo-Confucian synthesis. Nonetheless, although his ideas attracted the attention and admiration of many of his contemporaries, in the intellectual and political worlds of the Southern Song dynasty his teachings were not widely accepted as an undisputed orthodoxy. In fact, towards the end of Zhu Xi's life the government proscribed his school's teachings, following accusations that they constituted false learning propounded by an outlandish group of self-righteous literati. The subsequent rise to unmatched prominence of Zhu Xi's version of Neo-Confucianism was a gradual process and was closely linked with its incorporation into the government's system of civil service examinations. This was an immensely important development, since during the late imperial period the examination system was one of the defining institutions of Chinese society. Zhu Xi's editions and commentaries on the Confucian canon were first officially integrated into the core curriculum for the civil service examinations in 1313 under the Yuan dynasty, when the Mongol rulers reinstituted the examination system after a hiatus that lasted for half a century.

While the official examinations were not that important under Mongol rule—on the whole, the Mongols did not have high regard for Confucianism—they regained their central role after the reinstitution of native Chinese rule in 1368 under the autocratic and nationalistic Ming dynasty. Within the Ming system of official examinations, Zhu Xi's version of Neo-Confucianism became firmly entranced as state-sanctioned orthodoxy, a position it held until the abolition of the examination system in 1905. This helped establish Zhu Xi as a towering figure and ensure the wide diffusion of his teachings throughout the Chinese realm. His influence also spread beyond China, especially to Korea, after the conservative Chosŏn (Joseon) dynasty (1392–1910) embraced Neo-Confucianism as its official ideology, in the process transforming Korea into the most Confucian society in East Asia. To a somewhat smaller degree, the teachings of Zhu Xi and other Neo-Confucian figures also became popular in Japan during the Tokugawa period (1600-1868), especially among the samurai elites.

The system of official examinations was instituted in order to recruit talented candidates for positions in the imperial bureaucracy. It had an ancient history, with its early precursors going back to the Han dynasty. The examination system became a major mechanism for the selection and staffing of governmental posts during the Tang dynasty, and its scope and importance were greatly expanded during the Song era. At its core, the examination system was based on an ostensibly egalitarian principle: the sociopolitical elite that ran the Chinese state was to be chosen on the basis of individual merits and accomplishments—demonstrated by the passing of a sequence of demanding examinations—rather than according to birth and family status. In theory, the examination system was open to most males, including individuals from disadvantaged backgrounds, who were to be judged on the basis of their demonstrated intellectual acumen, literary abilities, and mastery of the canon. However, the rigor and the scope of academic preparations needed for passing the examinations meant that the vast majority of successful candidates were scions of gentry families, who could afford to provide their sons with the best educational opportunities.

The official examination system encompassed a series of exams, usually held every three years. The prevalent three-tiered scheme involved the candidates' participation in a sequence of increasingly more competitive and prestigious exams. Taking place at the prefectural, provincial, and national level, the exams entailed cut-throat competition for a very limited quota of successful candidates. The final exam was held at the capital under the auspices of the emperor himself. Success at the highest level opened highly desirable employment opportunities in the officialdom, which carried great social prestige. In pre-modern China such official postings were fervently sought-after or desired by most individuals with advantaged backgrounds, as entry into the higher echelons of the imperial bureaucracy served as the main avenue for the acquisition of social status and political power, and even to economic prosperity.

Accordingly, during the late imperial period the examination system was at the center of a sociopolitical nexus that linked educational attainment, governmental service, social status, and economic opportunity. It largely accounted for the exceptional unity of China's elites, who were molded on the prevailing prototype of scholar-official who have mastered the whole range of learning required for success in the examination system. The dominant position of Neo-Confucianism for over half a millennium was therefore principally based on its virtual monopoly of the educational system, by virtue of its established role as the government-approved standard for the official examinations. This greatly transformed the Neo-Confucian tradition, as the educational system, with its formulaic character and emphasis on rote learning, became increasingly identified with the pursuit of success in the civil service examinations and the worldly rewards that accrued from it. That led to charges of hypocrisy, as prevalent literati attitudes stood in contrast to the lofty ideals articulated by Zhu Xi. As we saw, Zhu Xi argued that genuine learning should be primarily undertaken for the sake of personal improvement and moral rectification, although he also endorsed the legitimacy and value of the examination system, and even made specific proposals for its reform.

The Confucian-based examination system embodied both the symbiotic relationship and some of the frictions between the imperial state and the social elites. On one level, it helped maintain the status quo and was a potent tool in the state's efforts at controlling society and literati culture. It was primarily accomplished by the methodical inculcation of specific values and ideas, which fostered the development of mind-sets attuned to imperial dominion. At the same time, the examination system also provided opportunities for the elites to acquire and maintain social status, accumulate wealth, and exert influence on public policy. These developments constituted a culminating chapter in the long-lasting marriage of convenience between Confucianism and Chinese imperial autocracy.

Figure 8.3   Shrine dedicated to Confucius, Confucian Temple, Gaoxiong, Taiwan

The infusion of Confucian ideals helped humanize existing social hierarchies and soften the exercise of political power and authority. At the same time, Confucianism was all too often used to legitimize inequitable—and at times openly tyrannical—systems of social stratification and exploitation, as well as buttress the foundations of the political institutions and cultural values that sustained them. Consequently, the imperial sanction of Neo-Confucian orthodoxy was linked with the prevalence of social rigidity and cultural conservatism, especially during the Qing dynasty. These traits were brought into sharp relief when China initially came in contact with the modern world during the nineteenth century, primarily via a series of uneasy encounters with colonial powers desirous of China's wealth and territory (for more on the examination system, see Elman 2000).

Dissenting voices and alternative perspectives

Even as the examination system buttressed the preeminent status of the Cheng-Zhu brand of Neo-Confucian orthodoxy, throughout the late imperial period its dominance was not complete and its tenets did not go unchallenged. Buddhism and Daoism, while not as vibrant as during their Tang heydays, continued to exert influence on Chinese culture and society. Among the literati who sat for the official examinations or occupied positions in the government many had diverse interests and affinities, as expressed by their patronage of Buddhist monasteries or interaction with Daoist clergyman. Moreover, there were some literati who contested the officially-sanctioned teachings from within Confucianism. Two prominent examples of such trends are the Neo-Confucian School of Mind and the School of Han Learning. Although adopting very different perspectives, they both offered compelling alternatives to a narrowly defined orthodoxy centered on the teachings of Zhu Xi.

The best-known representative of the School of Mind (Xinxue) is Wang Yangming (1472–1529; also known as Wang Shouren). He was the leading Confucian thinker of the Ming era and the principal challenger to the hegemony of Zhu Xi's thought. The basic ideas of the School of Mind—which is traditionally contrasted with Zhu Xi's School of Principle (Lixue)—go back to a strain of Neo-Confucian thinking that already existed during Zhu Xi lifetime, primarily associated with the ideas of his contemporary and main intellectual rival Lu Xiangshan (1139–1192; also known as Lu Jiuyuan). Lu argued that it is mistaken to focus one's energies on an external investigation of things or get bogged down in canonical exegesis. Instead, he taught that the mind of each person is identical with principle and is the fundamental source of all phenomena in the universe. Since mind and principle are inseparable, the quest for sagehood should revolve around reflection and illumination of the mind within, which leads to its purification and the elimination of selfish desires.

Building on Lu Xiangshan's ideas, in his philosophical discussions Wang Yangming placed emphasis on the mind as the fundamental locus of reality and highlighted the transcendental dimensions of Neo-Confucian spirituality. According to him, the mind of each person inherently possesses the capacity for intuitive knowledge of reality, and genuine wisdom is to be found within the mind itself. The quest for enlightenment should be based on inward-looking reflection and contemplation of the mind, not on intellectual study. Likewise, the attainment of sagehood, which entails extension and amplification of the inner goodness and the essential virtues that reside in each person, cannot be located anywhere else except within the human mind. These kinds of ideas clearly evoke similarities with Chan Buddhism, and Wang was taken to task by his critics as being tainted by Buddhist ideas. Another notable hallmark of his thought was the notion of unity of knowledge and action. According to Wang, knowledge of reality and inner virtue cannot be separated from their concrete manifestation in actions undertaken by individuals who are attuned to the Way. Ideally, authentic knowledge should guide and inform all actions, and there should be no separation between the two.

In contrast to the contemplative orientation of Wang Yangming's thought, the School of Han Learning (Hanxue) was firmly anchored in scholarly study and canonical exegesis. Also known as the School of Evidential Research (Kaozhengxue), this reaction to Neo-Confucian dominance became a prominent intellectual trend during the Ming-Qing transition (namely from the seventeenth century onward). Its

Figure 8.4　Entrance to the Confucian Temple, Tainan, Taiwan

proponents were sharply critical of the Neo-Confucians' penchant for metaphysical abstractions and subjective opinions. For them, thinkers such as Zhu Xi and Wang Yangming had strayed away from the central tenets and concerns of Confucius and his early followers. The Song and Ming philosophers were also seen as being guilty of incorporating numerous Buddhist and Daoist accretions into Confucianism. On the whole, they were proponents of heretical learning and were not genuine followers of the way of Confucius and the Duke of Zhou. The correct response to their errors, according to the proponents of Han learning, was a return to the timeless truths of the classics.

The School of Han Learning was grounded in classical studies and had a marked philological orientation, while also branching into archeology and the study of ancient history. Its proponents argued for a different kind of Confucian learning, based on empirical analysis and historical research into ancient texts. By carefully employing scholarly methodologies, especially newly developed techniques of philological study that involved detailed textual analysis and exhaustive comparisons of different manuscripts, scholars associated with this school endeavored to uncover the true words of the ancient sages. In the process they uncovered the composite nature of the Confucian canon, which included a number of later additions and even outright forgeries.

Status of women in Confucian society

In previous chapters we already noted the relatively open attitudes and participatory opportunities afforded to Chinese women by Buddhism and Daoism, even if the two religions at times succumbed to prevalent social mores in their treatment of women and were not immune to occasionally manifesting misogynic sentiments. Let us end this survey of Confucianism by briefly looking into its impact on the status of women in traditional Chinese society. To a large degree, Confucianism defined prevalent Chinese attitudes and discourses regarding gender. Consequently, Confucianism is often reproached for its significant roles in the systematic patterns of gender inequity that were predominant throughout Chinese history. Confucian teachings were a major ideological source of norms and rationalizations that sustained an entrenched patriarchal system, in which men took precedence over women and dominated the domestic and public spheres.

When looking at larger historical patterns and trajectories, it is undeniable that Confucian ascendancy and increase in the influence of Confucian norms correlate with lowering of the status of women (e.g. the Qing era), while women enjoy higher status and increased opportunities during periods when Buddhism and Daoism are dominant (e.g. the Sui-Tang period). The contrasts between the artistic representations and visual imagery of Chinese women from different periods can be quite striking. On one hand, we find Tang women depicted as playing football or riding horses as members of hunting parties. On the other hand, there are the images of memorial arches for chaste widows and bound feet from the Qing era (although the custom of foot binding can be traced back to earlier periods).

It is of course unfair to place the whole blame for women's oppression at the feet of Confucianism, as there were other factors that contributed to perpetuation of the patriarchal system. Nor is it necessarily reasonable to judge harshly traditional societies from the vantage point of present-day (Western) norms and values. Nonetheless, indubitably Confucianism was a major influence on the essentialist construal of gender roles in China (and the rest of East Asia) that buttressed prevalent forms of patriarchy, even if women's confinement to the domestic sphere and the emphasis on strict gender stratification were meant to foster social stability and harmony.

As was noted previously, prevailing Confucian models of social hierarchies and interpersonal relationships bestowed an inferior status on women and placed them in subservient positions vis-à-vis men. From birth until death, women were expected to show respect and obedience to the men in their lives, especially their fathers and husbands, as conveyed by the so-called "three forms of obedience" (see box overleaf). The rise of Neo-Confucian orthodoxy, with its absolutist attitudes and penchant for intransigent moralizing, further deepened and solidified deep-rooted patterns of gender inequity. A prime example of Confucian-influenced attitudes towards women is the cult of female chastity, which flourished in late imperial China with sanction from the imperial state. One of its core creeds was the stigmatization of female remarriage.

The stipulation that women must remain chaste and faithful to their husbands until death meant they should not remarry if they become widowed, even if that happened while they were still teenagers. In an oft-quoted passage, Cheng Yi states that it is preferable for a woman to die from starvation than lose her chastity by remarrying (see box). Striking symbols of such conception of femininity, and the

Cheng Yi on female chastity

Question: According to principle, it seems that one should not marry a widow. What do you think?

Answer: That is correct. Marriage is a match (made by Heaven). If a man takes a woman who has lost her integrity to be his own match, it means he himself has lost his integrity.

Additional question: There are cases in which the widow is all alone and poor, with no one to depend on. May she remarry?

Answer: This notion has come about only because people have come to be afraid to starve to death. But to starve to death is a trivial matter. To lose one's integrity, however, is a very serious matter.

Translation adapted from Chan 1967: 177.

Women's three forms of obedience

- To the father during one's early years.
- To the husband in one's marriage.
- To the eldest son after becoming a widow.

cultural norms that underscored it, were the aforementioned memorial arches for chaste widows. These monuments to idealized notions of female purity honored women who had lost their husbands at a young age, and then chose to remain widows until their death many years later. They celebrated the chaste widow as a heroic figure and an exemplar of key cultural values.

Without denying the impact of Confucian norms and ideals, as was already suggested we have to keep in mind that there were other social and cultural forces that shaped prevalent attitudes towards gender. There were also discrepancies between the rigid moralizing and seemingly oppressive mores propounded by noted Confucians on one hand, and the actual social practices and common modes of conduct on another. While famous Neo-Confucians such as Cheng Yi and Zhu Xi are often taken to task for their ostensibly harsh statements (see box on female chastity), which might offend modern sensibilities, historical sources also tell us that in some instances they treated women well. We also learn that they were capable of showing moral flexibility when faced with the predicaments of individual women. Still, there is no way of going around the fact that Confucian teachings and mores were major factors behind the inferior status of women during much of Chinese history, even if we account for the checks and balances inbuilt into prevailing Confucian tenets and norms, which regulated the status and the interactions between the two genders.

Key points

- Although in medieval China there was a relative decline in Confucian influence, in an age marked by the ascendancy of Buddhism and Daoism, Confucian learning continued to flourish within a cosmopolitan culture that fostered religious pluralism.
- There was a major reformation of Confucianism during the Song era, represented by the Neo-Confucian tradition that subsequently emerged as the officially-sanctioned orthodoxy.
- Zhu Xi, the best known and most influential of the Song-era reformers, created a grand Neo-Confucian synthesis that incorporated metaphysical speculation and spiritual cultivation.

- The emergence of Neo-Confucianism represented a creative response to the pervasive influence of Buddhism; although the Neo-Confucian thinkers were influenced by Buddhist teachings and practices, they offered trenchant critiques of the "foreign" religion.
- The concept of principle was central within the philosophical system formulated by Zhu Xi, which he paired with the ancient notion of vital force in his explanations of reality.
- The Neo-Confucians were involved in a radical recasting of earlier Confucian history, arguing that the true way was lost after Mengzi, only to be rediscovered by the great Neo-Confucian thinkers of the early Song era.
- Zhu Xi transformed the Confucian canon by focusing attention on the so-called Four Books, which came to be widely studied in light of his commentaries on them.
- The rise to supreme status of Zhu Xi's version of Neo-Confucianism unfolded gradually and was directly connected with the incorporation of his teachings into the government's system of civil service examinations.
- The hegemony of the Cheng-Zhu form of Confucian orthodoxy did not go uncontested, as evidenced by the rise of Wang Yangming's School of Mind and the School of Han Learning.
- The rise of Neo-Confucian influence during the late imperial period had a largely negative impact on the status of women in Chinese society.

Discussion questions

1. Explain the rise of Neo-Confucianism in relation to the extensive influence of Buddhism and Daoism and their appeal to the Chinese literati.
2. Describe Zhu Xi's interpretation of human nature and clarify how it influenced his views about spiritual cultivation.
3. Which were the main alternatives to the Cheng-Zhu version of Confucian orthodoxy in late imperial China, and what were the main points of disagreement between them and the teachings of Zhu Xi and his followers?

Further reading

See also the reading suggestions for Chapter 2.

Berthrong, John H. 1998. *Transformations of the Confucian Way*. Boulder, CO: Westview Press.

Chan, Wing-tsit, ed. 1963. *A Source-book in Chinese Philosophy*. Princeton, NJ: Princeton University Press.

Chan, Wing-tsit, trans. 1967. *Reflections on Things at Hand: The Neo-Confucian Anthology.* New York: Columbia University Press.

Chu Hsi. 1990. *Learning to Be a Sage: Selections from the Conversations of Master Chu, Arranged Topically.* Trans. by Daniel K. Gardner. Berkeley, CA: University of California Press.

Elman, Benjamin A. 2000. *A Cultural History of Civil Service Examinations in Late Imperial China.* Berkeley, CA: University of California Press.

Gardner, Daniel K. 2007. *The Four Books: The Basic Teachings of the Later Confucian Tradition.* Indianapolis, IN: Hackett Publishing Company.

Graham, A. C. 1992. *Two Chinese Philosophers: The Metaphysics of the Brothers Chêng.* La Salle, IL: Open Court.

Jensen, Lionel M. 1997. *Manufacturing Confucianism: Chinese Traditions and Universal Civilization.* Durham, NC: Duke University Press.

Knapp, Keith N. 2005. *Selfless Offspring: Filial Children and Social Order in Medieval China.* Honolulu, HI: University of Hawai'i Press.

McMullen, David. 1988. *State and Scholars in T'ang China.* Cambridge and New York: Cambridge University Press.

Taylor, Rodney. 1990. *The Religious Dimensions of Confucianism.* Albany, NY: State University of New York Press.

Tucker, Mary Evelyn and Berthrong, John. 1998. *Confucianism and Ecology: The Interrelation of Heaven, Earth, and Humans.* Cambridge, MA: Harvard University Center for the Study of World Religions.

Wechsler, Howard J. 1985. *Offerings of Jade and Silk: Ritual and Symbol in the Legitimation of the T'ang Dynasty.* New Haven, CT: Yale University Press.

Wilson, Thomas A. 1995. *Genealogy of the Way: The Construction and Uses of the Confucian Tradition in Late Imperial China.* Stanford, CA: Stanford University Press.

Yao, Xinzhong. 2000. *An Introduction to Confucianism.* Cambridge and New York: Cambridge University Press.

9 *Christianity, Islam, and other "Western" religions*

In this chapter

In the broad sweep of Chinese history, Buddhism was the most significant religion introduced from abroad, but by no means the only one. This chapter surveys the entry and growth of other religions whose faithful—following in the footsteps of the Buddhist missionaries that in earlier centuries made treacherous journeys to the Middle Kingdom—entered China from the "Western regions" during the cosmopolitan Tang dynasty. The focus of the chapter is on the historical transmission and growth of two of those religions, which established strong roots and to this day continue to be integral parts of the Chinese religious landscape: Christianity and Islam.

Main topics

- Entry of "Western" religions into China during the Tang dynasty.
- Early influxes of Christians during the Tang and Yuan dynasties.
- Jesuit missions and Catholic controversies over Chinese rites and terminology.
- Arrival of Protestant missionaries in the nineteenth century.
- Impact of Christian beliefs on the Taiping rebellion.
- Early transmission and growth of Islam.
- Muslim efforts at acculturation and conflicts with the Chinese state.
- Chinese Islam as a minority religion.

Entry of "Western" religions into Tang China

We already noted that Buddhism and Daoism reached their apogee during the Tang era, even as Confucian learning also thrived at the same time. While in the cosmopolitan environment of the Tang dynasty religious and intellectual life largely revolved around the "three teachings," there was an even greater religious diversity. Acceptance or tolerance of other cultures and traditions were among the hallmarks of that era, often characterized as the high point of Chinese civilization. Tang China's general openness to ethnic and cultural diversity, along with its embrace of religious pluralism, made it a welcoming destination for religious groups of all kinds. As a result, most of the important religious traditions in Eurasia that dominated the medieval world eventually found their way into the Chinese realm. In addition to Islam and Christianity (discussed in greater detail in the subsequent sections), that also included Zoroastrianism, Manichaeism, and Judaism.

Just as the pan-Asian expansion of Buddhism and its spread to China were closely linked with long-distance trade, merchant networks also played important roles in the transmission of other religions that came from areas that the Chinese called the "Western regions." That applied to the two Persian-originated religions of Zoroastrianism (also known as Mazdaism, especially in its early forms) and Manichaeism, as well as to Judaism. The ancient monotheistic religion of Zoroastrianism—named after the historically elusive prophet Zoroaster—was initially brought into China during the sixth century. Zoroastrianism became the state religion of Persia (present-day Iran) in the third century under the Sassanian Empire (224–651 CE). Its followers worshiped Ahura Mazda, the omnipotent creator and supreme deity. Its presence grew during the Tang era, when a few Zoroastrian shrines and temples were established in the capital Chang'an and elsewhere.

Zoroastrians saw the world in dualistic terms, as a battleground between the forces of good and evil, with each individual having the choice to side with either one. They also had eschatological beliefs about an end of times, when good will finally prevail over evil and when all virtuous people will be reborn in the heavenly realm of Ahura Mazda. In China the Zoroastrian community was primarily restricted to Persian merchants and émigrés, with its clergy not making conspicuous attempts to proselytize or win converts. Since the worship of sacred fire was a key feature of their rituals, Zoroastrians were also referred to as "fire worshipers" or "fire and God worshipers." The limited presence of Zoroastrianism in China was effectively obliterated during the persecutions instigated by Emperor Wu, which culminated in 845. Although primarily aimed at Buddhism (see Chapter 5), the persecutions also extended to other "foreign" religions.

The dualistic worldview of the syncretic religion of Manichaeism likewise postulated a timeless conflict between the forces of light and darkness, also expressed in terms of other related dichotomies: good and evil, spirit and matter. The religion was founded in Sassanian Persia by Mani (216–276 CE), who was said to have received new and final revelations as the last in a series of prophets, which included Zoroaster, Buddha, and Christ. While Manichaeism depicted ordinary persons as being entrapped in an imperfect corporal existence, it also held for its followers the promise of spiritual ascent to a primordial realm of light. That represented a return to each individual's real home, made possible by self-purification and acquisition of Gnostic knowledge.

Manichean theology postulated the existence of God, but he was seen as being remote and removed from everyday human concerns. Its teachings were an ingenious mixture of Zoroastrian, Christian, and Buddhist themes and doctrines, presented in accord with actual circumstances and tailored to meet the predilections of specific audiences. For instance, among people whose views and horizons of expectation were shaped by Christian teachings, the flowers of Mani presented their religion primarily in Christian—especially Gnostic—terms. Similar strategy was used in lands where Buddhism was prevalent, such as China, where Manichaeism had a distinctly Buddhist flavor. While Manichaeism ceded into oblivion and has not been a living tradition for long time, during the medieval period it was an influential religion. For almost a millennium it had many followers, in both East and West, even though it was often perceived as a dangerous heresy and suffered violent persecutions, especially at the hands of Muslims and Christians.

Manichaean merchants and missionaries seem to have traveled to China via the Silk Road as early as the fourth century, but the "official" entry of the religion into the Tang capital occurred at the end of the seventh century, during the reign of Empress Wu. While the religion's early following in China was restricted to Persians and some Central Asians, the number of faithful swelled considerably after the Uyghurs' mass conversion in 763. Before long, temples and monasteries were built to house the Manichaean clergy, and Manichaeism established a strong presence in the Chinese capital. Known as "the elect," its clerics were celibate, practiced vegetarianism, and observed the ideals of renunciation and poverty. In some ways they resembled Buddhist monks, whose religious order provided the main model for Manichaean monasticism. The religion's institutional presence in the capital and at other locations came to an end in 843 due to the persecution initiated by Emperor Wu, although some remnants of Manichaeism surveyed for a few additional centuries. The purge of Manicheans was especially harsh and violent, even more so than the anti-Buddhist persecution that followed it. A major reason for that was lingering Chinese animosity towards the Uyghurs, who were perceived as political rivals and were resented for their earlier raids and plunder of the two Chinese capitals.

The earliest tentative records of Jewish presence in China also take us back to the Tang era, although it is possible that Jewish merchants entered Chinese territory via the Silk Road before that. Small and isolated Jewish communities were established in several parts of China, some of them continuing to exist into the late imperial period. Best-known among them are the Jews of Kaifeng, the Chinese capital during the Northern Song dynasty, who originally emigrated from Persia. At the beginning of the seventeenth century the prominent Jesuit missionary Matteo Ricci (see p. 218) had amicable contacts with members of the Jewish community in Kaifeng, who worshiped together at a local synagogue and observed traditional Jewish customs and rituals. Some of the distant descendants of Chinese Jews were "rediscovered" during the twentieth century, although by that time they had become fully assimilated, after centuries of intermarriage and gradual neglect of traditional Jewish observances. There were also limited waves of Jewish immigrants during the nineteenth and early twentieth centuries, although most of them left China after the Communist takeover in 1949.

Early Christian missionaries

The first Christians to enter China were the Nestorians, who in 635 arrived at the Tang capital via the Silk Road. Nestorianism was a Christian movement that followed the teachings of Nestorius (died c. 451), the Syrian theologian and Bishop of Constantinople. His teachings about the two natures of Christ, the second person of the Holy Trinity (see box)—divine (Logos) and human (Jesus)—were condemned by the Roman ecclesiastical leadership and he was excommunicated as a heretic. Subsequently Nestorianism was suppressed by the mainstream church and its followers were pushed to emigrate to the Middle East, with many of them settling in Persia. The party that reached China was Persian and was led by a bishop called Aluoben. The Tang government was open-minded and receptive to the new religion, and the visiting prelates were welcomed at the imperial court. In a familiar gesture of religious toleration, the emperor allowed the Nestorians to proselytize, sponsored the building of a monastery for them in the capital, and permitted the ordination of new Christian monks.

Within a short period, a number of Nestorian monasteries were built in various parts of China. The growing acceptance of the foreign faith is indicated by an invitation that emperor Xuanzong extended to Christian monks to perform rituals at the imperial palace, something that was frequently done by the Buddhist and Daoist clergy. In 781 the Nestorian faithful in the capital erected a stele on which they recorded the history of their religion in China up to that point. The famous monument survived the ravages of history and can still be seen in Xi'an. In the course of the Tang dynasty the fortunes of the Nestorian community waxed and waned, depending on the patronage offered by various monarchs. As Nestorianism acclimated to the Chinese environment, its teachings and practices adopted syncretic tendencies, but they retained their distinctive Christian character. The Nestorian Church was decimated in 845 during the persecutions instigated by Emperor Wuzong and disappeared from China by the tenth century, although it revived during the Mongol period.

The Holy Trinity (one God revealed through three persons)

- Father
- Son (Jesus)
- Holy Spirit

The entry of the second wave of Christian missionaries into China was occasioned by the Mongol conquests of the thirteenth century. The Mongols' momentous rise to supreme military and political preeminence under Genghis Khan (r. 1206–1227) and his successors was marked with much bloodshed and brutality. However, once the Mongols conquered most of Eurasia and established the largest empire the world has seen, their rule provided unprecedented opportunities for transcultural interactions and movements of people, goods, and ideas. (The establishment of Pax Mongolica at the time was an early precursor of sorts, one might say, to the process of globalization we are witnessing today). The Mongols' dealings with the various religions that existed in their empire were often driven by pragmatic and political considerations, but overall they adopted an amicable policy of religious tolerance. This contributed to the substantial increases in long-distance missionary activities and interreligious interactions that occurred during that period.

In China, after establishing the Yuan dynasty the Mongols—who originally followed shamanic traditions—ended up embracing Buddhism (see Chapter 5), but their attitudes towards other religions, including Christianity, were on the whole benign and respectful. Kublai (r. 1279–1294), the Great Khan and first Yuan emperor, did not hesitate to employ as his advisers and government officials individuals with diverse religious backgrounds: Buddhist, Muslim, Christian, and Confucian. Most Christians in the Yuan empire were Nestorians, as attested in the writings of Marco Polo (1254–1324), who traveled to China during the reign of Kublai Khan. The largest concentration of Nestorians was in the Northwest. Most

The introduction of Nestorian Christianity into China

When the learned Emperor Taizong inaugurated the imperial fortune with splendor and magnificence, letting his gaze fall upon men with discernment and sagacity, there was in the kingdom of Daqin a person of superior virtue, called Aluoben. Having consulted the heavenly omens, he took with him the true scriptures. Having examined the musical tones of the winds, he faced difficulties and dangers. In the ninth year of the Zhenguan era (635) he reached Chang'an. The emperor ordered the minister of state, Duke Fang Xuanling, to proceed with the imperial guards to the western suburbs and, after greeting Aluoben as a guest, to welcome him to the imperial palace. The emperor had the (Christian) scriptures translated in the library. Within the forbidden quarters (of the palace), the emperor inquired about the (Christian) doctrine. He learned that the doctrine was correct and true, and he gave special order that it should be propagated.

From the Nestorian stele in Xi'an;
translation adapted from Charbonnier 2007: 29.

Nestorian faithful were not ethnic Chinese, with people of Turkish origin forming the predominant group.

During this period a historically significant development was the initial introduction of Catholicism into China. The first Catholic missionary to enter China was John of Montecorvino (c. 1246–1330), who reached Beijing toward the end of the thirteenth century after a missionary tour in Persia. He was a member of the Franciscan order, founded by St. Francis of Assisi (c. 1181–1226) in 1209. John started building churches and proselytizing, and later he was joined by other Franciscan missionaries sent by the Pope from Europe. Although the Catholics received financial support from the Yuan emperor and managed to win some converts, they were not successful in their efforts to Christianize China. By the end of the Yuan dynasty there were hardly any Christians in China, Nestorian or Catholic. The initial Catholic presence in China thus fizzled out within a few decades, and the situation did not change until the arrival of Jesuit missionaries almost a couple of centuries later.

Jesuit missions of the late Ming era

The efforts to spread Catholicism in China were revived with the advent of Jesuit missions towards the end of the sixteenth century, during the late Ming dynasty. Founded in 1534 in response to the Protestant Reformation, one of the primary tasks of the Jesuit order was service in foreign missions and conversion of indigenous populations. They were also renowned for their wide-ranging learning, which went beyond religious subjects, and their extensive educational work. The Jesuits represented a vanguard of the Counter-Reformation initiated by the Vatican, which aimed at reversing the spread of Protestantism and expanding the influence of the Roman church overseas, in an age when Europeans were eager to conquer foreign lands and evangelize their inhabitants (whom they pejoratively labeled as "pagans"). The best known Jesuit missionary in China was Matteo Ricci (1552–1610), an Italian who arrived in southern China in 1583. Prior to that he had a missionary stint in India, followed by a period of preparation for his Chinese mission in Macau, the Portuguese trading outpost located on the south coast of China, during which he studied Chinese language and culture.

After traveling across China, Ricci settled in Beijing and remained there until the end of his life. In the capital he was able to establish contacts with members of the Chinese elite; at the end of his life he even procured some limited support from the government, even though despite his efforts he was unable to gain an audience with the emperor. Ricci was greatly impressed by the sophistication of Chinese civilization and wrote favorably about China's greatness and wealth, as well as about its refined culture and orderly political institutions. He realized that in order to be successful in his missionary efforts, he had to be respectful of local customs and native sentiments. Accordingly, overall he presented a benign and accommodating version of Christianity, which was not threatening to the established order. To that end, he carefully studied classical Chinese texts and traditions, with an emphasis on Confucianism as the dominant ideology, although in some of his apologetics he sharply criticized Buddhism. He even translated the Four Books of Confucianism into Latin and strove to highlight the compatibility between traditional Chinese values and Catholic doctrine.

During the early years of their mission, Ricci and his associates adopted the appearance of Buddhist monks. By shaving their heads and donning monastic robes, they assumed familiar religious personas and tried to blend into the Chinese socioreligious milieu. However, in due course they realized that the social standing of the Buddhist clergy in Ming China was not that high. Accordingly, they altered their outer self-representation, adopting appearances and mannerisms more in tune with those of the Chinese sociopolitical elite: they took the garb of the Confucian literati. This outward transformation reflected Ricci's decision to focus his missionary efforts on elite circles.

The Catholic missionaries enthusiastically responded to the literati's interest in Western science, technology, and culture. They rendered their services in a number of practical areas valued by the imperial state, serving as court mathematicians, astronomers, translators, and geographers. Moreover, the Jesuits performed crucial roles as mediators between East and West, being a major source of information about China to Europeans. This contributed to a surge in European interest in Chinese thought, institutions, and art, evidenced in the writings of leading European intellectuals such as the French writer and philosopher Voltaire (1694–1778), who was a leading figure in the Age of Enlightenment.

Ricci and his fellow missionaries had some success in their efforts to spread their Gospel among the Chinese, as they converted a small number of Chinese literati. Furthermore, in some areas away from the capital, where Dominican and Franciscan missionaries became active, Catholicism started to gain a tentative foothold among the common people. By the end of the seventeenth century, the height of Catholic influence in imperial China, the missionaries were able to claim about a quarter million converts. However, the presence of the missionaries and their evangelization also caused an anti-Christian backlash among broad segments of the literati. Their staunchest critics were scholars and officials who subscribed to a conservative brand of Neo-Confucian orthodoxy, which increasingly came into vogue after the establishment of the authoritarian Qing dynasty.

Some of the Neo-Confucian intellectuals wrote harsh anti-Christian tracts, in which they denounced the foreign faith. They portrayed Christianity as a false teaching, incompatible with Chinese values and detrimental to the established sociopolitical order. These repudiations of Catholic doctrines and practices were also influenced by the presence of xenophobic sentiments among the Confucian-educated elites, in a manner that was somewhat similar to the situation faced by Buddhist monks when they arrived in China during earlier centuries. At times the verbal assaults led to actual harassments of Christian missionaries and converts. The situation was further exacerbated by a growing Catholic intransigence and dogmatic rigidity, which offended Chinese sensibilities and provoked additional anti-Christian hostilities, which led to an even lower rate of conversions.

Catholic debates over acculturation

Matteo Ricci's missionary strategy was based on a long-term vision, along with a willingness to acculturate and adapt Catholic teachings in light of prevalent Chinese norms and traditions. That meant presenting a form of Christianity that was not narrowly bounded by European culture. Ricci also deemphasized the ultimate goal of evangelizing China and shunned away from dramatic acts of conversion, while displaying sensitivity and respect towards Chinese culture. At the same time, he drew the Chinese literati's attention by showcasing his mastery of things they were interested in, namely Western science and secular learning. However, not everybody was in agreement with Ricci's accommodationist stance. Some of his successors, and even more their competitors, adopted increasingly aggressive strategies of proselytization and did not shy away from directly confronting ingrained Chinese beliefs and prevalent cultural practices. These differences in missionary strategy gradually developed into a full-blown dispute within the Catholic Church, known as the "rites controversy," which pitted the proponents of accommodation and acculturation against those who took the opposing view.

At the core of the rites controversy were deep-seated tensions and disagreements about the correct or preferable approach to missionary work and evangelization, especially as it related to the treatment of native customs and traditions. A key question faced by missionaries—in China as well as other places where Catholics were engaged in missionary endeavors—was whether they should adopt a stance of cultural accommodation towards local customs and observances, including those shaped by indigenous religious traditions. Some argued that an accommodationist approach and openness to acculturation were necessary, but others took a rigid exclusivist stance that emphasized the singular truth of the Catholic faith and the superiority of European culture. From the perspective of the second group, no accommodation was possible with the debased customs and ritual observances of "heathens" and "idolaters." Doing that would have negative effects on the distinctiveness of the singular Christian truth, they argued, and would compromise the integrity of the only true church that upholds and embodies it.

Within the Chinese context, the main issue under debate was whether it was allowable for converts to continue with traditional Chinese (particularly Confucian) observances, such as paying respects to Confucius, conducting customary funeral ceremonies, and performing ancestral rites. In a way, the issue hinged on the operative definition of "religious," since affirmation of the cultural origin and social function of Chinese rites or ceremonies made them more acceptable for Chinese coverts to Christianity, at least in the eyes of the Catholic proponents of acculturation. If their religious nature could be glossed over, presumed the Jesuits, the Chinese rites could be allowed as customary expressions of reverence rather than as acts of worship, which in its ultimate mode is reserved for God. Another related issue—sometimes dubbed the "terms controversy"—was the use of traditional Chinese vocabulary in the translation of important Christian terms. For instance, Ricci and other Jesuits argued for using long-established Chinese terms—Heavenly Lord (Tianzhu), Heaven (Tian), or Supreme Lord (Shangdi)—to render the Christian term for God. This was vehemently criticized by their adversaries, who perceived it as theologically unsound and as representing yet another unwarranted compromise.

The rites controversy unfolded over an extended period, involving not only missionaries in China but also the Roman curia. The whole debate was further complicated by the larger political contexts in which it took place. This included rivalry between the Jesuits—usually proponents of accommodation—and other missionary orders, especially the Dominicans and Franciscans, who (among other things) accused the Jesuits of allowing "pagan" practices. At times the internal strife among the missionary orders degenerated into acrimonious clashes and airing of public accusations in Rome. Another contributing factor was the ongoing competition among the European colonial powers—primarily Spain and Portugal, with France joining the fray at a later stage—which sought to carve their spheres of influence in Asia.

In the end, the battle was won by the opponents of acculturation and accommodation. After a series of papal decrees, which over the course of the controversy oscillated between the two opposing views, by the early eighteenth century the Roman Church decided to proscribe the Chinese rites and unequivocally condemn the strategy of acculturation. An official papal statement issued in 1742 was the last word of the debate, siding with the adversaries of accommodation and prohibiting further discussion of the topic. The intransigent and supercilious attitudes displayed by the Europeans led to an erosion of imperial support for the missions and alienated many among the Chinese literati.

The whole rites controversy brought into sharp relief key differences between the Christian faith and the literati's own cultural and religious traditions. It deepened perceptions that Christianity was a foreign religion and that Catholics placed submission to Rome ahead of obedience to the Qing emperor, a central theme that with minor variations continues to the present. Such concerns contributed to the government's intermittent prohibitions or restrictions on the spread of Christianity, evident in an imperial edict of 1724 that severely limited the scope of missionary activities. It was followed by a much harsher Christian persecution during the 1740s.

The Pope's disbanding of the Jesuit order in 1773 effectively marked the decline of the once promising Catholic mission, although small numbers of Catholics remained in China against all odds and the church revived during the nineteenth century.

Protestant missionaries in the nineteenth century

The Protestants were the final wave of Christian missionaries to enter China. They entered the Middle Kingdom in the nineteenth century, at a time when the Qing dynasty was experiencing protracted socioeconomic and political decline. It was a turbulent period in Chinese history, as the weakened and increasingly corrupt Qing empire faced the prospect of dealing with modernity on terms largely defined by the European colonial powers, with Japan and the US also entering the regional geopolitical scene (see Chapter 10). While officially Christian proselytizing was not allowed by the Qing government, during the early nineteenth century some Protestant missionaries began entering the country. Intent on spreading their Gospel, at times they used as their springboards missionary outposts located in British colonies in Southeast Asia, such as Malacca (now in Malaysia). One of the notable early missionaries was Robert Morrison (1782–1834). Originally hailing from England, in 1819 he produced the first complete Chinese translation of the Bible, although he was not very successful in gaining Chinese converts for the Christian faith.

The Protestant missionary influx increased considerably after China's defeat in the Opium Wars (1839–1842 and 1856–1860), when the Qing government was forced to end its isolationist policies and ease the restrictions on Western missionaries operating in China. After its second military defeat in 1860, the Qing government was forced into opening the door widely, giving Christian missionaries the freedom to operate throughout the empire. A major player in the missionary arena during this period was the independent and pan-denominational China Inland Mission, whose objective was to evangelize in interior areas where Christianity had not yet taken roots. Initially a pioneering effort of Hudson Taylor (1832–1905) and seventeen

Protestant perspective on what the Chinese really need

What, then, do the Chinese require from Europe? Not the arts of reading and printing; not merely general education; not what is so much harped on by some philanthropists—civilization. They require that only which St. Paul deemed supremely excellent, and which it is the sole object of the Missionary Society to communicate—they require *the knowledge of Christ*.

Robert Morrison (1824); quoted in Moffett 2005: 285.

other missionaries, who arrived from England intent on saving China's "perishing millions," the mission grew quickly and expanded its outreach considerably.

Taylor and his followers sought to convert the Chinese to their brand of evangelical Christianity, bringing the good news of redemption and life everlasting by faith in Christ. They emphasized the absolute authority of the Holy Scripture and preached strict morality. A noteworthy feature of the China Inland Mission was that many of its missionaries were female, and the organization was also successful in adding Chinese missionaries to its ranks. Women were also active participants in missions organized by mainstream Protestant denominations, including the Baptists, the Methodists, and the Presbyterians.

While publicly the main goal of the Protestant missions was evangelization and the saving of souls, the missionaries were also involved in efforts to modernize China by introducing Western knowledge, technology, and institutions. The Protestant missionaries saw themselves as positive agents of change that brought to China the benefits of progress and civilization. They were especially involved in the medical and educational arenas, along with humanitarian work like famine relief. The missionaries opened and operated clinics and hospitals that served local populations in various parts of China, and a good number of the missionaries themselves were medical doctors. They also established schools that accelerated the process of social

Figure 9.1   Protestant church in Guangzhou

change in China. Some of the schools gradually evolved into colleges, which became major places for the propagation of Western learning and influence.

Despite these positive developments, among many Chinese there was a lingering unease about the foreign missionary presence. The Chinese felt slighted by Western arrogance—often mixed with racist attitudes—and upset about the unequal treaties forced onto China by the threat of guns. The presence of colonial concession on Chinese territory, the granting of privileged extraterritorial status to Westerners, and their economic exploitation and ill-treatment of the Chinese further intensified the growth of anti-foreign sentiments. Much of that animosity was extended to the Christian missionaries, who were seen as a vanguard for the escalating encroachment into China by the Western colonizers and imperialists.

The simmering resentment of foreigners reached a boiling point during the violent Boxer Rebellion of 1899–1901. A number of missionaries were massacred by the fanatical rebels, who were determined to cleanse China of all foreign influences. The peasant-based, anti-imperialist rebellion—that received tacit support from the Chinese elites—was brutally suppressed by the Western armies (with Japan also joining the anti-Chinese alliance), which then turned their attention to the plunder and barbarous maltreatment of the local population. The reassertion of foreign dominance enabled the missionaries to regroup and continue with their work in China into the twentieth century.

Chinese Son of God

Some of the influences of Protestant Christianity and their intersections with local Chinese traditions are exemplified by the Taiping movement, whose rebellion against the imperial government in the mid-nineteenth century threatened to topple the Qing dynasty. Its leader Hong Xiuquan (1813–1864) came from a peasant family belonging to the Hakka minority, who had settled in southern China. Despite his humble circumstances, the young Hong was able to acquire some classical education, although he was unable to pass the official examinations at the provincial level. He then turned to religion, especially the Protestant teachings that at the time were filtering into China.

Having read some Christian tracts and passages from the Bible, Hong Xiuquan supposedly had a series of mysterious visions, which he understood to mean that God charged him with combating deviancy, including the falsehoods taught by Confucius, and destroying demonic forms of worship. Later Hong sought religious instructions from an American Baptist missionary. Before long, he embarked on a religious vocation as a messianic figure, preaching to ever increasing crowds of followers drawn to his personal charisma and egalitarian message of hope and redemption. The vast majority of his followers, who included some criminal elements, came from the underprivileged strata of southern Chinese society. During a time of social upheavals and economic depression, many of them were attracted to the promises of personal salvation, communal redemption, and universal peace.

Hong Xiuquan established a fellowship called Society for the Worship of God (Bai shangdi hui), which in a short time morphed into a sizeable movement, later called the Taiping (Great Peace). Hong's use of this messianic term—laden with rich political and religious overtones in Chinese history, going back to the Yellow Turban's rebellion in the second century—point to the fact that, notwithstanding the conspicuous Protestant influences, his ideas were also shaped by religious sentiments that were unmistakably Chinese. From early on, Hong proclaimed himself a son of God and younger brother of Jesus. Eventually he became the head of a theocratic state, in which his followers were tightly organized into groups, led by a hierarchy that blended religious, governmental, and paramilitary functions. In that capacity he assumed the title of Heavenly King (*tianwang*), claiming divine sanction to rule over a sanctified dominion, which he named the Heavenly Kingdom of Great Peace.

Hong and his cohorts proclaimed equality among all their followers; in a major departure from Chinese tradition, equality was also extended to women. Rejecting prevalent social attitudes and practices, the Taipings rallied against foot-binding and endorsed monogamy. They actively promoted gender equity, which among other things meant that women were able to serve as soldiers. In addition, their egalitarianism was reflected in the implementation of a communitarian ethos that included the proscription of private property and trade, along with the setting of institutional structures for the communal distribution of basic living necessities. (These guiding principles evoke comparisons with the ideals and policies implemented a century later by the Communist Party, when Mao and other revolutionary figures expressed admiration for Hong and the Taipings). Furthermore, the Taiping leadership vigorously promoted puritanical values, which they inculcated in their recruits with fanatical intensity. Their teachings and policies echoed creeds and practices promoted by Protestant missionaries, but also resonated with native Chinese mores. They preached modesty and frugality, and proscribed vices such as gambling, adultery, drinking, use of opium, and smoking. They were bent on cleansing China from its sins and were intolerant of other religions, with the harshest critiques reserved for Confucianism and Buddhism.

After careful military preparations, in 1850 Hong Xiuquan and his followers started an armed rebellion against the Qing government, which they perceived as a demonic power that had to be obliterated in order to establish their Heavenly Kingdom. From their original stronghold in Jiangxi the rebellion quickly spread to the surrounding southern provinces. By 1853 the rebels captured the ancient capital of Nanjing, which they renamed Heavenly Capital (Tianjing) and turned into their seat of government. From there they ruled a fairly large area that included much of southern China. While the initial responses of the Qing government and its military were ineffective, gradually a number of regional militias were organized by

The ten heavenly commandments of the Taipings

Honor and worship the Lord God

Do not worship false gods

Do not utter the name of the Lord God in vain

On each seventh day, worship and praise the Lord God for his grace

Be filial and obedient to your father and mother

Do not kill or injure other persons

Do not indulge in wickedness and lewdness

Do not steal or rob

Do not spread falsehoods

Do not think covetous thoughts

Translation adapted from de Barry and Lufrano 2001: 221.

local officials and the gentry, which initiated military campaigns against the Taiping armies. Eventually they were joined by mercenary units organized by Westerners.

The Western powers initially claimed neutrality in China's civil war, even as many Westerners were sympathetically inclined towards the Taipings and their ideas, especially in light of their perceived connection with Christianity. However, the Western colonial nations eventually decided that their political and economic interests were better served by propping up the weakened Qing government, which was seen as being preferable to the zealous and unpredictable rebels. As they learned more about Hong and his followers, Westerners also became dismayed by their fanaticism and outlandish theological positions, as evident in Hong's commentaries on the Bible. That led them to the conclusion that what he preached, after all, was not authentic Christianity. The combined Chinese and Western forces won a string of victories and finally recaptured Nanjing in 1864. In the wake of the final defeat, the Chinese son of God was said to have committed suicide, thus ending his dream of establishing a heavenly kingdom on earth.

Early transmission of Islam

The early growth of the monotheistic religion of Islam among the Arabs and its momentous spread across large areas of North Africa, the Iberian Peninsula, and the Middle East—and later to other parts of Asia—were seminal events that changed the course of world history. Soon after the death of Prophet Muhammad (c. 570–632), expansionist Arab armies moved into Persia and annihilated the Sassanian empire, whose rule during its heyday stretched from eastern Syria to Afghanistan. The conquering Arabs then incorporated Persia into the rapidly growing Islamic caliphate. By the early eighth century Islamic rule extended into Central Asia, parts of which were within the Chinese sphere of influence. In their quest for dominance in Central Asia the two empires clashed in the battle at Talas river (751), with the Arabs defeating the Chinese army.

The Arab conquerors brought with them the teachings and observances of their Islamic faith—which had unified the various Arabic tribes for the first time in history—along with its universalist truth claims. Military conquest was closely linked with religious expansion, although forced conversions were exceptions rather than the norm. Generally speaking, Muslims were not supposed to force other people to convert, since conversion to Islam should be a voluntary decision by each individual, once he or she becomes convinced of the truthfulness of its message. Missionary pressure or forced conversions were considered to be opposed to the trust or fate that God has in mind for each individual, which is supposed to bring everybody eventually to Islam. The military conquests initiated a gradual process of Islamization of Persia and Central Asia, thereby bringing the vibrant new religion to China's doorstep. The Islamization of Central Asia, whose population was predominantly of Turkish extraction, was to a large degree led by Sufi orders that were fairly open to religions syncretism and tolerant of local traditions.

The earliest Muslims to enter China were Persian and Arabic merchants and emissaries, who arrived via established trade networks in the seventh century, during the Tang dynasty. A major point of entry was the southern seaport of Guangzhou, which was home to a large community of expatriates, although Muslims also came to other ports in the South or entered from the northwest by way of the Silk Road. Later Islamic writers created a story about their faith's initial arrival in China being occasioned by the second Tang emperor Taizong (r. 626–649) sending a west-bound legation in search for Islam. The initial impetus for the sending of Chinese envoys, according to the legend, was a dream by the emperor (see box overleaf). The story goes on to tell how the Chinese legation brought back with them one of the Prophet's uncles along with a copy of the Qur'an, which were warmly received at the imperial palace. This trope is familiar from the story about the dream of Emperor Ming of the Han dynasty, which supposedly occasioned the initial arrival of Buddhism into China (see Chapter 5).

The Five Pillars of Islam (pious acts required of all Muslims)

1. Acceptance of the basic creed of Islam: that there is no god but Allah and that Muhammad is his messenger
2. Performance of five daily prayers, done at fixed times
3. Giving of alms to those in need
4. Fasting during the holy month of Ramadan
5. Performance of the Hajj pilgrimage to the holy city of Mecca

While most of the Muslim merchants were transient visitors, some of them settled in China, joining the sizable communities of immigrants from East and West Asia that thrived in some cities. There they established the earliest Muslim communities in China. Like other foreigners, the Muslims were mostly separated from the Chinese population, although some Muslim men married Chinese women. The lines of demarcation between the Muslim and native populations were reinforced by governmental regulations, which stipulated that foreigners should live in restricted urban zones and trade at specially designated markets. Muslim merchants retained substantial presence in China throughout the Tang-Song transition, especially in large urban centers that were involved in international trade. They enjoyed limited autonomy in the running of their communal affairs, and the Chinese government was not unduly concerned with micromanaging their lifestyles and religious observances. Despite the growing Muslim presence during this period, the native Chinese population, including the sociopolitical elites, had limited exposure to Islam and showed little interest in learning about it.

Adaptation and growth of Islam

The second wave of Islamic entry into China occurred under Mongol rule during the thirteenth century, when there was a large increase in China's Muslim population. The Mongols put an end to centuries of unified Islamic rule by their capture of Bagdad in 1258 and the destruction of the Abbasid caliphate. Many of the descendants of Genghis Khan that settled in Central Asia converted to the Islamic faith, along with their Mongol followers. Under the Yuan dynasty in China, the Mongols employed a number of Muslims in their administration and encouraged Arabic and Persian immigration. Their Muslim subjects worked in a number of important occupations,

Emperor Taizong's dream and the coming of Islam into China

One night Emperor Taizong of the Tang dynasty dreamt that a roof beam in his golden palace was collapsing. The roof beam nearly smashed his head, but it was intercepted and pushed back by a man standing on the right-hand side of his bed. The man wore a green robe and had a white turban wrapped around his head.... Alarmed, upon waking up the emperor immediately summoned his advisors. One of them, Xu Mao, immediately knew what the problem was: the empire was in danger. That was the meaning of the falling roof beam. The strange man was a Hui, a Muslim from the western regions. The great Tang empire needed the Hui people for its defense, he concluded.

Excerpt from *Huihui yuanlai*;
translation adapted from Ben-Dor Benite 2005: 205.

such as astronomers, architects, doctors, military engineers, and financial officers. Some of them rose to high ranks under Kublai Khan, like the provincial governor of Yunnan and the Yuan empire's financial minister.

There was a further increase in China's settled Muslim population during the Ming era, along with its improved integration into Chinese society. Many Muslims became fairly acculturated, coming to resemble the Han Chinese population by speaking Chinese and using Chinese names. Some Muslims had successful careers in the imperial bureaucracy, and there were many instances of intermarriage (which almost always involved a Muslim man and a Chinese woman). The best-known Muslim of the Ming era is Admiral Zheng He (1371–1433), who led the Chinese navy to a series of historic voyages. Born in Yunnan to Muslim parents, Zheng was brought to the court as a young man and entered governmental service as a eunuch. After gaining the confidence of the emperor and rising in the official ranks, he was entrusted to lead a large fleet (with as many as three hundred ships, according to some sources) in epochal sea voyages of unprecedented scale.

Zheng He's marine expeditions were meant to expand China's imperialist presence, glorify the reigning dynasty, facilitate long-distance trade, and establish diplomatic relations. The voyages were also important as sources of information about the world beyond China's vicinity. Zheng He undertook seven voyages during the 1405–1433 period, going to such far-flung lands as Southeast Asia, India, Ceylon (Sri Lanka), East Africa, the Persian Gulf area, and the Arabian peninsula. To this day Admiral Zheng remains an immensely popular figure not only in China but also in Southeast Asia; he is credited, among other things, with the growth of Islam in Southeast Asia.

A notable development during the Ming-Qing transition was the growth of Islamic educational institutions and the creation of Islamic scholarship written in the Chinese language. Sino-Muslim scholars steeped in Chinese intellectual traditions and Confucian learning—some of them holding official Chinese degrees and positions—made valuable contributions by translating from Arabic important classical texts and by creating original works of Islamic philosophy, which led to the formation of a Han Kitab (Chinese Islamic canon). In their writings scholars belonging to an informal Sino-Muslim intellectual network, based in the East China, made extensive use of Confucian vocabulary in their discussions of Islamic doctrine. In a way, they wrote about Islam from within the Chinese literati tradition, in an effort to fashion a hybrid identity that at the same time was both Muslim and (Confucian) Chinese.

The Sino-Muslim scholars developed and circulated a Chinese style or modality of Islamic learning that was congruent and coextensive with Confucian knowledge. For instance, in one of his popular books the renowned Sino-Muslim scholar Wang Daiyu (c. 1570–1650) correlated the Five Pillars of Islam (see box, p. 227) with the five Confucian virtues. In his writings Wang essentially used a Neo-Confucian conceptual framework in order to extol and explain Islam, as well as ascertain its rightful place as an integral part of Chinese tradition and learning (for more on these scholars, see Ben-Dor Benite 2005).

The seventeenth century also saw the initial influx of Sufi orders or brotherhoods (Tariqa) in northwestern China. Sufism represented a mystical strain or orientation within Islam. Its followers adopted ascetic lifestyles and engaged in contemplative practices, meant to lead to higher states of consciousness and spiritual union with God. There was always considerable diversity within the Sufi movement, with a variety of theological interpretations and practical methods of spiritual cultivation. Among the Sufi orders there was a shared emphasis on the master-disciple relationship, which led to the creation of spiritual genealogies. The diffusion of Sufi ideas, practices, and institutional frameworks in China led to considerable changes in local Islamic practice.

The westward expansion of the Qing empire, which by the eighteenth century came to incorporate large areas of Turkestan and other parts of Central Asia (what came to be known as the Xinjiang region), led to considerable increases in China's Muslim population and its ethnic diversity. This contributed to the emergence of competing visions and interpretations of the meaning of being a Muslim in China (or Chinese Muslim), which persist to this day. There were some strands or orientations within Chinese Islam, typically prevalent in the Muslim heartlands of Northwest China, that at times harbored militant, separatist, or revivalist tendencies. Nevertheless, there were also syncretic and accommodationist strands, usually representing urban-based versions of Islam that existed amidst the Han majority, which stressed the compatibility of their faith with mainstream Chinese culture.

Acculturation and conflict in Chinese Islam

Muslims in China often found (and still find) themselves in-between two worlds, having to balance dual loyalties: to Islam and to China. On one hand, over the centuries Muslims have had to cope with external pressures to adapt and acculturate, exerted by a state or a dominant Chinese majority that habitually expect conformity to their norms and mores. Often that is juxtaposed with a desire to fit in and become part of mainstream society. Conversely, there have been a propensity among Muslims to affirm their cultural distinctiveness and retain a clear sense of fidelity to their religious beliefs and traditions. This has often led to Muslims adopting different patterns of behavior, one for the home or with other Muslims, and another for public interactions with the Chinese majority.

In view of that, frequently there has been a dichotomy in Muslim responses to the domineering presence of Chinese civilization and the unavoidable pressure (or desire) to blend in. Muslims have made conspicuous efforts at acculturation and accommodation, especially during prolonged periods of peace and prosperity. On the other hand, often they have found themselves in conflict with Chinese culture and institutions, occasionally exhibiting a predisposition towards separatism. At times, such tendencies erupted into violent uprisings against the Chinese state and bold challenges to its authority.

Muslim attempts to demonstrate the compatibility between Islam and mainstream Chinese culture, principally as represented by Confucianism, are evident in the composition of apologetic tracts by the aforementioned scholars affiliated with the Sino-Muslim intellectual network. In large measure such texts were directed towards a broad spectrum of educated Chinese, including those who did not subscribe to the Islamic faith. Furthermore, Muslim acquiescence to acculturation is on visual display in the architectural styles of many of their mosques. Numerous mosques were built in the familiar layout and design of Chinese temples, with the minaret assuming the appearance of a Buddhist pagoda (see Figures 9.2 and 9.3). Further cultural intersections are observable in the spheres of artistic endeavor and visual representation, exemplified for instance by the hybrid calligraphic styles that juxtapose Chinese characters with Arabic script.

Notwithstanding such attempts at acculturation, there were also ongoing tensions and intermittent conflicts between the Chinese state and its Muslim populations. Muslims habitually resisted assimilatory pressures, especially the government's efforts to bring them into the fold of China's "civilizing" influence and make them accept mainstream mores. They were unwilling to adopt established Chinese values and cultural observances, such as ancestor worship and filial piety. At its core, the lingering sense of dissonance and disconnect from mainstream Chinese culture

Figure 9.2   The minaret of the Grand Mosque in Xi'an

Figure 9.3 The main prayer hall of the Grand Mosque in Xi'an

and institutions, felt by many Muslims, could be traced back to their distinctive worldview and unique way of life. Muslims had their own ceremonies, narratives, religious observances, dietary proscriptions, and dwelling arrangements. All of that led to the creation of exclusionary boundaries. Taken together, these fostered a sense of Muslim distinctiveness and led to the formation of communities that to a considerable degree were economically and socially disconnected from mainstream Chinese society.

Often Muslim discontent was intensified by ingrained assumptions that they should live under an Islamic regime and be subjected to Islamic laws. Traditionally, Islam is a totalistic system that aims at bringing together the diverse strands and facets of human life. This implies the abolition of barriers between the religious and secular realms, as we understand them in modern societies. As a self-confident religion with a strong center, in general Islam fosters a strong sense of self-identity. That usually makes Muslims disinclined to acculturate, even when they are in the minority and are surrounded by another dominant civilization, as was the case in China. In addition, many Chinese Muslims felt greater affinities with others of the same faith—those that belonged to the *umma*, or the Muslim community— regardless of nationality, than with the Han Chinese. The intermittent presence of such sense of alienation was (and to some degree still is) anchored in the acceptance of a pan-Islamic identity, which is universal and not bound to a particular place or country.

In the Chinese context, the sometimes taxing sociopolitical situation was exacerbated by the Chinese state's inveterate tendency towards totalitarianism and its aversion to accommodationist compromises. This went together with latent anti-Muslim biases, entertained by many Han Chinese, who stereotyped their Muslim countrymen as uncivilized and prone to violence. Other significant factors that led to Muslim disaffection were official corruption, incompetence, and mistreatment of Muslims at the hands of local administrators. During the late Qing era, greedy and dishonest officials regularly embezzled local tax revenues and misused public resources, which fed into widespread disaffection with imperial rule, leading to occasional Muslim revolts and insurgencies, such as those that occurred in the second half of the nineteenth century in areas with large Muslim populations, namely in the Northwest and Southwest (Gansu, Xinjiang, Shaanxi, and Yunnan).

The nineteenth century Muslim uprisings represent the bloodiest chapter in the history of Chinese Islam. At the time, they reflected widespread disaffection and frustration with Qing imperial rule, occasioned by adverse economic, political, and social circumstances that impacted the whole of China. The impact of these factors is also observable in the rise of other rebel movements such as the Taipings. The unstable and harsh conditions prevalent at the time contributed to the appeal of Islamic rebel groups that preached messianic and jihadist ideologies. Regional rebel leaders made concerted efforts to bring together and organize Muslim populations, which were usually fragmented. To that end, they also tapped into Islamic revivalist movements and ideologies that originated outside of the Qing empire. While religion was but one of the elements in the volatile mix that flamed the fires of revolt and violence, the stated aim of some Muslim leaders was the establishment of an independent Islamic state.

These developments greatly alarmed the Chinese government and the political elites, at both regional and national levels. The government did not tolerate any secessionist movement, but especially not those with capacity to rally masses of disaffected Muslims with their militaristic ethos and heterodox ideology. The rebellions and their suppression turned out to be exceedingly violent, with local non-Muslim militias also participating in the fighting. The large-scale violence resulted in many deaths, large refuge populations, and the devastation of huge areas. In the end the Qing armies destroyed the rebel militias, in the process executing and massacring thousands of Muslims. Long-term, the rebellions contributed to lingering feelings of mistrust between the Chinese state and its Muslim populations, which carried over into the twentieth century and the Communist era (for more on the history of Muslims in the Northwest, see Lipman 1997).

The Qing (and later Communist) government's capacity to control the Muslims was made easier by its ability to exploit centrifugal forces and deep divisions among the Muslim populace. While there was an element of group solidarity in Islamic communities, Chinese Muslims were fragmented, lacked an overarching religious or institutional authority, and were unable to formulate a unified strategy when confronting the Chinese state. In general, there was considerable competition for wealth, power, and religious authority among the leaders of different Sufi orders, some of whom commanded large followings and considerable riches, as well as between the Sufis and the clergy attached to conventional mosques. At times such competition turned violent, as rival Muslim groups turned against each other, with the government also entering the fray and taking sides in such disputes. Moreover, during the great rebellions of the nineteenth century some Muslim leaders collaborated with the Qing armies, joining them in the military campaigns against "disloyal" and seditious Muslims, and not shying away from killing their coreligionists.

Islam as a diverse minority religion

Although originating in an Arab milieu, from early on Islam took the guise of a universal missionary religion, with expansionist tendencies and stress on bringing new converts into its fold. That is not necessarily the case in China, where both in the past and at present Islam has primarily functioned as the religion of ethnic and cultural minorities. Within such context, religious identity is closely interwoven or tied up with discrete ethnic and cultural identities. On the whole, Islam has made little inroad among the ethnic (i.e. Han) Chinese. Facing the much more numerous and powerful Han majority, Muslims have by and large found themselves on the defensive, more concerned with safeguarding their identity and preserving their cultural and religious traditions, rather than with converting others to their faith. This minority predicament is further accentuated and complicated by the presence of considerable diversity within the ranks of China's Muslims, although the overwhelming majority of them belong to Sunni Islam and follow the Hanafi school of Islamic jurisprudence (one of the four orthodox traditions of legal interpretation, predominant in Central Asia and Turkey). We can hardly speak of a common identity that is universally shared by all Chinese Muslims, even though they are often stereotyped as a unified group with shared characteristics.

There is some Islamic presence throughout China, including Beijing, which has a thriving Muslim quarter and a number of mosques. Muslims are in the majority in some areas of the Northwest, especially the autonomous regions of Ningxia and Xinjiang, whose Muslim communities are most developed and distinctive. Substantial Muslim minorities are present in a few provinces, in particular Yunnan, Qinghai, and Gansu. Many of China's Muslims belong to the Uyghur and other Central Asian minorities (e.g. Uzbeks, Tajiks, and Kazakhs), which predominate in the Northwest. These groups are Turkic in terms of their ethnicity and language—with some exceptions like the Tajiks, whose language is close to Persian—with a distinctive appearance and unique culture that mark them as being quite different from the Han majority.

Another important part of China's Islamic mosaic are the Hui, whose ancestry goes back to early Muslim immigrants with varied backgrounds—Persian, Arabic, Mongolian, or Turkish—who settled in China and intermarried with local women. The Hui speak Chinese and can hardly be distinguished from the Han Chinese in terms of their appearance or ethnicity. They number into millions and are spread all over China, with major concentrations in the Northwest. On the whole, they are fairly heterogeneous and defy simple generalizations. Presently they are designated as one of China's national minorities, but such official identification is quite recent, being instituted by the communist regime in the 1950s (for details, see Gladney 1998). The Chinese term Hui itself is a cause of some confusion, as it is used both to refer to Muslims in general—Islam is known in Chinese as Huijiao, the "Hui teaching" (or religion)—and to a specific ethnic minority.

Presently there is no official or reliable demographic data on the number of Chinese Muslims. There is also the problem of defining what being a Muslim actually means. For instance, should all Hui be included, even if they are not observant Muslims

Figure 9.4   The Grand Mosque of Guangzhou

or even subscribe to the Communist Party's officially atheistic ideology? Various estimates put the total number of Muslims at between one and a half to three percent of China's population, with a total population of around twenty million being a reasonable educated guess. While Chinese Muslims are a relatively small part of the overall population, such numbers still puts China among the countries with large Muslim populations. To this day Muslims continue to be important actors in China's religious landscape, and their presence adds valuable dimensions to China's ethnic and cultural diversity.

Key points

- The open society and cosmopolitan culture of the Tang dynasty served as backdrops for the introduction of a number of important "Western" religions into China: Zoroastrianism, Manichaeism, Judaism, Christianity, and Islam.
- The first Christians to enter China were the Nestorians, who were welcomed at the Tang court in the seventh century.
- The Mongol conquests opened up new opportunities for long-distance missionary activities, which led to the initial introduction of Catholicism into China by Franciscan friars during the thirteenth century.
- During the seventeenth century Jesuit missionaries like Matteo Ricci made strides in the spread of Catholicism in China by showing respect towards Chinese culture and by adopting strategies of acculturation and accommodation in their presentation of Christianity.
- The so-called "rites controversy," which pitted opponents versus proponent of acculturations, was finally resolved by the Roman curia in favor of those who were against missionary orders' tolerance of traditional Chinese ceremonies and observances. That had negative impact on the Catholic church's fortunes in China during the eighteenth century.
- The influx of Protestant missionaries during the nineteenth century, occasioned by the forced opening of China by the Western colonial powers, contributed to the introduction and dissemination of Western ideas, technologies, and institutions into China.
- Hong Xiuquan, the leader of the Taiping rebellion, was greatly influenced by Protestantism; Christian themes and ideas were central in his theology and his institution of a theocratic state, which was supposed to lead to the establishment of a heavenly kingdom on earth.
- Islam was initially introduced into China during the Tang era by Arabic and Persian merchants and envoys, some of whom settled in trade cities with émigré populations and established the earliest Muslim communities.

- The Mongol rulers of the Yuan era employed many Muslims in their service and encouraged immigration from the Middle East; there was further growth and integration of the Muslim population during the succeeding Ming dynasty.
- Chinese Muslims made concerted efforts to acculturate to the dominant culture, but they also strove to highlight and safeguard their distinct identity.
- There were bloody Muslim revolts against the Chinese state, especially during the second half of the nineteenth century, which reflected widespread disaffection and frustration with Chinese rule, as well as yearnings for independence, among large segments of the Muslim population.
- Chinese Islam is fairly heterogeneous and primarily functions as the religion of diverse ethnic groups such as the Uyghur and the Hui.

Discussion questions

1. Compare the prospects and challenges faced by the early Buddhist missionaries with those of the Christian missionaries that arrived in Tang and Ming China.
2. What were the prime issues at stake in the Chinese rites controversies, which preoccupied the Catholic Church during the seventeenth and eighteenth centuries, and what were the pros and cons of the positions assumed by the two opposing sides in the debate?
3. Explain and contrast the whole range of Muslim responses to the pressures (and desires) for acculturation, focusing on their strategies of resistance and adaptation to Chinese mores and institutions.

Further reading

Bays, Daniel H., ed. 1996. *Christianity in China: From the Eighteenth Century to the Present*. Stanford, CA: Stanford University Press.

Ben-Dor Benite, Zvi. 2005. *The Dao of Muhammad: A Cultural History of Muslims in Late Imperial China*. Cambridge, MA and London: Harvard University Asia Center.

Brockey, Liam Matthew. 2007. *Journey to the East: The Jesuit Mission to China, 1579-1724*. Cambridge, MA: Belknap Press of Harvard University Press.

Charbonnier, Jean-Pierre. 2007. *Christians in China: A.D. 600 to 2000*. San Francisco, CA: Ignatius Press.

Dillon, Michael. 1999. *China's Muslim Hui Community: Migration, Settlement and Sects*. Richmond, Surrey: Curzon Press.

Dillon, Michael. 1996. *China's Muslims*. New York: Oxford University Press.

Foltz, Richard C. 2004. *Spirituality in the Land of the Noble: How Iran Shaped the World's Religions*. Oxford: Oneworld.

Feener, R. Michael, ed. 2004. *Islam in World Cultures: Comparative Perspectives*. Santa Barbara, CA: ABC-CLIO.

Gladney, Dru C. 1998. *Ethnic Identity in China: The Making of a Muslim Minority Nationality*. Forth Worth, TX: Harcourt Brace College Publishers.

Lipman, Jonathan N. 1997. *Familiar Strangers: A History of Muslims in Northwest China*. Seattle, WA: University of Washington Press.

Moffett, Samuel Hugh. 1998 & 2005. *A History of Christianity in Asia*. 2 vols. Maryknoll, NY: Orbis Books.

Murata, Sachiko. 2000. *Chinese Gleams of Sufi Light: Wang Tai-Yü's Great Learning of the Pure and Real and Liu Chih's Displaying the Concealment of the Real Realm*. Albany, NJ: State University of New York Press.

Polonskaya, Ludmila and Alexei Malashenko. 1994. *Islam in Central Asia*. Reading: Ithaca Press.

Standaert, Nicolas, ed. 2000. *Handbook of Christianity in China, Volume One: 635–1800*. Leiden: E.J. Brill.

Uhalley, Stephen, Jr. and Xiaoxin Wu, eds. 2001. *China and Christianity: Burdened Past, Hopeful Future*. Armonk, NY: M.E. Sharpe.

Xu, Xin. 2003. *The Jews of Kaifeng, China: History, Culture, and Religion*. Jersey City, NJ: Ktav Publishing House.

10 *Religion in modern China*

In this chapter

The last chapter brings the book's coverage of Chinese religions to an end by surveying the main historical trends and key influences that have shaped the religious terrain of modern China. The main focus is on significant developments that unfolded in the course of the chaotic twentieth century, although in order to provide overall historical context the discussion starts with crucial events that took place during the nineteenth century, and concludes with the prospects and challenges faced by the major religious traditions at the beginning of the twenty-first century. The chapter also considers the growth of some of the religious traditions discussed in this volume outside of the Chinese mainland, and takes note of the ongoing globalization of Chinese religions.

Main topics

- Key events and transitions that shaped modern Chinese history.
- Critiques of religion and traditional culture during the early twentieth century.
- Confucian responses to the challenges of modernity.
- Buddhist revival of the Republican era.
- Religious repression and persecution during early Communist rule.
- Growth of the cult of Mao.
- Religious revival of the post-Mao era.
- Intersections of religion and politics in present-day China.
- Contemporary growth of Christianity in China.
- Resurgence and global expansion of Chinese Buddhism.

Historical contexts

During the eighteenth century China was still among the richest and most powerful countries in the world. Under the adept and authoritarian early Manchu rulers, the Qing empire covered a huge area (roughly equivalent to the one controlled by the present-day Chinese state) and governed a very large and diverse population. During its heyday—especially the long reins of emperors Kangxi (r. 1662–1722) and Qianlong (r. 1736–1795)—the Qing dynasty enjoyed political stability, economic prosperity, and a general sense of social balance, reinforced by stringent laws and rigid norms that regulated socially acceptable behavior. The whole situation changed during the tumultuous nineteenth century, when the Chinese empire came close to unraveling under the combined burdens of internal problems and outside pressures. The domestic troubles included decaying political and social institutions, made worse by cultural conservatism that stifled China's capacity to change and adapt to new social and political predicaments, as well as a population boom that was not accompanied with adequate economic expansion, technological advance, or increase in productivity.

During this period the most formidable set of external challenges was harshly brought to China's doorsteps by the increasingly aggressive encroachment of Western colonial powers onto Chinese territory. This started with the Opium War of 1840–1842, when the British navy defeated the Chinese forces and imposed inequitable settlement on the hapless Qing government. This was then followed by other humiliations at the hands of the Western colonial powers, which extracted unequal treaties that included the privilege to set up foreign concessions on Chinese territory and gave their citizens extraterritorial rights. It set off a process of gradual erosion of Chinese sovereignty that continued into the early part of the twentieth century. By the end of the nineteenth century the Western powers were joined by Japan, which following the Meiji reformation of 1868 was emerging as a formidable colonial power. Japan's new ability to project power well into the Chinese dominion was made possible by its rapid economic development and technological modernization, which were accompanied with far-reaching social and political transformations that in important respects were tantamount to wholesale Westernization. To make things worse, during this period China also experienced a number of internal insurrections, including those instigated by the Taipings and the other rebellious groups with religious agendas, as discussed in the last chapter.

Amidst these internal difficulties and external pressures, the Qing government and the ruling elites were slow to adapt to the new situation and enact far-reaching reforms, particularly along the lines of those implemented in Japan. Notwithstanding the sporadic attempts to adopt Western science and technology, as well as reform the bureaucracy and the educational system, in the end the Qing empire collapsed under the combined weight of its decadent institutions, inept leadership, and entrenched cultural conservatism. The old imperial system was finally replaced with a new republican model based on Western sources, following the Republican revolution of 1911, led by Sun Zhongshan (1866–1925, often referred to as Sun Yatsen). While somewhat vague in its aims and confounded in its effects, the Republican revolution turned out to be an important historical event that ushered many changes. However, the twentieth century turned out to be as troubled and traumatic for the Chinese people as the one that preceded it, albeit in different ways. The early Republican period was marked by sociopolitical chaos and strong centrifugal forces, as various warlords ruled large areas of China and there was little in terms of a strong and effective central government.

The Chinese government was able to establish a semblance of central governmental control under the leadership of Jiang Jieshi (1888–1975, often referred to as Chiang Kaishek), the military strongman who in 1926 led the Northern Expedition that brought about reunification of the country. Subsequently Jiang and his Nationalist party initiated a series of reforms that aimed at modernizing the army, expanding the economy, and developing public institutions. During the early 1930s there were some successes in the government's efforts to modernize the country, and there was a growth of vibrant urban middle class in some of the major cities. The lives of most people, however, especially the lives of the vast majority of people living in the countryside, hardly improved. The situation was made worse by the protracted civil war between the Nationalist government and the Communists, who after the establishment of the Chinese Communist Party in 1921 initiated a long-lasting struggle with the ultimate goal of wrestling political power and establishing a new state based on Marxist and Leninist principles. If that was not bad enough, there was also the Japanese invasion that initiated China's early entry into the Second World War. After years of gradual Japanese encroachment onto Chinese territory, in 1937 the long-simmering hostilities flared into open warfare that initially pitted both the Communists and the Nationalist in a united front against the superior Japanese imperial army.

The defeat of Japan and the end of the Second World War in 1945 brought about only a temporary lull in the warfare. Before long, the Communists and the Nationalists turned against each other, thereby initiating a bloody civil war. While the Nationalist army had superior armaments and many more soldiers, by that time Jiang Jieshi's corrupt and inept government had lost support from most of the populace. In contrast, under the leadership of Mao Zedong (1893–1976) the Communists were much better organized and had a broad base of popular support, especially among the rural population. By 1949 the Communists were able to militarily defeat the Nationalists, who retreated to Taiwan and reconstituted their government on the island. Consequently, in Beijing Mao was able to proclaim the founding of the People's Republic. In the immediate aftermath of the bloody civil war the new government faced an array of enormous problems, as the county desperately needed to develop strong and stable public institutions that would finally bring about the changes that were needed in order to modernize China and strengthen its standing in the world.

The early years of Communist rule were marked by the creation of a strong central government controlled by the Communist Party, which instituted new social, political, and economic order. The Communist government initiated a number of bold reforms that aimed at modernizing the economy, building new infrastructure, and redistributing wealth and power in accord with its egalitarian ideology. There were marked improvements in healthcare, which led to a decrease in infant mortality and an increase in life expectancy, as well as an overall rise in the standard of living. However, Mao's poorly conceived economic policies aimed at bringing about rapid modernization, especially during the Great Leap Forward that was ushered in 1957, backfired and ended up in disaster, creating massive famine that caused the deaths of tens of millions of poor people in the countryside.

During the early years of Communist rule there were also numerous rectification campaigns and large scale purges of intellectuals. That was followed by further social and political upheavals, which reached a crescendo during the violent excesses of the Cultural Revolution (1966–1976), a disastrous period of violent conflict, social anarchy, and cultural cataclysm that arguably constitutes one of the darkest chapters in China's long history. While the revolution was supposedly initiated for the sake of protecting the "proletariat" from the corrupting influences of reactionary "bourgeoisie" elements that have supposedly infiltrated the government and the party, at its core it involved internal power struggles that pitted Mao and his cohorts against moderate elements within the party leadership.

After Mao's death in 1976, the new party leadership, eager to lay to rest the revolutionary fervor and social unrest of the previous decade, instituted a number of far-reaching political and market reforms that led to rapid economic growth. The transition to a new and more productive economic system, which for all practical purposes involved the introduction of capitalist structures and market principles into China's purportedly socialist society, was the centerpiece of the moderate policies, which before long also led to greater social and cultural openness. During this period of societal liberalization and accelerated economic change—helped by massive infusion of foreign capital and know-how—the Chinese people experienced remarkable improvement in their living standards, lessening of governmental control over their everyday life, development of more liberal social and cultural attitudes, and expanded educational opportunities. By the end of the chaotic twentieth century, these momentous developments were accompanied with greater openness towards the outside world, as amidst numerous challenges, including far-reaching environmental degradation, China was able to incrementally strengthen its position as a key player in the global community.

Facing the challenges of modernity

The collapse of the imperial state roughly coincided with China's entry into the modern era. The Qing empire's inability to adequately respond to the challenges of modernity led to the disintegration of age-old social and political institutions. However, in the aftermath of the Republican revolution the initial efforts at creating a strong and modern state ended in abject failures. The bleak situation was exacerbated by the moribund economy, political uncertainty, and rampant corruption. There was a pervasive sense of disillusionment with China's weakness and backwardness, coupled with resentment of its low standing in the international arena, brought into sharp relief by a series of traumatic encounters with the Western powers and Japan. That led to a sense of national emergency and a crisis of confidence, as Chinese leaders and intellectuals faced an uncertain world, in which a weak and humiliated China had to deal with a host of monumental challenges.

During the early twentieth century many educated Chinese, especially those who have received a Western education, came to trust incipient notions about the desirability of social progress and to have faith in the power of reason and science. The prevalent trend was to romanticize the West and to glorify science, under the modernist conviction that science had the power to solve most pressing human problems. Many among the urban elites shared a somewhat naïve belief that modern ideas and institutions, derived from Western paradigms, could be readily appropriated by the Chinese, as they discarded their burdensome traditions and embarked on a crash course of modernization. This kind of progressive and anti-traditionalist trajectory was perceived as being part of a larger process of epochal civilizational change, spearheaded by the irreversible ascendancy of science and technology.

These kinds of liberal ideas, combined with fervent nationalist sentiments, found an especially receptive audience among segments of the urban youth, who were perturbed with past failures and present struggles, but also hopeful for a better future. All of these trends were given a potent political expression by the May Fourth Movement, which was initiated by patriotic students in Beijing on May 4, 1919. The students, along with their supporters among the intellectuals and the general public, were frustrated with the social and political status quo, although the immediate cause for their anti-imperialist demonstrations was the transfer of German concessionary rights in Shandong province to Japan, negotiated by the Western powers at the Versailles Peace Conference in the aftermath of the First World War.

While political makeover and modernization were on the top of the national agenda, a number of intellectuals argued that political transformation had to be accompanied with corresponding changes in the cultural sphere. That led to a reevaluation of central aspects of traditional Chinese civilization, including religion. A prime expression of that was the New Culture Movement, initiated in 1915 by reform-minded intellectuals disenchanted with the perceived shortcomings of

China's traditional culture. Proponents of the New Culture Movement sought to introduce new cultural frameworks that would challenge prevalent ways of thinking and reshape dominant social values, thereby putting an end to the decadent cultural traditions of old China. Within that context, Confucianism was identified as the main culprit, as it was perceived as constituting the core of China's traditional culture, although there were also anti-religious sentiments directed at other traditions, which were dismissed as dated superstitions. Many Western-educated intellectuals decried the continuing influence of Confucian principles and mores on Chinese life, which persisted even after the collapse of the imperial system and the official death of Confucianism as governing political ideology.

Radical reformers saw Confucian values as being completely irrelevant to life in modern China, useless artifacts that could safely be discarded into the dustbin of history, along with other aspect of traditional life associated with the discredited Manchu rule. Even worse, Confucianism symbolized an oppressive and burdensome past that impeded progress, freedom, and creativity. Confucian ideology was completely discredited, argued the reformers, due to its close ties with the oppressive feudal system and the autocratic form of government that sustained it. Consequently, one of the rallying slogans of the young revolutionaries that spearheaded the May Fourth Movements was "smash the shop of Confucius." China's ability to turn the corner and enter the modern world stage as a powerful and stable nation necessitated a thoroughgoing rejection of all vestiges of outdated thought and action, especially those shaped by Confucian norms and ideals. The culture of the new China the revolutionaries sought to establish was to be based on science and democracy, and the reactionary teachings of Confucianism had no place in it (see box).

Chen Duxiu's (1879–1942) critique of Confucianism

In China, the Confucians have based their teachings on their ethical norms. Sons and wives possess neither distinct individuality nor personal property. Fathers and elder brothers bring up their sons and younger brothers and are in turn supported by them. It is said in chapter thirty of the *Record of Rites*: "While parents are living, the son dares not regard his person or property as his own." This is absolutely not the way to personal independence.... Confucius lived in a feudal age. The ethics he promoted were the ethics of a feudal age. The social mores he taught, and even his own mode of living, were teachings and models of a feudal age. The objectives, ethics, social norms, mode of living, and political institutions (he advocated) did not go beyond the privilege and prestige of a few rulers and aristocrats, and had nothing to do with the happiness of the great masses.

Excerpts adapted from de Bary and Lufrano 2001: 353–56.

Among the purportedly dated cultural attitudes and mores associated with Confucianism, which were inimical to the modern society that the Westernized reformers yearned for, especially open to critique were the manifold abuses and discriminatory practices directed towards women, who were habitually victimized by the prevalent patriarchal system. Instead of adhering to Confucian morals that demanded from women submission to men and promoted the cult of female chastity, symbolized by the injunction against the remarrying of widows (see Chapter 8), modern Chinese should embrace Western-inspired ideas about gender equity. Furthermore, in contrast to traditional Confucian teachings that promoted social conformity and blind respect for established authority, the reformers advocated new Western values such as individualism, democracy, and materialism.

While most of the modernist critiques centered on the shortcoming of Confucianism and its incompatibility with the modern world, similar criticism was also directed towards a whole range of "superstitious" religious beliefs and practices prevalent among the common people, which included those of Buddhism, Daoism, and popular religion. All of these are evident in some of the popular writings from the Republican period, which were composed in vernacular Chinese and in genres influenced by Western literature. Under the influence of a literary revolution launched in the 1910s by Hu Shi (1891–1962) and other intellectuals critical of the prevalent use of classical Chinese, the formal language of scholars and officials in imperial China, during this period the vernacular language emerged as the main medium of literary communication and creative expression. In his "Diary of a Madman" and other short stories, Lu Xun (1881–1936), arguably the most famous writer from this period, presents a forceful indictment of traditional Chinese culture and society; an important theme of that is the hypocrisy and decadence of Confucianism. Another good example of the use of literature as a form of social critique is "New Year's Sacrifice," where Lu Xun presents a compelling condemnation of the outmoded outlooks, restrictive mores, and coldhearted attitudes observable among the scholarly elites that still adhered to Confucian norms and rituals, along with a passing indictment of popular religious beliefs.

Revitalization of Confucianism in Republican China

During the Republican period proponents of progress and radical change argued that the advent of modernity in China required iconoclastic break with tradition and thorough liberation from the burdens of the past. Others, however, rejected this kind of militant anti-traditionalist stance and argued for the continuing value and relevance of age-old cultural or religious traditions. After becoming better acquainted with Western civilization, a number of influential Chinese expressed dismay with what they perceived to be its serious shortcomings, particularly the self-indulgent individualism, crass materialism, and mindless consumerism. While not necessarily promoting wholesale rejection of the modernization program, traditionalist intellectuals and politicians decried a prevalent tendency towards unreflective Westernization, which in their estimate had the pernicious effects of undermining the fundamental values of traditional Chinese civilization, including those transmitted by Confucianism.

As it has often happened in the past, the most powerful and visible support for Confucianism came from the top. Jiang Jieshi, the leader of the Nationalist regime, in the mid-1930s initiated a government-sponsored program that aimed at the restoration of traditional values and virtues, known as the New Life Movement. In order to foster national unity and uplift the morale of the Chinese people during a period of great uncertainty, Jiang called for a nationwide return to traditional values, which he basically equated with the fundamental principle of traditional Confucian morality. Within that context, restoration of traditional values meant renewed emphasis on ritualistic decorum and adherence to established cultural norms, concern for social harmony and communal wellbeing, and emphasis on respect for law and authority. Accordingly, Confucian values and ideals were promoted as essential elements of China's cultural legacy, as well as vital forces that could unify the country and install a sense of purpose and discipline among its people (see box).

It is perhaps easy to dismiss Jiang's program of moral reform as being motivated by a desire to shore-up party discipline and strengthen his grip on power, as well as to increase the popularity of the Nationalists by positioning them as upholders of order and morality, in contrast to the supposedly immoral and treacherous Communists. Nonetheless, it is undeniable that his traditionalism resonated with many Chinese, especially those interested in a moral revival along traditional lines, as they tried to resist the threat of Western "spiritual pollution" and reassert a sense of patriotic

Jiang Jieshi on the essential principles of the New Life Movement

The New Life Movement aims at the promotion of a regular life guided by the four (Confucian) virtues: ritual (*li*), righteousness (*yi*), integrity (*lian*), and sense of shame or humility (*chi*). These virtues must be applied to ordinary life in the matter of food, clothing, shelter, and action. The four virtues are the essential principles for the promotion of morality. They form the major rules for dealing with men and human affairs, for cultivating oneself, and for adjusting to one's surroundings. Whoever violates these rules is bound to fail, and the nation that neglects them will not survive .... By the observance of these four virtues, it is hoped that social disorder and individual weakness will be remedied, and that the people will become more military-minded.

Excerpts adapted from de Bary and Lufrano 2001: 341–44.

pride in their own culture. In a way, Jiang's program harked back to perspectives that were prevalent among some late nineteenth and early twentieth century intellectuals, who acknowledged the utilitarian functions of Western science and technology, but continued to argue for the primacy of Confucian learning and values, which they construed as the essence of Chinese culture. The basic paradigm promoted by them, based on the traditional Chinese philosophical dyad of essence (*ti*) and function (*yong*), underscored that Chinese/Confucian learning should be applied to the essential sphere of fundamental principles and ethical norms, while Western learning (i.e. modern science and technology) should be used in the functional sphere of practical problems and everyday applications. The famous scholar and politician Kang Youwei (1858–1927) even went as far as to suggest that Confucianism should be instituted as China's state religion, in a manner analogous to Christianity's established position in the West, while most of the temples of other religions were to be converted into public schools.

At some distance from the central political arena, during the same period we also witness the beginning of a new movement of intellectual revival within scholarly Confucian circles. For some traditionalist intellectuals, the restoration of China as a strong nation and the revival of its culture were closely linked with the revitalization of Confucianism. While not necessarily opposed to progress and modernization, they argued against simply equating modernization with Westernization. These trends led to the formation of a new tradition of Confucianism with modern orientation, usually referred to as "New Confucian Learning" or "New Confucianism" (Xin ruxue). Highly intellectualized and philosophically oriented, this new version of Confucianism was supposedly adapted to the spirit of the new era; nonetheless, it was essentially a modern extension or reinterpretation of Neo-Confucianism, even as it introduced new philosophical perspectives and expanded the field of Confucian discourse.

Basic realignments within the New Confucianism movement roughly replicated the earlier two-fold division of Neo-Confucianism into the School of Mind and the School of Principle (see Chapter 8), with the first strain becoming more influential among the modern intellectuals. Many of the scholarly proponents of New Confucianism secured academic positions, even as they pursued activist agendas aimed at reconstituting Confucianism and reestablishing its central place in Chinese life. They claimed to be retrieving the genuine insights and timeless spirit of the ancient Confucian way, while expressing them in contemporary idiom and presenting them as humanistic philosophy with deep relevance for modern life. According to them, the humanistic principles of Confucianism were not only essential for reconstituting the moral system and revitalizing the culture of China, but they were also capable of making singular contributions to the development of unity and harmony throughout the world.

A noteworthy aspect of the New Confucianism movement during its formative period—especially among the proponents of the New School of Mind—was its engagement or recourse to Buddhist and Western philosophical systems, even if the main agenda of its leading figures involved the repackaging of Confucianism as the essential core of Chinese culture, bolstered with selective reading of Chinese history. For instance, Xiong Shili (1885–1968), widely regarded as one of the leading Chinese philosophers of the twentieth century, integrated the idealistic metaphysics of the Buddhist doctrine of Consciousness Only (Weishi) into his philosophical speculations. In a similar vein, his disciple Mou Zongsan (1909–1994) undertook studies of Daoism, classical Buddhist thought, and Western philosophy (especially Kant). After the Communist victory of 1949, many thinkers associated with New Confucianism moved to Taiwan, where Jiang Jieshi's military dictatorship continued the policy of promoting Confucianism, an important part of which was the introduction of Confucian ethical studies as part of the official school curriculum during the 1950s.

Buddhist revival of the Republican era

During the tumultuous Republican period the adverse social and political circumstances also affected Buddhist institutions—already in poor shape at the end of the Qing period—as traditional beliefs and practices were rejected by many educated Chinese as outdated superstitions. Furthermore, Buddhism and its monastic order received harsh criticism from Protestant missionaries engaged in aggressive proselytization. The Christian missionaries were able to make their anti-Buddhist arguments from a position of relative strength, as at the time they enjoyed privileged status in China and had the financial backing of their home churches in Europe and America. To make the situation more difficult for Buddhism, some of the policies and actions of both the Qing and the Nationalist governments had negative impact on the social standing and economic wellbeing of Buddhist institutions. That included the expropriation of monastic lands and other properties (without due compensation), which the government used to redress its financial troubles. There were also the involuntary conscription of monks into the Nationalist army and the military occupation of a number of monasteries, despite the existence of various laws that guaranteed religious freedom. In response to the new predicament, Buddhist leaders engaged in varied efforts to protect and revitalize their religion. Despite the difficult circumstances, Buddhism even managed to stage a minor revival.

In some quarters, the revitalization of Buddhism took the form of renewed interest in traditional intellectual pursuits and religious activities. It included philosophical reflection on various aspects of Buddhist doctrine, which preoccupied a number of intellectuals, along with renewed interest in the practice of Chan meditation. There was also an increased participation in devotional activities among the laity, the forming of a variety of Buddhist associations, the undertaking of charitable activities, and the publication of various kinds of Buddhist literature, including new editions of canonical texts, philosophical studies of Buddhist doctrines, and popular journals. A notable exemplar of some of these trends is Xuyun (1840–1959), the most famous Chan teacher of the twentieth century, who was very active in the propagation of traditional Buddhist teachings and whose followers numbered into the tens of thousands.

Other segments of the Buddhist community took a different approach, promoting comprehensive self-reform and trying to reconstitute Buddhism along modern lines. Reflecting the general sense of urgency and uncertainty that engulfed China during this period, the leaders of the nascent Buddhist modernization movement argued that the very survival of Buddhism depended on its capacity to successfully reform itself and meet the challenges of modernity. Some reform-minded monks were so carried by the revolutionary spirit that they became heavily politicized, becoming actively involved in efforts at nation-building and defense against foreign aggression. The progressive agenda of the reformers included establishment of educational institutions where the clergy received modern education. In some of the modern Buddhist colleges the curriculum included secular learning and the study of foreign languages.

The best-known example of a reformist leader is Taixu (1890–1947), the most influential Buddhist activist and modernizer from the Republican period. Generally speaking, Taixu and other likeminded reformers promoted a this-worldly ethos, popularly known as "humanistic Buddhism." Taixu called for redirecting Buddhist practice away from otherworldly concerns, particularly funerals and memorial services for the dead. Instead, modern Buddhists were to leave their mark on this world by improving the social and economic conditions of their compatriots. In addition, efforts were made to internationalize Chinese Buddhism by establishing contacts with other Buddhist traditions. To that end, Taixu traveled abroad—including trips to Japan, Europe, and America—while his and other Buddhist groups invited monks from other countries to come to China.

Religious repression under early Communist rule

With the Communist victory in the civil war and the establishment of the People's Republic in 1949, all religions in China had to contend with a governing ideology that had little sympathy for traditional religious beliefs and practices. The stated goals of the Communist revolutionaries involved thoroughgoing rejection and forceful overthrow of the repressive old order. Their rise to power allegedly marked a radical break with a backward past and opened the door for writing a completely new chapter in Chinese history. Having finally established peace after decades of conflict and turmoil, during the 1950s the new regime was mainly concerned with consolidating its grip on power and bringing about industrial development and economic expansion. They also initiated reforms that radically remade the sociopolitical landscape of

China by reallocating wealth, restructuring the distribution of power, imposing revolutionary values, and politicizing all aspects of public and private life. Within that context, the cultural sphere was to be brought under the firm control of the Communist Party. For instance, art and literature were politicized and were made to serve the cause of the Communist revolution.

From the outset, the Party adopted the negative stance towards religion that is emblematic of Marxism, according to which religion is "the opium of the people." The Communist state asserted its control over religion by instituting policies that restricted the activities of the clergy, expropriated religious properties, and imposed state supervision over religious organizations, amidst a general atmosphere infused with intimidation and fear. Notwithstanding the deteriorating situation in regard to religious freedom, during the early period of Communist rule the state and the party largely abstained from directly engaging in brutal repression of religion. In certain instances they even tried to use religious groups—which increasingly came to be represented by government-controlled associations such as the National Daoist Association, founded in 1957—to realize party goals or harness public support for certain policies.

The relative lack of open hostility towards religion during the earliest years of Communist rule reflected the social and political realities that existed at the time, but it was also in accord with Mao's ideas about the revolution, which he already expressed well before his ascent to the peak of power as China's paramount leader. For instance, in his famous "report" on the peasant movement in Hunan, written in 1927, Mao included religion as one of the four main embodiments of the decadent feudal-patriarchal system he hoped to destroy. The four, according to him, constituted the main sources of traditional authority that Communist revolutionaries had to contend with: the state's political authority, the authority of the clan system (that encompasses ancestor worship), the various sources of religious authority (that includes the belief in divinities and supernatural realm), and the authority of the patriarchal system that subjugates women.

While asserting that these four sources of traditional authority are insidious forms of bondage, from which the Chinese people will only become free in the new society that will be born out of the communist revolution, Mao stressed that the main focus should be on political change, which was to be closely followed by economic change. Once that is accomplished, the clan system, the various kinds of religious superstitions, and the final vestiges of gender inequity will disappear naturally, without the party having to do anything special about them. Such assumptions were very much in tune with orthodox Marxist ideology, according to which changes in the economic system will naturally bring about corresponding changes in the cultural sphere. Once the peasant masses see the light, argued Mao, they will spontaneously abandon their religious idols and do away with everything else linked with the repressive feudal system, under which they have suffered for so long.

Despite the efforts of the Communist Party to educate its populace about the worthlessness of religion, many people continued to hold on to their faith and engage in traditional religious observances. The disappearance of religion, which according to orthodox Marxist dogma was to follow the establishment of socialist society, was not exactly happening. Accordingly, not only was there an intensification in the anti-religious rhetoric and propaganda, but gradually more repressive actions were introduced in order to stamp out the persistent presence of "superstitious" beliefs and practices among the Chinese populace.

The religious situation rapidly deteriorated during the 1960s, and reached its lowest point with the violent suppression of all religions during the worst excesses of the Cultural Revolution (1966–1976). During this chaotic and turbulent period of perpetual revolution—ostensibly meant to stamp out the influence of "bourgeois" social elements that threatened the putative dictatorship of the proletariat—there was a wholesale attack against all ideas or things that could be construed as conveying traditional values or being linked with foreign influence. Mao called on his followers to completely obliterate the "four olds"—old customs, habits, cultures, and ideas—and they responded massively and enthusiastically, often with violent ferocity. As one would expect, the traditional ideas and things that needed to be eradicated included all religious institutions, objects, and practices, which were to be exterminated once and for all as conspicuous remnants of an old order that hampered revolutionary change.

The revolutionary fervor and the violent war against religious traditions waged during the Cultural Revolution led to the closing or destruction of all monasteries, temples, churches, and mosques, along with the forced laicization of the clergy. No religious sect or tradition was spared from violent persecution. In the process of cleansing China from bourgeois elements and old-fashioned superstitions, countless religious artifacts, including statues, books, and paintings, were destroyed. The anti-religious repression was extended to people's homes and their private lives. All expressions of faith, public and private, were proscribed. Individual instances of noncompliance with these guiding principles, which could simply mean the mere possession of a religious symbol or artifact, carried serious consequences, including harassment and imprisonment.

The cult of Mao

The indiscriminate anti-religious suppression and the sweeping inhumanity of the Cultural Revolution were accompanied with the growth of a cult centered on Mao's revolutionary persona. Ironically, at its height the cultic veneration of Mao adopted many of the elements of organized religion, notwithstanding the official atheistic ideology espoused by Mao and the party. The image of Mao assumed mythical proportions, as he effectively became deified. Within the mass hysteria that prevailed at the time, his eager followers, who were subjected to methodical propaganda and systematic indoctrination, worshiped him as if he were a living god. Unlimited love and devotion to Mao and the party were to supersede everything, even the feelings of filial affection and the natural bonds between children and parents.

The cult of Mao had its own scripture, in the form of the ubiquitous *Little Red Book*, a collection of Mao quotations that was fervently read and memorized by the Red Guards, the youthful units assembled to serve as the revolution's vanguard, and other devoted followers of the Great Helmsman. The recitations of the red book, which effectively functioned as a "bible" of sorts for the Red Guards, assumed forms reminiscent of religious rituals (see Figure 10.1). In terms of practice, the cult's followers were taught to cultivate revolutionary virtues and self-sacrifice, study the thought of Mao, and work for the common good and the welfare of the people. It is also possible to draw parallels between the utopian belief in a perfect communist society and the various millenarian beliefs promoted by different religious groups throughout Chinese history. Finally, there was a pronounced puritanical streak in Communist outlook and practice, already observable before Mao's grasp of supreme power. That was manifested in the proscription of an array of vices, such as gambling, prostitution, and drinking, which evoked the puritanical attitudes of the Taipings and other religiously-inspired rebel movements.

Figure 10.1 Chinese peasants gather in a field around a portrait of Mao and read collectively his *Little Red Book* (May 1969) (AFP/Getty Images)

While the cult of Mao officially came to an end with the conclusion of the Cultural Revolution, the deified image of Mao remained a part of his legacy. During the 1980s and 1990s there was a popular resurgence of interest in Mao. The great revolutionary was even unofficially incorporated as a protective deity of sorts into the popular religious pantheon, the very kind of folk superstition that Mao tried to uproot. This is evident in the Mao talismans that are hung on the rearview mirrors of taxis, with the hope that they will bring good luck and protection from traffic accidents. Ongoing interest and veneration of Mao are also evident in the numerous examples of Mao memorabilia that can be found all over China. These include Mao statues and portraits that are often placed for good luck in homes and business, or even carried in religious processions during local festivals, along with a variety of items that have Mao's image emblazoned on them.

Contemporary religious revivals

With the institution of more liberal policies by the new Communist leadership during the late 1970s, religion began to stage a slow comeback. Over the last three decades the main focus of the Chinese government has been on economic development and modernization, especially industrial growth, scientific and technological modernization, restructuring of the agricultural sector, and the upgrading of national defense. The phenomenal economic boom that followed the comprehensive financial and industrial restructuring and the introduction of capitalist elements into China's supposedly socialist society, the likes of which the world has hardly ever seen before, has been studied extensively and has received ample media attention. Somewhat less noticed are the remarkable changes occurring in the religious arena, which have been gradually unfolding against the larger backdrop of multifaceted changes in the social and cultural spheres. Those changes involve a growing sense of cultural openness, improved educational opportunities, relaxing of political controls, and increases in social mobility and personal freedoms, including the ability to travel across China and abroad. Other contributing factors are the decreases in the influence of Marxist ideology and the ability (or willingness) of the Chinese government to engage in outright repression of its people, as well as the exponential increase in the flows of information and opportunities to communicate with the external world, which are further enhanced by the extensive use of internet technology.

Recently China has been experiencing a remarkable revival of traditional religious beliefs and practices, often recast in new forms that reflect contemporary social realities and cultural predilections. All of the main religions described in this volume—Buddhism, Christianity (in its Catholic and Protestant forms), Confucianism, Daoism, Islam, and popular religion—are experiencing institutional renewals, along with resurgent interest in their teachings and practices. There are even new entrants into the multifarious and increasingly vibrant religious scene, exemplified by Falun gong and other popular groups or movements (see next section). Once again, across China there are festivals dedicated to popular deities; traditional burials and memorial services are also being revived, along with a variety of public rituals that are officiated by ordained clergy and attended by throngs of pious worshipers.

These dramatic changes were in large part made possible by a dramatic shift in the government's attitudes towards traditional Chinese culture. Starting during the 1980's, the party leadership decided to move away from the kinds of trenchant critiques and violent rejections of traditional culture associated with the May Fourth movement and the Cultural Revolution. Instead the Communist Party, driven in part by concerns about perceived moral decline and eager to shore up its nationalist credentials, adopted a policy of tolerance or even support for traditional culture, especially for values and traditions it deemed helpful in its ongoing quest for legitimizing its rule. The tolerant attitude was also extended to Confucianism, which for much of the twentieth century was vilified by the Communist Party and by reform-minded intellectuals. This was especially the case in regard to those aspects of Confucianism that offer support to authoritarian rule and promote social harmony.

The reappearance of respect for Confucius, along with acknowledgement of his central role in Chinese history, are evident in the government's sponsorship of a variety of organizations and undertakings—local, national, and international in scope—that in some way are linked with Confucianism. A case in point is the establishment of a government-sponsored, global network of centers dedicated to the promotion of Chinese language and cultures—somewhat analogous to France's Alliance Française and Germany's Goethe Institute—under the designation of "Confucius Institute." That effectively turns Confucius into a potent symbol of Chinese culture. Within a very short period of time, after the establishment of the first Confucius Institute in South Korea in 2004, the Chinese media reported that over two hundred Confucius Institutes have been set up in over seventy countries or regions, including Australia, Bulgaria, Canada, Germany, Indonesia, Ireland, Israel, Japan, Pakistan, Poland, Russia, Thailand, the US, and many more. There have even been public discussions about establishing as many as a thousand such institutes by 2020.

Another example of increasing interest in the teachings of Confucius is the growing number of Confucian schools, where some eager parents send their young children with the intent of exposing them to traditional Chinese values and culture. Then there is the rise to best-seller status of a popular book on Confucianism (also forthcoming in an English translation in 2009). Based on a widely-watched series of TV lectures on the *Analects of Confucius* that was aired in 2006, the book made publishing history by selling over four million copies within a year; in the process it turned its female author, Yan Du, originally an obscure college professor with no formal training in Confucian studies, into a national celebrity and a millionaire.

Important impetus to the gradual revival of religious beliefs and practices during the post-Mao era was provided by the restoration of religious establishments—for example Buddhist monasteries, Daoist temples, or Islamic mosques—many of which were destroyed or had their building put to different use during the Cultural Revolution. Much of it was undertaken with funds provided by the Chinese government, which was eager to portray itself as the guardian of China's rich and varied cultural heritage. Substantial funds were also donated by Chinese living abroad. For instance, many Buddhist and Daoist temples were rebuilt with financial contributions coming from outside, especially from religious devotees in Hong Kong, Singapore, Taiwan, and elsewhere. With the growth of personal wealth, an outcome of China's recent economic boom, religious institutions increasingly depend on the economic support that they receive from local devotees and patrons.

The rebuilding or refurbishing of temples and other religious sites, especially those with notable historical significance, are often linked with the growth of the tourist industry, which has recently exploded amidst the rise in personal incomes and the newfound freedom of movement. At present many famous temples and pilgrimage sites—including those located at famous Buddhist and Daoist mountains, such as Emeishan and Longhushan—are major tourist destinations, although the lines of demarcation between tourism and pilgrimage are not always clearly drawn (see Figure 10.2). The same applies to other important sites, such as the birthplace of Confucius in Qufu, which encompasses the temple of Confucius, the cemetery of Confucius and his descendants, and the mansion of the Gong family. On the other side of the religious spectrum, increasing numbers of Chinese Muslims have been able to make the traditional pilgrimage to Mecca. Often local governments are keen to restore and promote religious establishments in their area in order to bring income from tourism, as well as with the intent of engendering among their population a sense of pride in their local culture.

The rejuvenation of religious sites and establishments across China is accompanied with a growing concern about the preservation of religious artifacts, especially those with historical significance, as the Chinese people recover a normal sense of respect and pride in their long history and rich culture. Chinese museums, many of which have recently been refurbished or expanded, are full of wonderful objects of religious art, such as bodhisattva images or Daoist steles. Other notable developments include an upsurge in the participation in a variety of religious activities, both formal and informal, and a notable increase in the number of people who identify themselves as followers of a particular religious tradition. This is accompanied with increases in the numbers of the clergy and other religious professionals that serve particular religious denominations, along with reestablishment of the Buddhist and Daoist monastic orders and the reinstitution of formal ordination procedures.

In conjunction with the revival of ancient liturgies and other kinds of religious observances, there has also been increased emphasis on the training and education of

Figure 10.2 Pilgrims and tourists at Shaolin Monastery, Songshan, Henan

priests, although the curriculum of religious educational institutions is still subject to governmental approval and supervision. There has also been a sharp increase in the publication of magazines and books on religious subjects, from popular religious tracts to new editions of canonical works such as the Confucian classics and the Buddhism scriptures. There is even a flourishing Bible industry, with millions of copies being printed both for the Chinese and the international markets. While the status of religious studies in the Chinese academy remains a sensitive subject, there have also been modest advances in the scholarly study of religion. At present courses on Buddhism, Daoism, and other religions are offered at a number of Chinese universities, and there are even academic institutes dedicated to such study. Notwithstanding the relative progress in such areas, on the whole the educational system is still set up in a way that marginalizes and even downgrades religion.

Outside of China, we can trace related developments in the growth of various religious groups and organizations among the Chinese diasporas. For instance, in Malaysia and Singapore there are longstanding patterns of participation in popular religious rituals and observances (see Figure 10.3), and recently there has been a notable resurgence of interest in Buddhism (see below). There has also been a growing interest in Chinese religions in the West, as well as expansion of their local

Figure 10.3 Entrance of a Chinese temple in Malacca, Malaysia

presence as integral parts of increasingly multifaceted and diverse religious milieus. Such interest is reflected in the publication of numerous popular and academic books that deal with various aspects of Chinese religious teachings, history, literature, etc. The last few decades have also witnessed the establishment of a variety of temples and centers, especially in the US and other parts of the world that have received considerable influxes of ethnic Chinese immigrants. These developments are part of the ongoing globalization of religion, which is among the central themes of our time and is projected to have manifold ramifications for the world's future.

Intersections of religion and politics

In contemporary China there is an official policy of freedom of worship—with some important caveats—that is enshrined in the Chinese constitution (see box overleaf). For the most part, nowadays the Chinese people have relative autonomy to practice any of the officially approved religions, as long as that does not pose a challenge to the established social order or the political status quo. An increasing number of people are availing themselves to the varied opportunities for religious engagement and expression. On the whole, there is a discernible trend towards greater religious

Article 36 of the Chinese Constitution

Citizens of the People's Republic of China enjoy freedom of religious belief. No state organ, public organization or individual may compel citizens to believe in, or not to believe in, any religion; nor may they discriminate against citizens who believe in, or do not believe in, any religion. The state protects normal religious activities. No one may make use of religion to engage in activities that disrupt public order, impair the health of citizens or interfere with the educational system of the state. Religious bodies and religious affairs are not subject to any foreign domination.

participation, although China still comes across as being much more secular when compared to other countries with high levels of religious belief and affiliation, such as the US or India. On the other hand, there is probably more religious participation in China than in much of Europe.

Notwithstanding the greater openness and freedom of the post-Mao era, there continues to be state supervision and control over religious groups and institutions, which is exercised both from the political center in Beijing and at the regional level. The Chinese government is engaged in a balancing act: it tries to present itself as being tolerant and supportive of religious freedom, but at the same time it is greatly concerned with maintaining social stability and political control. Typically, the overarching concern with maintaining control still trumps the growing sense of religious liberty. At critical junctions, the government has shown itself to be quite capable of engaging in forceful repression of religiously-inflected challenges to its authority. Within such a framework, the government has the prerogative—or even the duty—to use coercive measures and stamp out religious heterodoxy, especially when it deems it to be inimical to the party's conception of public interest and social progress.

The prevailing strategies used by the Chinese government in its efforts to control religion have ample precedents in the annals of imperial China, even though they are presented as constructive efforts aimed at facilitating accommodation between socialism and religion. In that sense, China still lacks full-fledged religious freedom, as understood in Western liberal democracies. On the other hand, prevalent notions about the state's right to exert control over religious organizations, as well as interfere with the religious beliefs and practices of its citizens, have longstanding precedents throughout Chinese history. The government remains eager to channel religious participation via state-approved forms and organizations. These are primarily constituted by the official intuitions of the five main religions recognized by the Chinese state: Buddhism, Catholicism, Daoism, Islam, and Protestant Christianity. These are represented by a number of officially approved associations, which operate at the regional, provincial, and national levels, while the main governmental agency responsible for the supervision and control of religion is the State Administration for Religious Affairs (until 1998 known as the Religious Affairs Bureau). That leaves popular religion in a sort of limbo or gray area, as it lacks the formal sanction and legal protection afforded to the officially-recognized religions.

Notwithstanding the somewhat tenuous status of popular religion, for the most part traditional religious observances are tolerated by various local authorities. In many areas on the Chinese mainland there are significant revivals of popular religious beliefs and practices, which also continue to flourish in Taiwan and among the Chinese diasporas in Singapore, Malaysia, and elsewhere. Examples of such revivals include the rebuilding of communal religious networks in rural China and the widespread worship of a host of popular deities such as Nuwa, Shennong, Mazu, and Guandi. Recently there has also been a revival of the cult of the Yellow Emperor; his worship as the putative ancestor of the Han people and the father of the Chinese nation has become tied-up with an upsurge in Chinese nationalism. Concrete examples of the cult's revival are the huge public ceremonies staged at the Yellow Emperor's mausoleums in Shaanxi and Henan—both of which claim to be his birthplaces—that have been organized under official auspices and have been attended by various politicians and other celebrities.

The Chinese government's ongoing concerns about the intersections of religion and politics, as well as its willingness to undertake hard measures when it feels that a particular religious group has crossed the line and has undermined its authority, are evident in the ongoing suppression of Falun gong. In the aftermath of a silent and large-scale demonstration, staged by Falun gong in 1999 at the Communist Party's headquarters in Beijing—said to have involved ten thousand followers—the government undertook a comprehensive persecution of the group, which it labeled as a subversive movement and deviant or evil cult. Subsequently the group reconstituted itself abroad, where it still occasionally instigates anti-government demonstrations (see Figure 10.4). The rise of Falun gong can be traced back to the growing popularity of *qigong*, the ancient system of healing techniques and spiritual exercises, the practice of which initially received the blessings of communist officials during the post-Mao era. The *qigong* fad reached its peak during the 1990s when various *qigong* masters, some of them making extravagant claims about their special powers and esoteric knowledge, attracted millions of followers (see box overleaf).

The Chinese government is also concerned with the potentially subversive role of religion in outlying regions with restive minority populations, especially in places with nationalist and secessionist movements like Xinjiang and Tibet. The Communist government is keen to be seen as promoting regional autonomy and supporting local culture, which among Xinjiang's Uyghurs is deeply rooted in traditional Islam, while the Tibetans have a unique Buddhist culture. Nonetheless, the government remains gravely concerned about any possible convergences between nationalist agendas

Figure 10.4   Falun gong followers protesting in front of the Chinese consulate in San Francisco

Li Hongzhi (1951–), the founder of Falun gong, on his powers and his teachings

This is transmitting a practice that leads to high levels, and it wouldn't work if I didn't guide you like this—that would be irresponsible, and it'd be asking for trouble. We're giving you so much, we let you know so many truths that everyday people shouldn't know, I'm imparting the Great Law to you, and I'll give you lots and lots of things, your bodies are purified for you, and there are some other things involved.... There were a lot of sages in the past, and they could only teach one disciple—it was okay if they protected just one disciple. Doing that on this large a scale, though, the average person wouldn't really dare to do that. But here I'm telling you that I can do that, because I have countless Law Bodies which have my enormous divine Law-power, and they can display their great divine powers and great Law-power. Also, what we're doing today isn't as simple as it looks, and I didn't just come out to do this on some kind of impulse. I can tell you that a lot of Great Enlightened Beings are watching this event.... If you're asking me what your teacher gives you, this is what I give you. My Law Bodies will protect you all the way until you're able to protect yourself, and at that point you'll be on the verge of going beyond Triple-World-Law cultivation and you'll have attained the Dao.

Excerpted from Li's "Second Talk" in *Zhuan Falun* (Turning the Law Wheel), online edition (2003).

and religious sentiments, and it has shown itself to be ready to come down hard on those who are using religion in connection with indigenous aspirations for political independence. The case for Tibetan independence—or autonomy, according to a different formulation—has also become an international cause célèbre, bolstered by the worldwide renown of the current Dalai Lama (1935–) and the considerable popularity of Tibetan Buddhism in the West and elsewhere.

Growth of Christianity

For reasons of space, it is impossible to offer a detailed survey of all the main religious traditions that comprise the diverse and multifaceted religious scene in contemporary China. Instead, in this and the next section I will briefly survey Christianity and Buddhism, two key traditions that are perhaps best positioned to shape the religious future of China. It seems clear, however, that in the foreseeable future China's overall religious milieu will remain quite diverse and will involve a number of other traditions. Presently China is undergoing rapid and multifarious changes, and it faces many obstacles on the way to what many informed observers consider to be its reemergence as a major (perhaps even the major) world power. While that makes predicting the future very difficult, by looking at longstanding historical patterns and existing trajectories, I would venture to speculate that (1) religion will continue to play increasingly important functions in Chinese social and cultural life, and (2) there will be a fairly open system of religious pluralism, which in key respects will resonate with some of the past models discussed in previous chapters.

The present-day situation facing Christianity exemplifies some of the crucial challenges that arise from the aforementioned intersections of religion and politics; it also sheds light on the impact of religious traditions on the ways in which contemporary Chinese negotiate key areas of modernity. During the post-Mao era, both Catholic and Protestant Christianity emerged as important participants in China's religious resurgence. While to some degree Christianity retains the stigma of being associated with the unsavory history of Western colonialism and imperialism, its teachings resonate with the spiritual needs and predilections of many people, as they cope with constantly changing economic and social realities. Over the last few decades there has been a considerable growth in the popularity of Christianity and a notable increase in the number of Chinese who identify themselves as Christians, although accurate data about the number of Chinese Christians is not available. Various surveys and other sources put the number anywhere between ten and hundred million. The approximate number is probably somewhere in between the two, perhaps in the ballpark of fifty million (or roughly 4 % of the total population), as indicated by some recent surveys, with Protestants probably outnumbering Catholics by a ratio that is close to three to one. The Christian population is not evenly distributed across the whole country. Areas with the highest numbers of

Protestants include the adjacent eastern provinces of Anhui, Zhejiang, Jiangsu, and Henan. Both the Catholic and the Protestant churches are further divided between official churches, which are closely regulated by the government, and underground or house churches, which lack official status and are occasionally subjected to harassment or repression.

The position and fortunes of Catholicism in China are to a large degree shaped by a longstanding conflict between the Roman Curia in the Vatican and the Chinese government. The conflict started as early as 1949, when the Pope prohibited Chinese Catholics to cooperate with the new Communist government. At the same time, the Communists were bent on bringing the church firmly under their control. To that end, in 1957 they organized the Catholic Patriotic Association, which to this day remains the only official Catholic organization acknowledged by the Chinese government. Recently there have been some improvements in the antagonistic relationship between Beijing and the Vatican, made possible in large part by the Chinese government's readiness to give greater autonomy to the official church and by the Vatican's increased willingness to be flexible.

The Vatican's newly-found flexibility is exemplified by its tacit approval of some bishops appointed by the official church in China, who were first cleared by the Chinese government. In 2007 Pope Benedict XVI wrote a special letter to China's Catholics in which he urged reconciliation between the followers of the official and the underground churches. There are also ongoing rumors about the reestablishment of full diplomatic ties between China and the Vatican, which were cut off in 1951. Nonetheless, there is still no final agreement on such key issues as the appointment of bishops and the ordination of priests. The Vatican continues to assert its tradition of the Pope naming all bishops, while the Chinese government continues to interpret that as interference in its internal affairs. Consequently, the loyalties of Chinese Catholics remain contested (see box).

While the Vatican insists on the Pope's sole authority to appoint bishops, the Chinese government rejects the notion of an organized church led by clergy that owes its foremost allegiance to a foreign religious institution, as it conflicts with its expectation that all religions must follow the norms and dictates of the Chinese state. These conflicting priorities are evident in the deep splits that divide the Catholic community, pitting those who worship at official churches against those associated with the underground churches. The underground churches generally reject the authority of the Catholic Patriotic Association, which they perceive as a tool of governmental control over their religion; instead, they have their own religious network, with clergy that is trained in underground seminaries. The ongoing confrontation between the two groups has sometimes taken violent turns. The government also continues to undertake occasional raids on underground churches and to imprison some of their clergy. The situation is exacerbated by the government's perception of foreign influence within the ranks of the underground

Aloysius Jin Luxian (1916–), the Bishop of Shanghai, on the Catholic Church in China

I want to share with you my joys and my sorrows. My joys stem from the revival of the Catholic Church in China, with 140 seminarians at Sheshan, the thirty or so churches in the municipality of Shanghai, the publications of the Guangqi Catholic Research Centre, and the brand new printing works... My sorrows are due to the internal divisions between patriotic and underground Catholics and the separation of the Church in China from the Holy See. Let us pray for the unity of the Church in China and for the unity between the Church in China and the Holy See; then I will be able to sing my *Nunc dimittis* (Canticle of Simeon)—"Lord, now lettest thou thy servant depart in peace."

Quoted in Jean-Pierre Charbonnier 2002: 522.

church, which is said to be receiving support from right-wing elements in the US and elsewhere. On the other hand, there are signs of increased rapprochement and reconciliation between the two groups. These underlying tensions unfold amidst a considerable religious fervor that is characteristic of many Chinese Catholics. Furthermore, the majority of Catholics are villagers that practice a syncretic form of Catholicism that is infused with elements from popular religion, including cultic worship, primarily focused on the Blessed Virgin, exorcism, and spiritual healing.

The social and political predicaments faced by Chinese Protestants are similar to those confronted by the Catholics. There is also analogous division between the official churches (see Figure 10.5), represented by the government-controlled Three-self Patriotic Movement and China Christian Council, and the underground (or house) churches, although the Protestant churches are much more decentralized and diverse. Protestants do not have to deal with the aforementioned issues of priestly appointments and ordinations, or with the kinds of divided loyalties that pit the Rome-based Catholic Church against the Chinese state. There also seems to be less open hostility and greater overlap between the official and underground churches, with many parishioners attending religious services at both. Theologically Chinese Protestants tend to be fairly conservative, subscribing to evangelical and fundamentalist strands of Protestantism, which primarily focus on fervent faith and personal experience, usually at the expense of intellectual study and theological reflection. There are also strong Pentecostal undercurrents that intersect with major aspects of popular Chinese religion, which tend to be more predominant in the underground churches. Such tendencies are manifested in the prevalence of healing practices, utilitarian concern with the procurement of this-worldly benefits, pervasive sense of anti-intellectualism, and focus on dramatic conversion experiences.

Figure 10.5 Sermon at a Protestant church in Shanghai

These features of Chinese Protestantism are closely related to the fact that the majority of believers live in rural areas and have little education (with a large number of them being illiterate). Consequently, the form of Christianity they practice is influenced by their local culture and traditional religious practices, which differ considerably from those of many urban congregations. As a result, Christian teachings and practices are refashioned by recourse to indigenous religious templates and systems of values. These include beliefs in karmic recompense and reciprocal relationship between the human and divine realms, as well as traditional notions about morality that encompass the virtue of filial piety. Another related development is the emergence of quasi-Christian sects or cults that are rejected by the Protestant mainstream, which are often led by charismatic leaders that profess to perform miracles and propound an array of millenarian doctrines. Some of these sectarian groups evoke comparison with the Taipings and other millenarian movements that sprang up in late imperial China (see Chapters 7 and 9). These trends have led some scholars to suggest that the prevalent patterns of local or village-based expressions of Christianity in China could be looked upon as peculiar variations or alternative forms of Chinese popular religion.

Buddhist resurgence

The recent resurgence of Buddhism involves many of the general elements noted in the above discussion about the current religious revival that is taking place in China: restoration of temples and monasteries, ordination of clergy, and resumption of traditional beliefs and practices. Since the early 1980s there has been considerable growth in the numbers of monks and nuns. The lack of leadership and other structural problems related to the serious generational gap between the senior and junior clergy—especially notable during the 1980s, when monastic ordinations resumed after the break caused by the Cultural Revolution—have to a large extent been ameliorated, even if in many instances prominent monks owe their leadership positions more to their administrative skills and political acumen than to their meditative prowess or scriptural learning. Advances have also been made in the formal education of monks and nuns, many of whom are now able to enroll in Buddhist academies that are functionally equivalent to secular colleges, although political indoctrination remains part of the official curriculum. Some of the famous public monasteries have also reinstituted traditional programs of monastic training, which depending on particular establishments might place greater emphasis on Chan meditation or Pure Land rituals and other devotional practices. In some locales there has also been a resurgence of traditional eremitic practices, undertaken by monks and nuns desirous of solitude and predisposed towards contemplative lifestyle.

Presently not only have most of the well-known monasteries been rebuilt, but a good number of Buddhist establishments have undertaken significant expansions or upgrades of their compounds. In many instances improvements in the physical setting are accompanied with ambitious growth of education programs and outreach activities. Alongside with the growth of the Sangha, there have been even greater increases in the number of the laity, although reliable data about it is not available. (Recently the official press has on a number of occasions stated that there are around a hundred million Buddhists in China, but the sources for that figure remain unconfirmed). Increasingly donations from the local laity, along with fees they pay for particular services (such as memorial rituals for the dead), are becoming the main sources of economic support for temples and monasteries. Other common sources of funding for monastery upkeep and Buddhist activities include financial contributions from overseas Chinese, grants from the government, and income from tourism. In addition, Japanese Buddhist sects have contributed substantially to monasteries and sites that are historically linked with the lives of their founding patriarchs.

Another important development is the growing popularity of Buddhism among urban professionals. Recent public declarations of faith by popular celebrities have also directed media attention towards Buddhism. Moreover, some (Han) Chinese laity (as well as a few monastics) have expressed interest in the teachings and practices of a Tibetan Buddhism, which offer distinctive alternatives to the more familiar forms of Chinese Buddhism. These kinds of intersections and rapprochements with Tibetan Buddhism are often driven by mixtures of romanticized imagery, genuine piety, and penchant for exoticism or adventure. Tibetan Buddhism has recently also grown in popularity in Taiwan, Singapore, and among overseas Chinese elsewhere.

In contemporary China the clergy and the laity participate in a wide range of traditional Buddhist practices and observances, including daily rituals, repentance ceremonies, memorial services, sutra lectures and recitations, meditation sessions, and an array of devotional practices. There has also been a surge of interest in the study of Buddhism as an integral part of traditional Chinese culture, as well as a significant increase in the availability of Buddhist texts and related literature, both popular and scholarly. On the whole, in many respects the present Buddhist revival is a continuation of trends that were already present during the Republican period. It combines traditionalist orientations with modernizing tendencies, which at times clash with each other, even if they are both meant to strengthen Buddhism. While there is strong interest in reviving traditional teachings and practices, notable efforts are also directed towards modernizing Buddhist intuitions and presenting the religion in formats that resonate with contemporary inclinations and sensibilities.

Chinese forms of Buddhism are also thriving in other parts of Asia, often more so than in China itself, where Buddhism still remains under governmental control. Notable examples of Buddhist growth and flourishing include the numerous temples and organizations established by ethnic Chinese communities in Southeast Asia. For instance, over the last few decades there has been considerable expansion and flourishing of Buddhism in Singapore (see Figure 10.6). That is reflected in the notable increase in the number of Singaporeans that identify themselves as Buddhist, with the latest census data showing that Buddhism has become the largest religion in the city-state. Buddhists now outnumber both Christians and Muslims by a ratio of about three to one; they constitute an even more imposing majority among the Chinese population of Singapore (75% of the total population), more than half of whom identify themselves as being Buddhist (see box opposite). Moreover, Buddhism has made significant inroads among the better educated and wealthier segments of Singaporean society, thereby making a dent in the customary association of Christianity with high social status, which is among the vestiges of Singapore's colonial legacy. There has also been an increased penetration of Buddhism among the younger generations, as evidenced by the flourishing of Sunday study groups, the establishment of Buddhist schools, and the active presence of Buddhist student organizations on college campuses. Similar trends are also observable among the ethnically Chinese population in neighboring Malaysia.

Arguably the most vital and far-reaching revival of Chinese Buddhism is currently underway in Taiwan. Ever since the ending of military dictatorship by the Nationalist government in 1987, Taiwan has undergone a radical transformation that includes

Figure 10.6 Vesak celebration at Phor Kark See Monastery, Kong Meng San, Singapore

Religious breakdown of the Chinese population of Singapore, 1980–2000

Religion	1980	1990	2000
Buddhism	32.3%	39.4%	53.6%
Daoism	38.2%	28.4%	10.8%
Christianity	10.9%	14.3%	16.5%
Other religions	0.2%	0.3%	0.5%
Non-religious	16.4%	17.7%	18.6%
Total	100%	100%	100%

Based on official statistics of the Singapore Government; adapted from a table in the Census of Population 2000 Advance Data Release, p. 36.

The four main Buddhist organizations in Taiwan

- Foguangshan (Fo Guang Shan, Buddha Light Mountain), founded by Xingyun (Hsing Yun, 1927–).
- Ciji (Tzu Chi Foundation), founded by Zhengyan (Cheng Yen, 1937–).
- Fagushan (Fa Gu Shan, Dharma Drum Mountain), founded by Shengyan (Sheng Yen, 1931–2009).
- Zhongtaishan (Chung Tai Shan), founded by Weijue (Wei Chueh, 1928–).

rapid economic growth and modernization, development of democratic values and institutions, increased social openness and mobility, and ingenious cultural flowering. The recent emergence and growth of large, highly organized, and multifaceted Buddhist organizations—exemplified by groups such as Foguangshan and Ciji—is an especially noteworthy feature of religious life in contemporary Taiwan (see box). Led by charismatic monastic leaders, despite their varying emphases these groups all combine modern approaches with traditional mores and practices, which are often recast in ways that reflect contemporary predilections and realities. All of these Buddhist organizations incorporate a range of modernizing elements and adopt activist stances; they are also responsive to present-day concerns, and every so often they blur the distinctions between secular and religious endeavors. This includes their running of a range of charitable organizations, educational institutions (from nursery schools to universities), medical facilities, sophisticated fundraising operations, publishing houses, and other kinds of media outlets.

The advent and expansion of such large-scale and multifaceted Buddhist organizations can be interpreted as ingenious religious responses to the momentous social, economic, and political changes that accompanied Taiwan's rapid modernization, including its development of democratic institutions and its integration into the networks of global capitalism. Instead of bringing about a decrease in religious participation, as one might expect on the basis of the secularization theory (which postulates that modernization entails a decrease in religiosity), over the last few decades the embrace of global capitalism and the increased rationalization of social life have brought about a resurgence of interest in religion. Within that context, Chinese forms of Buddhism have emerged as the most vital and widely practiced religious traditions in places like Taiwan and Singapore. Accordingly, the study of Taiwan's and other similar Buddhist revivals can be interpreted as potentially fecund entry points for conceptualizing the various ways in which religious traditions interact with globalization in its economic, political, and cultural dimensions.

A particularly striking feature of the growth of the Taiwanese Buddhist organizations is their ongoing global expansion, which over the last couple of decades

Figure 10.7 The main hall of Xilai monastery, Hacienda Heights, California

has come to include the setting up of local temples and centers in many parts of the world. Their presence is especially evident among ethnically Chinese communities in Asia and North America, but Foguangshan and Ciji have been able to establish their presence on all major continents. Their primary membership in North America consists of first and second generation Chinese immigrants from Taiwan, along with other immigrants from China and Southeast Asia. Some of their American branches, such as Xilai (Coming West) monastery in Southern California, which is the largest and architecturally most distinctive Buddhist establishment in America (see Figure 10.7), are also making efforts—albeit with limited success—at reaching out towards people with diverse ethnic and cultural backgrounds. For instance, some of them are offering retreats or classes on Chan (or Zen) meditation that are primarily geared towards non-Asian audiences.

The global outreach of these Buddhist organizations is also characterized by enthusiastic adoption of modern technologies, willingness to engage with other systems of values, and responsiveness to the concerns of varied constituencies. All these factors encourage experimentation with multiple approaches to marketing Buddhism. They also contribute to the fashioning of new kinds of hybrid religious identities that at times are fraught with subtle tensions and ambiguities. In important respects, the religious identities fostered by these Buddhist groups are global, evoking the traditional role of Buddhism as a transnational religious tradition that obviates ethnic divisions and cultural boundaries. At the same time, in other areas the newly forged identities are also distinctly Chinese (or perhaps Taiwanese-Chinese), embracing select aspects of a range of Chinese religious and cultural traditions, including Confucian values.

Key points

- In the course of the late nineteenth and throughout most of the twentieth century China experienced a series of monumental political changes and social upheavals. During this tumultuous period the age-old structure of imperial governance was replaced with a (largely dysfunctional) republican model in 1911, that after the bloody civil war in 1949 gave way to a communist system of one-party rule.
- Many Western-influenced Chinese intellectuals of the Republican period, eager to strengthen China and usher it on a new path of progress and modernity, became deeply disillusioned with traditional Chinese culture, with Confucian values and ideals becoming the central objects of their critiques.
- A number of traditionally-oriented intellectuals, politicians, and religious leaders of the Republican era rejected the iconoclastic stance of the radical reformers and argued for the continuing relevance of longstanding cultural or religious traditions. Among them, especially prominent were the New Confucians and the proponents of the government-sponsored New Life Movement, which attempted a nation-wide restoration of traditional Confucian values.
- Buddhist leaders of the Republican era tried to revive their religion by revitalizing traditional teachings and practices, as well as by introducing modern ideas and reforming Buddhist institutions.
- During the early years of Communist rule the new government adopted a negative attitude towards religious beliefs and practices, and instituted policies aimed at imposing state control over religious organizations. With the onset of the Cultural Revolution the religious situation deteriorated drastically, as there were violent persecutions and thoroughgoing suppression of all forms of religion.
- One of the striking occurrences during the Cultural Revolution was the development of a cult centered on Mao, which came to adopt many elements that are strongly evocative of organized religion.
- During the post-Mao era there has been a remarkable religious revival all over China, as numerous temples, churches, mosques, and monasteries have been restored or refurbished, and new clergy have been ordained. Once again, many Chinese subscribe to age-old beliefs and practices, while various religious traditions provide moral values and spiritual solace to growing segments of the Chinese population.
- Officially in China there is a policy of freedom of worship and the Chinese people have the choice to practice any of the officially approved religions. Nonetheless, the government is still very much involved in the control of

religious institutions, and is ready to suppress or proscribe any religious group it deems to be subversive or detrimental to the established sociopolitical order.

- Over the last few decades there has been considerable growth in the number of Chinese Christians, with Protestants greatly outnumbering Catholics. Both Protestant and Catholic Christianity remain divided between official churches, supervised by the government, and house or underground churches, which face occasional harassment and persecution.
- The last few decades have also seen a significant revival of Chinese Buddhism. On the Chinese mainland monasteries have been rebuilt, often on an impressive scale, and many monastics and laypeople now follow traditional Buddhist beliefs and practices. There have been even greater Buddhist revivals in Taiwan and Southeast Asia, as well as global expansion of Chinese Buddhism as numerous temples and centers have been established in North America and other parts of the world.

Discussion questions

1. What was the impact of new modernizing or Westernizing trends, which swept across Chinese intellectual circles during the early twentieth century, on critical perceptions of religion, especially in urban settings and among educated Chinese?
2. How did Marxist ideology and actual sociopolitical circumstances on the ground influence the general status and staying power of religion in China, both during the 1949–1966 and the 1966–1976 periods?
3. Examine the main causes that are behind the deep divisions that presently characterize Chinese Christianity, including important historical factors, key articles of faith, and dominant political issues.

Further reading

Bell, Daniel A. 2008. *China's New Confucianism: Politics and Everyday Life in a Changing Society*. Princeton, NJ: Princeton University Press.

Bell, Daniel A. and Hahm Chaibong, eds. 2003. *Confucianism for the Modern World*. Cambridge and New York: Cambridge University Press.

Chandler, Stuart. 2004. *Establishing a Pure Land on Earth: The Foguang Buddhist Perspective on Modernization and Globalization*. Honolulu, HI: University of Hawaii Press.

Chang, Maria Hsia. 2004. *Falun Gong: The End of Days.* New Haven, CT: Yale University Press.

Clarke, J. J. 2000. *The Tao of the West: Western Transformations of Taoist Thought.* London and New York: Routledge.

Clart, Philip and Charles B. Jones, eds. 2003. *Religion in Modern Taiwan: Tradition and Innovation in a Changing Society.* Honolulu, HI: University of Hawai'i Press.

DuBois, Thomas. 2005. *The Sacred Village: Social Change and Religious Life in Rural North China.* Honolulu, HI: University of Hawaii Press.

Kuah-Pearce Khun Eng. 2003. *State, Society and Religious Engineering: Towards a Reformist Buddhism in Singapore.* Singapore: Eastern University Press.

Lawrance, Alan, ed. *China since 1919: Revolution and Reform. A Sourcebook.* London and New York: Routledge, 2004.

Luo Zhufeng, ed. 1991. *Religion under Socialism in China.* Translated by Donald E. MacInnis and Zheng Xi'an. Armonk, NY: M.E. Sharpe.

MacInnis, Donald E, ed. 1989. *Religion in China Today: Policy and Practice.* Maryknoll, NY: Orbis Books.

Madsen, Richard. 1998. *China's Catholics: Tragedy and Hope in an Emerging Civil Society.* Berkeley, CA: University of California Press.

Madsen, Richard. 2007. *Democracy's Dharma: Religious Renaissance and Political Development in Taiwan.* Berkeley, CA: University of California Press.

Miller, James, ed. 2006. *Chinese Religions in Contemporary Societies.* Santa Barbara, CA: ABC-Clio.

Ownby, David. 2008. *Falun Gong and the Future of China.* London and New York: Oxford University Press.

Palmer, David A. 2007. *Qigong Fewer: Body, Science, and Utopia in China.* New York: Colombia University Press.

Pittman, Don Alvin. 2001. *Toward a Modern Chinese Buddhism: Taixu's Reforms.* Honolulu, HI: University of Hawaii Press.

Tarocco, Francesca. 2006. *The Cultural Practices of Modern Chinese Buddhism: Attuning the Dharma.* London and New York: Routledge.

Tuttle, Gray. 2005. *Tibetan Buddhists in the Making of Modern China.* New York: Columbia University Press.

Xue Yu. 2005. *Buddhism, War, and Nationalism: Chinese Monks in the Struggle against Japanese Aggressions, 1931-1945.* London and New York: Routledge.

Appendix

Chinese festivals and anniversary celebrations

All dates follow the traditional Chinese lunar calendar, unless noted otherwise; the first number refers to the month, the second to the day.

Major Chinese festivals

- Lunar New Year or Spring Festival (Nongli xinnian 農曆新年 or Chun jie 春節), 1/1.
- Lantern Festival (Yuanxiao jie 元宵節 or Deng jie 燈節), 1/15.
- Qingming Festival or Tomb Sweeping Day (Qingming jie 清明節), on the fifteenth day after the Spring Equinox, which corresponds to 4/4 or 4/5 of the solar calendar.
- Dragon Boat Festival (Duanwu jie 端午節), 5/5.
- Double Seventh or Night of Sevens Festival (Qixi 七夕), 7/7.
- Hungry Ghosts Festival (Zhongyuan jie 中元節), 7/15.
- Mid-Autumn or Moon Festival, (Zhongqiu jie 中秋節) 8/15.
- Double Ninth or Double Yang Festival ([Jiujiu] Chongyang jie [九九]重陽節), 9/9.
- Ancestors' Sacrifice Festival (Song hanyi 送寒衣, lit. "sending of winter clothes [to the dead]"), 10/1.
- Water Lantern Festival (Xiayuan jie 下元節), 10/15.
- Mid-Winter or Winter Solstice Festival (Dongzhi 冬至), on the day of the winter solstice, usually on 12/22 of the solar calendar.
- Day the stove god reports to heaven (Xiaonian 小年), 12/23.

Important birthdays and commemorative celebrations

- Birthday of the Jade Emperor, 1/9.
- Birthday of the earth god, 2/2.
- Birthday of Wenchang (文昌), the god of literature, 2/3.

- Birthday of Laozi, 2/15.
- Nirvana of the Buddha, 2/15.
- Birthday of bodhisattva Guanyin, 2/19.
- Birthday of the god of medicine, Baosheng (Baosheng dadi 保生大帝), 3/15.
- Birthday of goddess Mazu, 3/23.
- Birthday of the Buddha, 4/8.
- Birthday of immortal Lu Dongbin, 4/14.
- Birthday of god Guandi, 6/24.
- Birthday of bodhisattva Dizang, 7/30.
- Birthday of Confucius, 8/27.
- Birthday of Chan patriarch Bodhidharma, 10/5.
- Enlightenment of the Buddha, 12/8.

Glossary

Aluoben 阿羅本
Amituo 阿彌陀
Anyang 安陽

bagua 八卦
Baopuzi 抱朴子
Bai shangdi hui 拜上帝會
Bailian jiao 白蓮教
Baimasi 白馬寺
baojuan 寶卷
bianwen 變文
bigu 避穀
Bo Juyi 白居易
Budai 布袋

Caoxi 曹溪
Chan (Zen) 禪
Chang'an 長安
Chen Duxiu 陳獨秀
Cheng Hao 程灝
Cheng Yi 程頤
Chengguan 澄觀
chenghuang shen 城隍神
chi 恥
Chogye (Jogye) 曹溪
Chongxuan 重玄
Chosŏn (Joseon) 朝鮮
Chunqiu 春秋
Ciji 慈濟

dantian 丹田
Dao 道
Dao'an 道安
Daode jing 道德經
Daojia 道家
Daojiao 道教
Daotong 道統
Daozang 道藏
Daoxue 道學
Daxue 大學
de 德
Dihuang 地皇
Dilun 地論
Dizang 地藏
dong 洞
Dong Zhongshu 董仲舒
Dongshen 洞神
Dongxuan 洞玄
Dongzhen 洞真
egui 餓鬼
Emei shan 峨嵋山
Fagushan 法鼓山
Fajia 法家
fajie 法界
Falun gong 法輪功
fangshi 方士
Faxian 法顯
Fazang 法藏
fengshui 風水

Foguangshan 佛光山

foxing 佛性

fu 福

Fujian 福建

Fuxi 伏羲

Ge Chaofu 葛巢甫

Ge Hong 葛洪

Ge Xuan 葛玄

gewu zhizhi 格物致知

geyi 格義

gong'an (kōan) 公案

guan 觀

Guan Yu 關羽

Guandi 關帝

Guanding 觀頂

Guangming shan 光明山

Guangxiao monastery 光孝寺

Guanyin 觀音

gui 鬼

guwen 古文

Han Feizi 韓非子

Han Yu 韓愈

Hanxue 漢學

He Qiong 何瓊

He Xiangu 何仙姑

Hong Xiuquan 洪秀全

Hongshan (culture) 紅山 (文化)

Hongzhou school 洪州宗

Hu Shi 胡適

Huahu jing 化胡經

Huainanzi 淮南子

Huangdi 黃帝

Huanglao 黃老

Huayan 華嚴

Hui 回

Huijiao 回教

Huineng 慧能

Huiyuan 慧遠

hun 魂

Jiang Jieshi 蔣介石

jiao 醮

Jin Luxian 金魯賢

jing (essence) 精

jing (scripture) 經

Jingtu 淨土

jingzuo 靜坐

jinshi 進士

Jiuhua shan 九華山

Jizang 吉藏

junzi 君子

Kaifeng 開封

Kang Youwei 康有為

Kangxi 康熙

kaozhengxue 考證學

Kong fuzi 孔夫子

Kongzi 孔子

Kong Meng San; see Guangming shan

Kou Qianzhi 寇謙之

Kunlun mountain 崑崙山

Laozi 老子

li (principle) 理

li (rites) 禮

Li Hongzhi 李洪志

Li Si 李斯

lian 廉

Lianzhu (culture) 良渚(文化)

Liji 禮記

Lin Moniang 林默娘

Lin Zhaoen 林兆恩

Lingbao 靈寶

Linji 臨濟

Lixue 理學

Longhushan 龍虎山

Longmen 龍門

Longshan (culture) 龍山(文化)
lu 祿
lü (Vinaya) 律
Lu Xiangshan 陸象山
Lu Xiujing 陸修靜
Lu Xun 魯迅
Lunyu 論語

Ma Yu 馬鈺

Mao Zedong 毛澤東

Maoshan 茅山

Mazu (goddess) 媽祖
Mazu Daoyi 馬祖道一
Mengzi 孟子
Miaoshan 妙善
Mile 彌勒
Mo Di 墨翟
Mou Zongsan 牟宗三
Mozi 墨子

Namo Amituo fo 南無阿弥陀佛
Nanjing 南京
neidan 內丹
nianfo 念佛
Nuwa 女媧
panjiao 判教
Phor Kark See; see Pujue chan
    monastery
po 魄
Pujue chan monastery 普覺禪寺
Putuo shan 普陀山
qi 氣
Qianlong 乾隆
qigong 氣功
Qing (dynasty) 清(朝)
qinggui 清規
Qiu Chuji 丘處機
Qu Yuan 屈原

Quanzhen 全真
Qufu 曲阜
ren 仁
Renhuang 人皇
Rinzai; see Linji
ru 儒
Rujia 儒家
Rujiao 儒教
rulaizang 如來藏

sanbao 三寶

Sanhe hui 三合會
sanhuang 三皇
sanjiao heyi 三教合一
Sanli 三禮
Sanlun 三論
sanxing 三星
Sanyi jiao 三一教
Shangdi 上帝
Shanghai jing 山海經
Shangqing 上清
Shao Yong 邵雍
Shaolin monastery 少林寺
Shelun 攝論
shen 神
shengren 聖人
Shengyan 聖嚴
Shennong 神農
Shenxian zhuan 神仙傳
shi (event) 事
shi (scholar-official) 士
Shiji 史記
Shijia mouni 釋迦牟尼
Shijing 詩經
shou 壽
shouyi 守一
Shujing 書經
Shun 舜
Sima Qian 司馬遷
Sima Tan 司馬談

Song (dynasty) 宋(朝)
Songshan 嵩山
Su Shi 蘇軾
Sui (dynasty) 隋(朝)
Sun Buer 孫不二
Sun Zhongshan 孫中山
sushi 素食
taiji 太極
Taiji quan 太極拳
Taiping 太平
Taiping dao 太平道
Taishang Daojun 太上道君
Taishang Laojun 太上老君
Taixu 太虛
Taizong 太宗
Tang (dynasty) 唐(朝)
Tao Hongjing 陶弘景
ti 體
tian 天
Tiandi hui 天地會
Tianhou 天后
Tianhuang 天皇
Tianjing 天京
tianming 天命
Tianshi dao 天師道
Tiantai 天台
tianwang 天王
tianxia 天下
tianzi 天子
Tianzhu 天主
Tōdaiji 東大寺
Tudi gong 土地公

waidan 外丹

Wang Bi 王弼
Wang Daiyu 王袋輿
Wang Wei 王維
Wang Yangming 王陽明
Wang Zhe 王喆
Wei Huacun 魏華存

Weijue 惟覺
Weishi 唯識
Wenshu 文殊
wu (nothingness) 無
wu (shaman) 巫
Wu Zetian 武則天
wudi 五帝
Wusheng Laomu 無生老母
Wutai shan 五臺山
wuwei 無為
Wuzong (emperor) 武宗

xian 仙
xiao 孝
Xilai monastery 西來寺
xin (mind/heart) 心
xin (faithfulness) 信
Xin ruxue 新儒學
xing 性
Xingyun 星雲
Xinxue 心學
xinzhai 心齋
Xiong Shili 熊十力
Xiwangmu 西王母
Xuanxue 玄學
Xuanzang 玄奘
Xuanzong 玄宗
Xunzi 荀子
Xuyun 虛雲

yang 陽
Yang Xi 楊羲
Yangshao (culture) 仰韶 (文化)
Yanluo 閻羅
Yanwang 閻王
Yao 堯
Yaoshi (fo) 藥師 (佛)
yi 義
Yiguan dao 一貫道
Yijing (name) 義淨
Yijing (book title) 易經

Yili 儀禮
Yin 殷
yin 陰
yong 用
Yu 禹
Yuan (dynasty) 元(朝)
yuanqi 元氣
Yuanshi tianzun 元始天尊
Yudi 玉帝
Yuejing 樂經
Yuhuang 玉皇
Yun'gang 雲崗
zaoshen 灶神
zhai 齋
Zhang Daoling 張道陵
Zhang Zai 張載
Zheng He 鄭和

Zhengyan 證嚴
Zhengyi dao 正一道
zhenren 真人
zhi (wisdom) 智
zhi (calmness) 止
Zhiyi 智顗
zhong 忠
Zhongtaishan 中台山
zhongyuan 中元
Zhou Dunyi 周敦頤
Zhouli 周禮
Zhu Xi 朱熹
Zhuangzi 莊子
Zhuanxu 顓頊
zong 宗
zu 祖
zuowang 坐忘

Bibliography

This bibliography includes titles that are not included in any of the lists of recommended readings that appear at the end of each chapter. It primarily consists of general books on Chinese religion or history, along with a few volumes on related topics, such as Chinese art and the general study of religion.

Adler, Joseph A. 2002. *Chinese Religions*. London and New York: Routledge.

Barnhart, Richard M., Yang Xin, Nie Chongzheng, and James Cahill. 1997. *Three Thousand Years of Chinese Painting*. New Haven, CT: Yale University Press.

Blunden, Caroline and Mark Elvin. 1998. *Cultural Atlas of China*. (rev. edn). New York: Checkmark Books.

Chan, Wing-tsit. 1963. *A Source-book in Chinese Philosophy*. Princeton, NJ: Princeton University Press.

Ching, Julia. 1993. *Chinese Religions*. Maryknoll, NY: Orbis Books.

Cua, Antonio S., ed. 2003. *Encyclopedia of Chinese Philosophy*. London and New York: Routledge.

de Bary, Wm. Theodore and Irene Bloom, eds. 2000. *Sources of Chinese Tradition, vol. 1: From Earliest Times to 1600*. (2nd edn). New York: Columbia University Press.

de Bary, Wm. Theodore and Richard Lufrano, eds. 2001. *Sources of Chinese Tradition, vol. 2: From 1600 through the Twentieth Century*. (2nd edn). New York: Columbia University Press.

Ebrey, Patricia Buckley. 1996. *The Cambridge Illustrated History of China*. Cambridge: Cambridge University Press.

Ebrey, Patricia Buckley, ed. 1993. *Chinese Civilization: A Sourcebook*. (2nd edn). New York: The Free Press.

Ebrey, Patricia Buckley, and Peter N. Gregory, eds. 1992. *Religion and Society in T'ang and Sung China*. Honolulu, HI: University of Hawai'i Press.

Hansen, Valerie. 2000. *The Open Empire: A History of China to 1600*. New York: Norton.

Hucker, Charles O. 1975. *China's Imperial Past: An Introduction to Chinese History and Culture*. Stanford, CA: Stanford University Press.

Gernet, Jacques. 1982. *A History of Chinese Civilization*. Cambridge: Cambridge University Press.

Jochim, Christian. 1985. *Chinese Religions: A Cultural Perspective*. Upper Saddle River, NJ: Prentice Hall.

Jones, Lindsay, ed. 2005. *Encyclopedia of Religion*. Detroit, MI: Macmillan Reference USA.

Li Hongzhi (2003) *Zhuan Falun [Turning the Law Wheel]*. Online edition: http://www.falundafa.org/book/eng/zfl_new.html

Liu, JeeLoo. 2006. *An Introduction to Chinese Philosophy: From Ancient Philosophy to Chinese Buddhism*. Oxford: Blackwell Publishing.

Lopez, Donald, ed. 1996. *Religions of China in Practice*. Princeton, NJ: Princeton University Press.

Mair, Victor H. 2001. *The Columbia History of Chinese Literature*. New York: Columbia University Press.

Mair, Victor, Nancy S. Steinhardt, and Paul R. Goldin, eds. 2005. *Hawai'i Reader in Traditional Chinese Culture*. Honolulu, HI: University of Hawai'i Press.

Moeller, Hans-Georg. 2004. *Daoism Explained: From the Dream of the Butterfly to the Fishnet Allegory*. Peru, IL: Open Court.

Mote, Frederick W. 1999. *Imperial China, 900-1800*. Cambridge, MA: Harvard University Press.

Overmyer, Daniel. 1998. *Religions of China: The World as a Living System*. Long Grove, IL: Waveland Press (orig. edn: HarperSanFrancisco 1986).

Pals, Daniel L. 1996. *Seven Theories of Religion*. Oxford and New York: Oxford University Press.

Reischauer, Edwin O. 1955. *Ennin's Travels in Tang China*. New York: Ronald Press Company.

Smith, Jonathan Z., ed. 1995. *The HarperCollins Dictionary of Religion*. San Francisco, CA: HarperSanFrancisco.

Sommer, Deborah, ed. 1995. *Chinese Religion: An Anthology of Sources*. Oxford and New York: Oxford University Press.

Thompson, Laurence. 1995. *Chinese Religion: An Introduction*. (5th edn). Belmont, CA: Wadsworth Publishing.

Thorp, Robert L. and Richard Ellis Vinograd. 2001. *Chinese Art and Culture*. New York: Abrams.

Wen, C. Fong, and James C. Y. Watt. 1996. *Possessing the Past: Treasures from the National Palace Museum, Taipei*. New York: Metropolitan Museum of Art.

Yang, C. K. 1961. *Religion in Chinese Society: A Study of Contemporary Social Functions of Religion and some of their Historical Factors*. Berkeley, CA: University of California Press.

Yu, Anthony C. 2005. *State and Religion in China: Historical and Textual Perspectives*. Chicago, IL: Open Court.

Zhang, Dainian. 2002. *Key Concepts in Chinese Philosophy*. New Haven, CT: Yale University Press.

Index